Music and Memory

Music and Memory

An Introduction

Bob Snyder

The MIT Press
Cambridge, Massachusetts
London, England

This book was set in Sabon by Best-set Typesetter Ltd., Hong Kong and was printed and bound in the United States of America.

Library of Congress Cataloging-in-Publication Data

Snyder, Bob, 1946–
    Music and memory: an introduction / by Bob Snyder.
        p. cm.
    Includes bibliographical references (p.) and index.
    ISBN 978-0-262-19441-9 (hc. : alk. paper)—978-0-262-69237-3 (pbk. : alk. paper)
    1. Music—Psychological aspects. 2. Memory. 3. Music—Theory, Elementary. I. Title.
ML3830 .S56   2000
781′.11—dc21

                                                                        99-086731

10 9 8 7 6

For Roger Gilmore, who gave me a chance

Contents

Preface

What we call music in our everyday language is only a miniature, which our intelligence has grasped from that music or harmony of the whole universe which is working behind everything, and which is the source and origin of nature.

—Hazrat Pir-O Murshid Inayat Khan (1882–1927)

I began writing this book because I needed a text to use in my undergraduate musical composition classes at the School of the Art Institute of Chicago. Few of my students were trained musicians, and there was little available on the subject that did not require a knowledge of music theory and notation. Wanting to talk about music from a somewhat less Eurocentric perspective, I went outside music theory, to the discipline of cognitive psychology. Here I found at least tentative answers to many of the "why" questions my students would ask as they grappled with the mechanics of music (Why are there phrases? Why is downward movement often closural? and so on).

When the book began to circulate outside of my class in manuscript form, I realized that music and memory was a subject of interest to a wider audience than I first imagined. Other artists who dealt with time, in film and video, for example, were also interested in memory and its effects on the construction of sequences of information.

The idea for the form of this book came from reading Robin Maconie's compilation of lectures and interviews of the German composer Karlheinz Stockhausen (1989). It struck me that a distinction Stockhausen made about levels of musical structure might be related to the nervous system's ability to process information. I felt that there was a relationship between a fairly standard three-part model of memory and a three-level description of musical structure. (Things turned out to not be quite that simple, as we shall see.) Delineating the three types of memory and then exploring the structural features of music that are related to each of these types seemed like an interesting way to proceed. Hence the book's two-part form, with the psychological ideas introduced in part I linked to their musical manifestations in part II.

Because the book directly reflects the way my class is taught, I have left out several topics that might otherwise be expected to appear. There is, for instance, no section on harmony. Many of my students use monophonic instruments, and at present there is no component of the course that deals directly with harmony. (It is also worth pointing out that the theory and use of harmony, especially as it relates to modulation between different harmonic centers, is primarily a European phenomenon.) There is also no detailed treatment of timbre here, partly because timbre is still only a partly understood parameter, and partly because exploring what *is* known about timbre in detail presumes a considerable knowledge of acoustics, which is outside the scope of my course. Also, I have not used standard music notation (with one exception) because many of my students are not familiar with it and because many of the sounds that they produce on their own improvised instruments have only approximate pitch anyway. I consider only very generalized types of melodic contours, and for this, I think that my nonspecific pitch notation is adequate. More detailed works with many specific notated examples are cited throughout the text and notes. (I have also avoided using certain "standard" plural forms, preferring "schemas" and "tempos" to "schemata" and "tempi.")

Another subject not dealt with here is emotion. Although an important factor, one that can interact with the type of phenomena described in this book, emotion is simply too big a subject to include within the limits of an introductory book.

The chapter on metaphor also grows directly out of my class. My students, who for the most part do not have much musical training, nonetheless enjoy music, and find meaning in it. Their explanation of what a particular piece of music means to them is often couched in terms of some personal metaphor (see Sibley, 1993). These metaphorical explanations sometimes have common features (see Guck, 1981). It is often useful to explore the metaphors, and to discuss other cultures' metaphorical systems for describing musical experience and structure. It also encourages students to consider the idea that composition can be approached as a metaphorical transformation of their own experience into sound.

A number of ideas in this book are taken from cognitive linguistics. Since the publication of Stephen Handel's book *Listening* (1989), I have come to see music and language as more closely related. Moreover, recent work in cognitive semantics—specifically the idea of perceptual representations in memory—may shed light on some types of musical meaning. Perceptual representations may be a basic form of thought that precedes and forms part of the meaning of both language and music. The indeterminacy of the relations between these representations and language might explain why subjective accounts of the meaning of music can be so variable. The ideas of Stevan Harnad (1993) and Lawrence Barsalou (1993) have strongly influenced me in this regard. The work of Mark Johnson (1987), and George Lakoff (1987) on image schemas has also been importrant to the ideas presented here.

This book provides an overview of predominant theories in a field that is quickly evolving. I am well aware that presenting information about a field such as cognitive psychology entails taking theoretical positions, and that many of the ideas current in the field are hypothetical to varying degrees and have not been completely established empirically. For example, models of how human cognition works, and especially how it is implemented neurologically, are still in early formative stages. Even basic phenomena such as the operation of neurons are by no means understood completely. Nevertheless, I have included some basic theoretical ideas from contemporary neuroscience in a few chapters. These ideas are speculative at this point, and exactly how the musical processes mentioned in the book are implemented neurologically is not yet clear. What I have given is a brief description of some general kinds of theoretical models that seem appropriate for the processing of music.

One of the features of cognitive psychology is that most of its constructs are theoretical—their existence is inferred indirectly through experiment. No one has ever seen an echoic memory or a schema; rather, these theoretical constructs have been created to explain and predict aspects of people's behavior. They are what Ronald Langacker has called "convenient reifications" (Langacker, 1987: 100). As such, there are different theoretical perspectives on these entities, and even on what the relevant entities are. Readers interested in empirical data on these issues may consult the references in the text and notes.

It seems to me that there is a conflict in cognitive psychology between two paradigms. One is an older "classical" information-processing paradigm, which grows out of metaphors from serial digital computing and information theory. The second is a newer connectionist paradigm, which comes from models of the nervous system based more on parallel computing. This text presents ideas from both lines of thought. While I am sympathetic to the newer view, many of the classical concepts have some explanatory power. Indeed, what is referred to as psychological "theory" is a constantly shifting perspective, and, as John Jahnke and Ronald Nowaczyk

(1998: 13) point out in their recent cognitive psychology textbook, "All [such] theories should be taken with a grain of salt. They all contain many elements of truth regarding cognition, although none may tell the whole story."

Cognitive structure creates constraints on possibilities for musical structure, and these ideas can be useful for both understanding and formulating compositional strategies. In summarizing important recent ideas in music cognition, cognitive psychology, and cognitive linguistics, I have tried to make them comprehensible to my students. Many of the important books and papers in these fields were virtually unreadable to my students. To make these materials more comprehensible, I have had to generalize; no doubt at least minor exceptions could be raised to many statements in this book. Some of these generalizations may offend experts in the fields involved, and for this I apologize in advance. I have made abundant use of parenthetic references and endnotes—to guide interested readers wishing to explore the subjects dealt with in this book in greater depth; to show the scholarly basis for particular theoretical ideas; and to explain my use of particular terms, as well to present alternative terms.

Whether there are any such things as psychological musical universals is debatable, and I would be the last to deny that music exists within a cultural context. Nevertheless, it seems clear that the human nervous system is subject to universal cognitive constraints, some of which impinge on possibilities for musical structure. This book takes a position between the extremes of autonomous music perception, unaffected by cultural construction, on the one hand, and purely cultural construction of all levels of musical order, on the other. I believe there are bottom-up (perceptual) effects that, while not completely autonomous from top-down (cognitive) influences like culture, are relatively predictable, and that these processes are necessary for the perception of patterns in the first place, especially unfamiliar patterns (Bregman, 1990: 403–405).

As one begins to look at "higher-level" musical structure, especially in relation to memory, the influence of an individual's personal and cultural knowledge becomes greater. That music perception (especially at higher levels) is not totally autonomous from culture does not mean, however, that absolutely any possible kind of musical structure is comprehensible. Certainly, cultural constructs will be constrained by bottom-up factors. The question is, to what extent? The answer will hinge on much more research into the musical conceptual systems of other cultures, and how these systems affect the experience of listeners in those cultures. However, the experiments that could determine the effects of cultural construction are difficult to design, and are full of contextual effects so carefully eliminated in many music psychology experiments.

While the concepts introduced in this book are clearly Western, it is my belief that they also can be applied to the music of other cultures. Many of the phenomena mentioned here can be found in much music of different cultures, and the list of listening examples in the appendix reflects this. Whether the music is conceptualized in this way by the people who make it is another matter entirely.

Clearly, one of the most complex problems at this stage in the development of the cognitive sciences is understanding the conceptual systems of other cultures, and how this affects perception and memory. How far "down" do "top-down" factors extend? Thus, many of the effects described in this book are probabilistic to varying degrees. I make no pretense in this book to having a complete understanding of how other cultures conceptualize their music. Music cognition studies have not yet tended to go very far into an ethnomusicological perspective.

Nonetheless, my own experience has led me to believe that there are certainly levels on which cross-cultural enjoyment and even understanding of music are possible. The structure of our bodies and to some extent our minds are what we all have in common (Langacker, 1997). We all use the same tools to understand music and the world. Today's musicians have the music of the whole world to draw on. What needs to be done is to construct theoretical tools to deal with that diversity.

Structure of the Book

Readers who would rather not read through the detailed review of cognitive ideas in part I may read "Auditory Memory: An Overview" (chapter 1), and then skip to part II, returning to look up unfamiliar ideas whenever necessary. All readers should note that measurements of time and frequency or tempo are approximate unless otherwise stated.

Part I presents basic ideas about memory and perception from cognitive psychology and, to some extent, from cognitive linguistics. Central to the introductory chapter on memory is a full-page modular diagram that attempts to illustrate some functional aspects of memory, in the tradition of Broadbent (1958) and of Atkinson and Schiffrin (1968).

As Nelson Cowan (1995) points out, however, it is hard for such a diagram to clarify both the cognitive processes involved in memory and the temporal sequence of memory processing because the processes are almost certainly used recursively. This means that there are many loops where information actually travels backward and affects processes it has already passed through. Another problem is that a modular diagram may suggest that these processes are mechanistic and determinate, whereas in reality they are highly fluid. I am also aware that using rectangular imagery is reminiscent of flow diagrams and the information-processing mindset in general. Unfortunately, although I needed the third dimension to get in all of the information I wanted to include, my graphic skills were such that I could not produce convincing blobs in three dimensions, although they might have been more appropriate. Especially difficult to depict are the different memory *states*. Thus, for graphic clarity, short-term memory is diagrammed as a separate box, although described in the text as a probable subset of long-term memory.

Moreover, students of memory will notice that I lean toward "proceduralism" in describing memory, locating memories where the relevant processing occurs, rather than in some other generalized "place," thus implying thousands of "locations" for memory. There is probably no way of making a simple diagram that represents this view of memory. Thus, in order to indicate a rough time sequence for the different memory processes, I have used essentially a nonprocedural diagram, noting in the text, however, that what the diagram really represents are processes, not places.

Many issues about exactly what happens in echoic memory and the early stages of processing have not been settled. Chapter 2 presents my own take on such consensus as exists in the field at this time. As it explores grouping, the basic organization of perception into units, which influences memory a great deal (especially in relation to the phenomenon of "chunking"), chapter 3 considers the perceptual results of early processing.

Chapter 4 deals with short-term memory, whose limitations form many important constraints on perception and memory. These constraints in turn determine some aspects of music. Chapter 5 discusses closure, one way humans have attempted to overcome short-term memory limitations by forming various kinds of links between memory "chunks."

Chapter 6 summarizes recent thinking about types and structures of long-term memory, while chapter 7 deals with category structure, particularly important for understanding many of the limitations long-term memory places on basic musical materials such as tuning systems and systems of durational proportions.

Chapter 8 considers schemas, larger abstract memory representations that allow us to have expectations about the progress of musical events and about many other aspects of musical organization. Much of listeners' schematic organization of musical memory constitutes what could be called their "musical culture." Chapter 9, the final chapter of part I, deals with another cognitive construct, metaphor. Much of the language used to describe the structures and processes of music is metaphorical, although this is not always acknowledged in books on music. Recent work in cognitive semantics suggests that our descriptions of many abstract aspects of our experience may be based on image schemas, cognitive structures that are thought to form a basis for metaphors (Johnson, 1987). While I am well aware that there is a great deal of debate about the actual cognitive operation of metaphor, by including material on image schemas, this book suggests one way music might be related to the rest of our cognitive structure and our everyday experience.

Part II shows, in detail, how the concepts of part I are exemplified in music, proceeding through the three levels of musical experience: (1) event fusion (chapter 10); melody and rhythm (chapters 11 and 12); and (3) form (chapter 13). In each of these four chapters, memory distinctions and cognitive concepts are used to explain the possible origins of some kinds of basic musical structures.

Chapter 10, on event fusion—the formation of single musical events from acoustical vibrations on a timescale too small to consider rhythm—introduces the basic musical concepts of pitch and interval (with special attention to the octave).

Chapter 11, on melody, defines other basic musical concepts such as tuning system, scale, and tonality, and relates these to cognitive concepts from part I, which are shown to often impose constraints on musical materials. It points out that many aspects of musical structure create centers or landmarks that allow us to have some sense of "where we are" in the music, and ends with a discussion of melodic schemas, a kind of melodic archetype.

Chapter 12, on rhythm, defines beat, pulse, tempo, accent, meter, and the like, relating these structural concepts to our sense of orientation in music, and touching on more complex kinds of rhythmic organization, such as polyrhythm, and freer kinds of rhythmic organization not organized in relation to a regular pulse.

Chapter 13, the final chapter, deals with the psychological conditions necessary for making large-scale (i.e., formal) boundaries clear in music, rather than with particular traditional musical "forms." It discusses parameters, the basic variables used to define higher-level musical "shapes," and linearity, the construction of large-scale continuity and progression in music, as well as ways musicians can structure music to elude memory through various uses of time scale and the creation of memory interference effects.

Included at the end of the book are a glossary of important terms and an appendix of listening examples available on compact disc, taken from the materials I use in my class and meant to exemplify the concepts presented in the book.

Acknowledgments

First of all, I would like to thank Robert Gjerdingen, who gave the manuscript a very thorough reading, and whose thoughtful suggestions resulted in important changes to the book. My thanks also to Lawrence Barsalou, Fred Lerdahl, Stephen McAdams and John Corbett, and three anonymous readers for MIT Press for their helpful comments; to Amy Brand, Carolyn Gray Anderson, and Katherine Almeida of MIT Press for answering my many questions, and for seeing the book through to publication; to Jeanine Mellinger for helping me solve my problems with fonts, graphics, and printing; to Robb Drinkwater for his help with all sorts of computer problems; to my students, especially Scott Alan Godoy, Mike Moses, Shanna Linn, Melissa Levin, Petra Klusmeyer, Olivia Block, Danielle Smith and Mike Filimowitcz for asking such provocative and productive questions; and to my former students Don Meckley and Robert Mazrim for their help with an earlier draft. Finally, I want to thank my friend and companion Sara Livingston, who read many parts of the manuscript countless times, and who was always helpful and encouraging.

List of Illustrations

I

Some Cognitive Concepts

1

Auditory Memory: An Overview

This book is about memory and how it affects our perception of the world and our experience of music. The organization of memory and the limits of our ability to remember have a profound effect on how we perceive patterns of events and boundaries in time. Memory influences how we decide when groups of events end and other groups of events begin, and how these events are related. It also allows us to comprehend time sequences of events in their totality, and to have expectations about what will happen next. Thus, in music that has communication as its goal, the structure of the music must take into consideration the structure of memory—even if we want to work against that structure.

First, we shall look at a simplified model based on current ideas about how memory is organized. In this model, memory consists of three processes: echoic memory and early processing; short-term memory; and long-term memory. Each of these three memory processes functions on a different time scale, here referred to as a "level of musical experience."[1] These time scales are then loosely related to three corresponding time levels of musical organization, which I have called the "level of event fusion," the "melodic and rhythmic level," and the "formal level," respectively. I say that the timescales and time levels are "loosely related" because the three memory processes do not function altogether independently of each other.

Indeed, the memory processes are *functional* rather than structural—that is, people's use of memory seems to divide itself up in this way, but so far no one has definitely established that distinct anatomical structures in the brain correspond to these particular processes. Thus they are probably best thought of as different memory *states*: current theory (Edelman, 1989, 1992; Fuster, 1995) suggests that at least two of these processes (short-term and long-term memory) may use some of the same anatomical structures in different ways.

From the current physiological perspective, memory is the ability of nerve cells (neurons) in the brain to alter the strength and number of their connections to each other in ways that extend over time.[2] Because activity at the connection between any two neurons can cause chemical changes that outlast the activity itself, memory could be said to be a characteristic of virtually all nerve cells (Black, 1991: 18).

Although we often speak of "memory" as though it were one thing, different kinds of memories seem to affect the function of different brain systems over time. In this book, we will be primarily concerned with auditory memory.[3]

In the first process of the memory model, *echoic memory and early processing*, the inner ear converts sounds into trains of nerve impulses that represent the frequency and amplitude of individual acoustical vibrations (see Buser and Imbert, 1992: 156–171). This information persists as an *echoic memory*, which usually decays in less than a second, like an echo.[4] Current theory is that sensations at this point are not categorized in any way; they are thought to persist as raw, continuous sensory data. During *feature extraction*, individual acoustical features (e.g., pitch, overtone structure, presence of frequency slides) are extracted from the continuous data of echoic memory by many specialized groups of neurons (see Bharucha, 1999: 413–418). During *perceptual binding*, these features are then bound together, with different features that are simultaneous, covarying, or both and correlated into single, coherent auditory *events* (see Bregman, 1990: 213–394). At this point, events have been encoded into relatively discrete categories (see, for example, Burns, 1999: 226–228); the information is no longer continuous, and the amount of data present has been reduced substantially, although there may also remain a residue of continuous information left over after the categorization process. Feature extraction and perceptual binding together constitute what Gerald Edelman (1989, 1992) has referred to as "perceptual categorization."

After separate features have been bound into events, these events are themselves organized into groupings based on similarity and proximity, that is, events similar in some way, close together in time, or both are grouped together. (More will be said about these processes in chapter 3.)

The events then activate those parts of long-term memory (LTM) activated by similar events in the past. Called "conceptual categories," these long-term memories comprise knowledge about the events that evoked them and consist of content usually not in conscious awareness (not activated), which must be retrieved from the unconscious. This can take place either in an unconscious and spontaneous way (recognizing and reminding) or as the result of a conscious effort (recollecting). The actual formation and consolidation of these permanent long-term memories can take weeks or even months (Squire and Kandel, 1999).

Not all long-term memories activated at this point become conscious; indeed, many are thought to remain unconscious, forming a *context* for current awareness (see Baars, 1988: 137–176). This context takes the form of expectations, memory of the recent past, and other related knowledge that can influence the direction that current consciousness takes, even though it is not itself conscious. Memories that are a part of this ongoing context are said to be "semiactivated," that is, they are neurologically active and can affect consciousness, but are not so active as to actually be in consciousness themselves.[6] Thus a large part of our mental activity at any given time remains unconscious.

Some of the information from long-term memory is in the highest state of activation, and is said to be "in the focus of conscious awareness," as may be information from current perception (see Baars, 1997: 90–91). Information in the focus of conscious awareness is *our immediate conscious experience*. This means that the current consciousness can consist of two parts; a vivid perceptual aspect, and a conceptual aspect from long-term memory.

Long-term memories that have reached this higher state of activation can then persist as current *short-term memory* (STM). If not displaced by new information, short-term memories may be held for an average of 3–5 sec (sometimes longer). They will then decay (disappear from consciousness) if not repeated or *rehearsed* internally, which involves bringing the information back into the focus of awareness from STM. If rehearsal takes place consciously, or if the information is particularly striking or novel in some way, it may be passed back to LTM and added to or cause modifications of similar memories already established. It may then become part of permanent LTM. There is a constant interchange between long-term and short-term memory.

Memory Diagram

Figure 1.1 is a schematic diagram of the functional arrangement of the three kinds of auditory memory described above. Remember that the different parts of this diagram represent different *processes*, rather than different *places*, and that the diagram's purpose is to illustrate certain relationships between those processes.[7] The time order in which these processes occur is roughly represented in the diagram by

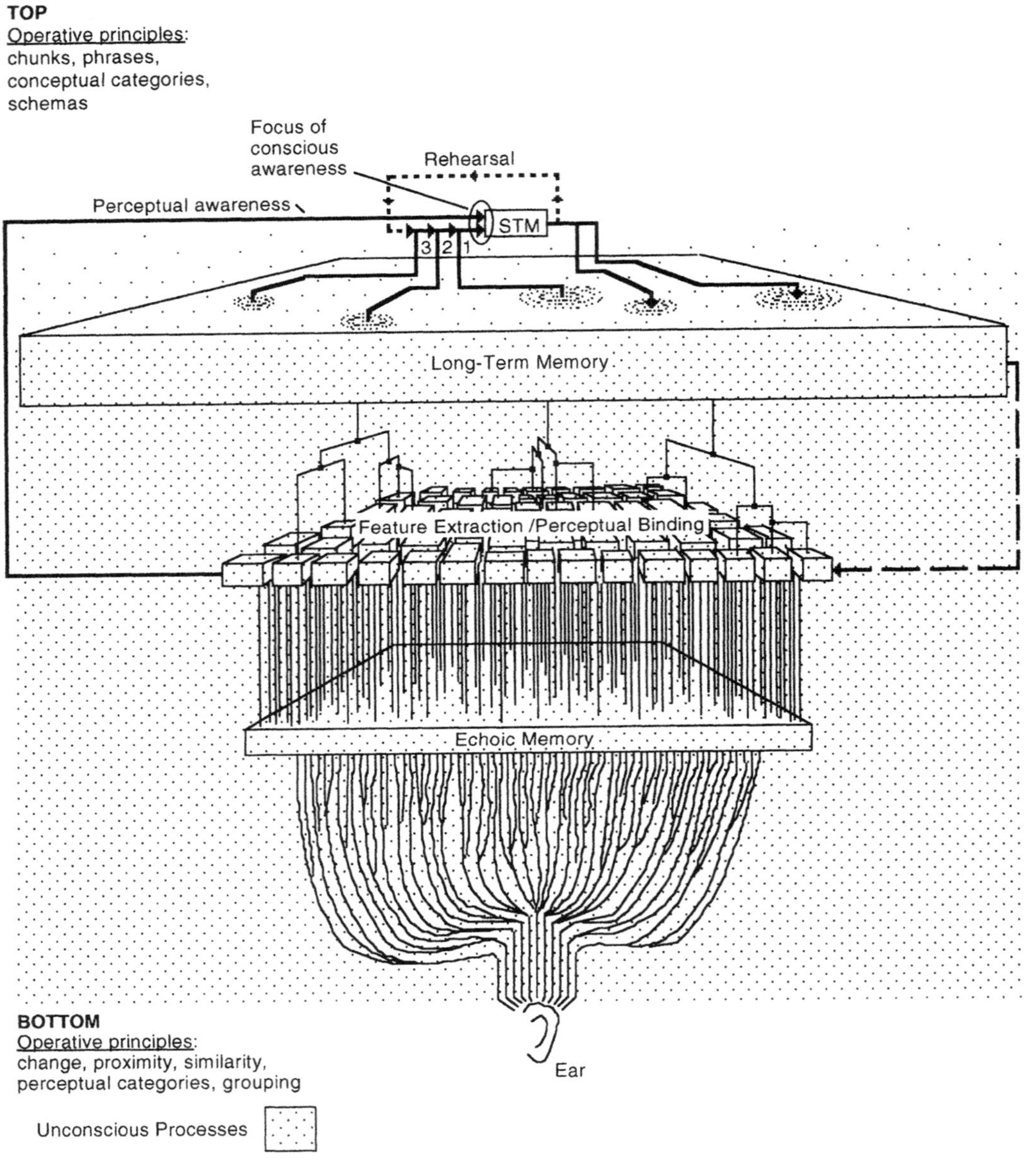

TOP
Operative principles:
chunks, phrases,
conceptual categories,
schemas

Focus of
conscious
awareness

Rehearsal

Perceptual awareness

STM

3 2 1

Long-Term Memory

Feature Extraction / Perceptual Binding

Echoic Memory

BOTTOM
Operative principles:
change, proximity, similarity,
perceptual categories, grouping

Ear

Unconscious Processes

Figure 1.1
Some aspects of auditory memory. Note that this represents a "snapshot" of a few milliseconds' duration and that connections would not be "hard-wired," but would be constantly changing.

moving from the bottom to the top. There are, however, thought to be many feed-back loops (not shown for the sake of simplicity) where information may recirculate back through previous stages of processing.[8] In this diagram, information is represented as moving primarily upward, through successively higher levels of processing. This is an attempt to illustrate the distinction, common in information processing terminology between "bottom-up" (perceptual) and "top-down" (cognitive) processing.

At the bottom of the diagram is the ear and lines that represent the auditory nerves that are connected to it. These nerves (about 30,000 from each ear; see Barlow and Molon, 1982: 273) carry trains of electrochemical nerve impulses derived from mechanical vibrations from the middle and inner ear that were originally caused by sounds in the environment impinging on the eardrum. These trains of impulses encode the frequency and loudness of all of these environmental sounds.

This information then persists as echoic memory, which lasts briefly, but long enough so that it can be processed by various types of feature extractors, represented in the diagram by a layer consisting of many separate boxes. Each box represents a group of neurons that are "tuned" to extract a particular type of feature of a sound.

During *feature extraction/perceptual binding*, fundamental acoustical features of sounds are extracted; features having various types of correlation or synchronization in time are then bound together into coherent events. These processes together constitute what has been previously referred to as "perceptual categorization." In the diagram, there are many lines connecting echoic memory to the feature extraction stage, because the amount of information that persists as echoic memory can be large. Note that these lines are parallel to each other, indicating that the output of many neurons is processed simultaneously, in parallel. Note also that the feature extraction stage consists of many separate modules, each of which has a specialized function, such as detecting frequency change, sliding pitch change, or noise content.[9]

The thick line in the diagram that connects feature extraction directly to short-term memory represents the fact that perceptual information can be brought directly into awareness.[10] This perceptual information is continuous and can be perceived, but not well remembered, because it exists outside of the categorical structure of long-term memory. This is what is referred to as "nuance" (explored further in chapter 7).

Perceptual binding is represented in the diagram by horizontal connections between the vertical lines coming out of the feature extractors. These connections are illustrated as coming together at small black squares. At this point various types of acoustical features that happen simultaneously or are correlated in other ways are thought to be combined to produce coherent *events* (Bregman, 1990), discrete entities whose information has lost much if not all of its continuous character through the process of *perceptual categorization*. Notice that there are many fewer lines connecting feature extraction/perceptual binding to long-term memory than there are lines connecting the ear to echoic memory. This is because perceptual categorization reduces the large amount of continuous sensory information of echoic memory into a small number of discrete categories. These categorized events then activate previously established representations in long-term memory.[11] The presence of several lines connecting the bound features to LTM indicates that several perceptual categorizations can move to LTM in parallel simultaneously. It is probably at this point that the identification of names occurs, with the spread of activation to other memories of the words that stand for particular kinds of sounds, particular pitches, and other musical knowledge. Also note that the direct connection between perceptual categorization and LTM raises the possibility of unconscious perception and memory. Remember that at any given time most of the contents of LTM are unconscious. If indeed perception interacts with LTM before becoming conscious, we can on occasion see or recognize something without it necessarily entering consciousness completely, as in "subliminal" perception. We can even learn things about our environment without being consciously aware of it (Reber, 1993), through "implicit memory" (a process dealt with in greater detail in chapter 6).

Long-term memories activated by perceptual categories, *conceptual categories* are much larger networks of memories than perceptual categories, involving the past to a greater extent and possibly also different kinds of memories (see Edelman, 1992: 108–110). They constitute knowledge about the perceptual categories that activate them. The combination of such knowledge with vivid current perception constitutes our experience.

All of the processes described in the diagram thus far are unconscious, indicated by a dot screen. At this point, some concepts become fully activated; along with current perceptions, they move into the focus of conscious awareness, represented by a small oval, and become conscious (the rest of currently semiactivated long-term memories remain part of unconscious context, as mentioned above). Like a "window of consciousness," the oval represents the *only* point in the diagram where processing that is occurring is *completely conscious*, and thus is the only part of the diagram not covered by a screen of dots. That long-term memories may be semi-activated is indicated in the diagram by the decreasing density of the dot screen as we move upward toward the very top of the diagram; the degree of unconsciousness decreasing as we approach consciousness in the focus of conscious awareness. To repeat, a large percentage of the long-term memory in use at a given time is only semiactivated, and remains unconscious, although it has a large effect in guiding what we are conscious of—indeed, constitutes the meaning of what we are conscious of.

Information that has just been in the focus of conscious awareness may then persist as short-term memory, where it is no longer in conscious awareness, but is still immediately available for recall. This immediate availability lasts only about 3–5 sec on the average, after which time the information in STM is forgotten if not rehearsed, that is, recycled through the focus of conscious awareness.

That the number of lines connecting feature extraction to long-term memory is much larger than the number of lines connecting LTM to the focus of conscious awareness and short-term memory indicates that not all of the information that is perceptually and conceptually categorized makes it into conscious awareness. The very few lines connecting the LTM function to the focus of conscious awareness and STM indicate that the amount of information that can be activated from LTM and persist as STM at any given time is very small. The number of items in the encircled focus of conscious awareness is even smaller. Conscious awareness is a *reductive* process (see Baars, 1988: 120). Much of what our experience activates in memory becomes unconscious background or context, especially if it is not changing, novel, or subjectively important in some way.

Information may flow in both directions between short-term and long-term memory; indeed, it is probably best to think of LTM and STM as two memory *states*—two processes taking place within one memory system—rather than as two completely independent memory systems. Short-term memory may be the part of long-term memory currently most highly activated.

It has been mentioned that long-term memories activated by experience can come into awareness, represented in the diagram by the three thick arrows pointing upward from LTM into the focus of conscious awareness. The dotted circular ripples on the unpointed (back) ends of these three arrows represent semiactivated long-term memories about to become conscious. These might be thought of as memory associations that are becoming more highly activated, "condensing" into conscious thoughts as they move into the focus of conscious awareness and short-term memory. Also entering the focus of conscious awareness at this point is vivid current perceptual information, represented by the arrow from the feature extraction stage labeled "Perceptual awareness" at its pointed end.

Modifications to long-term memory can be made from short-term memory, represented by the two thick arrows pointing downward from STM back into LTM. The dotted circular ripples on the pointed (front) ends of these two arrows represent the spreading activation of new memory associations that are the result of current consciousness. These might be thought of as rippling outward into new areas of memory associations. Some of the memories activated here may influence or enter consciousness at a slightly later time.

Note that all of the parts of the diagram up to the focus of conscious awareness depict information as moving along multiple lines in parallel, and roughly at the same time. When it reaches the focus of conscious awareness and short-term memory, however, information moves *horizontally* across the diagram. This is to indicate that the events in consciousness are experienced serially in a definite time order. This is also indicated by the numbers next to each of the arrows. The first three arrows, numbered 1, 2, and 3 (pointing to the right) represent information "chunks" from long-term memory sequentially entering short-term memory from a semiactivated state. Perceptual information that is entering consciousness directly at this time is also indicated here with a second (upper) arrow, labeled "Perceptual awareness," that originates in the early processing stage of perception. The last two arrows (pointing downward) represent information leaving STM and causing new spreading activation of further associations in LTM.

The process just described forms the basis for *recognition*, essentially the automatic activation of some particular contents of long-term memory that have some relation or association with current perception. (Language reflects this comparative aspect of recognition when we say that we want to see what something looks or sounds "like".) Recognition occurs whenever what we see or hear seems familiar, which is much of the time. The recognition mode of consciousness consists of information from the environment entering short-term memory through the activation of long-term memory.

Identification occurs when we not only recognize something, but are able to connect it with memories of its name and associated with its concept. Conscious *recollection*, on the other hand, takes place when we purposefully try to retrieve something from long-term memory.

Long-term memory is thus an important factor in the selection of material coming from echoic memory, letting only a small fraction of the memory activated by the original sensory input into the focus of conscious awareness.[12] Which incoming information actually gets selected for our consciousness is determined by factors such as its novelty, and its relation to our goals, values, and so on. (Many of these factors could be described as "schemas," a memory structure we shall deal with later.) This means that LTM acts as something like a filter, determining which aspects of our environment we are aware of at a given time.[13] The presence of this type of connection between the early stages of perception and LTM essentially means that perception and memory are often impossible to separate; there may be little differ-ence between memory processing and memory storage.[14]

The selection of incoming information is important because the information capacity of the focus of conscious awareness and short-term memory is very small, represented in the diagram by the small number of lines connecting long-term memory to STM. In fact, there are five of these lines, which appears to be roughly the number of "chunks" of information that can be accessed from LTM at a time.

In conscious *memorization*, information is recirculated repeatedly (rehearsed) through the focus of conscious awareness and short-term memory. This rehearsal greatly increases the chances that the information being recirculated in STM will cause modifications in permanent long-term memory. Rehearsal is represented in the diagram by the dotted loop going out from and returning back to STM.

Thus we see that the contents of long-term memory are a factor in the control of what enters conscious awareness, which in turn controls what enters long-term memory. This is essentially a feedback loop. In other words, all of the knowledge and categories stored in long-term memory (including experience, values, goals, models, etc.) have control over which parts of the enormous amount of informa-tion coming in through our senses actually enters our awareness, and only a frac-tion of this is ultimately stored in LTM. What we already know literally determines what we see and hear, which means that we see and hear what we look *for* more than what we look *at*.[15]

The three memory processes just described (echoic memory, short-term memory, and long-term memory) are related to three different time levels of musical experi-ence, which I will refer to, respectively, as the "level of event fusion," the "level of

Table 1.1
Three Levels of Musical Experience

	Events per second	Seconds per event
EVENT FUSION (early processing)	16,384	1/16,384
	8,192	1/8,192
	4,096	1/4,096
	2,048	1/2,048
Functional units = individual *events* and *boundaries*; pitches, simultaneous intervals, loudness changes, etc.	1,024	1/1,024
	512	1/512
	256	1/256
	128	1/128
	64	1/64
	32	1/32
MELODIC and RHYTHMIC GROUPING (short-term memory)	16	1/16
	8	1/8
	4	1/4
Functional units = *patterns*; rhythmic and melodic groupings, phrases.	2	1/2
	1	1
	1/2	2
	1/4	4
	1/8	8
FORM (long-term memory)	1/16	16
	1/32	32
Functional units = large scale *constancies*; sections, movements, entire pieces.	1/64	1 min 4 sec
	1/128	2 min 8 sec
	1/256	4 min 16 sec
	1/512	8 min 32 sec
	1/1,024	17 min 4 sec
	1/2,048	34 min 8 sec
	1/4,096	1 hr 8 min 16 sec.

melodic and rhythmic grouping," and the "level of musical form" (see table 1.1).[16] The three types of processing define three basic time scales on which musical events and patterns take place.

Memory and Time Levels of Musical Experience 1: Level of Event Fusion

Repeating acoustical vibrations that occur closer together than 50 msec (which is referred to as a frequency of 20 events per second) fuse together to form *pitches*, and constitute the *event fusion* level of musical experience.[17] (I refer to this as the "level of event fusion" because, even though we shall be talking primarily about pitched events in this book, it is possible for acoustical vibrations to fuse together into events that do not have the property of pitch.) Changes in pitch and loudness are detected in the early stages of processing of acoustical information. Differences in pitch are described in Western (and some other) musical cultures with the spatial metaphor of "higher" and "lower."

The event fusion level of experience is associated with information processing that takes place early in the chain of neural processes leading from the ear to the higher brain centers (auditory cortex), and the boundaries of this level are the result of limits on the speed at which these neurons can process incoming information. Note that the level of event fusion as here defined is the only time level in which the most basic events—individual acoustical vibrations—are *not* directly perceptible. That is, the individual vibrations that make up a pitch are not individually accessible to consciousness (because they happen too quickly, and fuse together like a temporal blur), although any change in their frequency is. The lowest perceptible grouping at the event fusion level is a single *pitch event*, a perceptual category that is the result of the fusing together of many individual vibrations. The pitch of this event is determined by how many of these individual vibrations occur in a given amount of time—more vibrations produce a higher pitch; fewer vibrations, a lower pitch. Changes in frequency form the boundaries of individual pitch events, and are detected and experienced as changes in pitch. Other changes in basic parameters such as loudness, timbre, and the like are also detected at this point.

Memory and Time Levels of Musical Experience 2: Level of Melodic and Rhythmic Grouping

Events that are farther apart than 63 msec (16 events per second), therefore individually discriminable but still not so far apart as to exceed the time limit of short-term memory (average 3–5 sec per event), constitute the *melodic and rhythmic* level of musical experience. Differences in the frequency of events are metaphorically described as "faster" and "slower." Speed or tempo at this level corresponds to frequency at the event fusion level (see Monahan, 1993). The main characteristic of the melodic and rhythmic level is that separate events on this timescale are grouped together in the *present*. This time level has two dimensions, which we perceive as two separate aspects of musical experience: (1) *melodic grouping*, where sequences of pitches are grouped according to their similarity of range, "rising and falling motion," and reversals in that motion; and (2) *rhythmic grouping*, where events are grouped according to their timing and intensity.

Because the melodic and rhythmic level and its boundaries are associated primarily with short-term memory, which is our memory of the immediate past, melodic and rhythmic groupings, which consist of multiple separate events in a time order, nonetheless have something of the character of all being available at once. This is how we can make the comparisons across the short lengths of time necessary to perceive melodic and rhythmic patterns. The primary difference between the melodic and rhythmic level, on the one hand, and the event fusion level, on the other, is that at the event fusion level, we detect boundaries between *single* events, whereas at the melodic and rhythmic level, we detect temporally extended patterns consisting of *multiple* events. The difference is one of time scale. Event boundaries are immediate and momentary, not exceeding the length of echoic memory, whereas patterns are more extended in time, requiring short-term memory for their comprehension. Note, however, that these time differences are not absolute, and that the time lengths of echoic and short-term memories may overlap.

Memory and Time Levels of Musical Experience 3: Level of Form

Large groupings of events that occur over a time span longer than the limits of short-term memory constitute the *formal* level of musical experience.[18] Units on the formal level consist of entire sections of music. Just as the timing and pitch of individual events define the shape of groupings and phrases, so the character and distribution of sections define the shape of entire pieces of music.

Groupings of events on the formal level are usually described as "earlier" and "later," or with the metaphor of being "in" a particular "place" (see Brinner, 1995: 195–196). We also speak of "getting lost" and of "losing our place" in the music. Most frequently we describe this level of experience with metaphors of moving through physical space.[19] Moving through large physical spaces requires that we use long-term memory in much the same way that moving through "long stretches" of music does. Indeed, the very notion of a musical "piece" is physical and spatial.

The formal level and its articulation are associated with the structure and limits of long-term memory. Unlike those on the melodic and rhythmic level, patterns on the formal level exist on a time scale that is too large for them to all be grasped in the present. In addition, large-scale sequences of events on this level do not automatically retain their time order. Rather, this order has to be reconstructed—it is not a given, as it is in short-term memory. Discovering relations between events on the formal level requires that those events come at least partially back into consciousness (through recollecting or reminding) from long-term memory.

The important thing to notice about the distinction between these three time levels is that our language describes what in reality is a uniform continuum of event frequencies as qualitatively different levels of experience and uses different metaphors to describe them. All of our experiences of these three levels are actually of temporal relationships. These different levels of experience are really just differences in our own *modes* of information processing and memory.

It has been pointed out that most of the language we use to describe musical events is metaphorical. It is important to note that the metaphors used in Western European musical culture to describe musical experience are by no means universal. I shall use these particular metaphors in this text, however, because of their familiarity to most of my readers, while making reference to metaphoric systems from other cultures when appropriate.

At the event fusion level, we speak of "pitches," a word that in its literal meaning refers to physical position. Tones are referred to as being pitched "higher" and "lower," and intervals between successive pitches are referred to as "steps" or "leaps." Even the terms *sharp* and *flat* are physical in their original literal meanings. At the melodic and rhythmic level, we refer to sequences of events "rising" and "falling," "moving faster" or "slower," and to rhythms as having a "smooth" or "jerky" quality, and so on. At the formal level, architectural and spatial metaphors are often used. We speak of large formal structures as "arches," and of "losing" and "finding our place" in the music. (We shall examine the use of metaphor in relation to music more closely in later chapters.)

Thus all three of the memory processes mentioned above contribute to our experience of music. Echoic memory and early processing provide our immediate experience of the present moment of music in the focus of conscious awareness, and help to segment it into manageable units; short-term memory establishes the continuity and discontinuity of that moment with the immediate past; and long-term memory provides the context that gives it meaning, by relating the moment to a larger framework of ongoing experience and previous knowledge. We shall now examine the characteristics of each memory process and its effect on the structure of music.

Notes

1. I am aware that modeling these three types of memory as completely independent functions would not be an accurate representation of current theory. I nonetheless think that because these three memory states operate on different timescales, a main concern of this book, it is useful to distinguish between them. For an overview of memory research, see Cowan, 1988; for a recent review of the evidence, and an affirmation of the continued usefulness of a three-part model of memory, see Pashler, 1998, pp. 319–356.

2. Individual nerve cells connect at gap junctions called "synapses." The chemical changes that take place at these connections, referred to as "long-term potentiation" (LTP), are currently believed to constitute a possible basis for long-term memory, although this has not been definitively proven. For a concise summary of current theory on LTP, see LeDoux, 1996, pp. 213–224.

3. Memory systems similar to the auditory one discussed here probably exist at least for vision, touch, language, and physical movements, although the memory system for smell is somewhat different. All of these different memory capabilities are tied together by the principle of associative memory.

4. Although echoic memory may persist as long as several seconds under some circumstances, overlapping with the time persistence of auditory short-term memory, the two memory processes are nevertheless distinct. Echoic memory is a precategorical auditory "image" (an actual sensory persistence of a sound in memory), whereas short-term memory is a categorized conceptual memory. See Pashler, 1998, p. 321.

5. The time order of feature extraction and perceptual binding has not been established definitively, and it is possible that some eventlike characteristics are derived before some individual features. See Howard and Ballas, 1981, pp. 181–195; and Fuster, 1995, pp. 26–36. By no means are all the particular features that might comprise a sound known at this time.

6. Current theory has it that when the level of electrical activity of a particular group of neurons exceeds a certain threshold (there appears to be a constant background of low-level random activity), activation of memory represented by that group of neurons begins, but is not conscious; only when the level exceeds a higher threshold does the memory become conscious. See Fuster, 1995, pp. 288–294.

7. A recent view of memory, often referred to as "proceduralism," proposes that memories are formed at the actual sites where particular kinds of perceptual processing take place. That is, sensory memories consist of a kind of residue in the sensory processing neurons themselves; memories would thus reside in many different places, and types of memory would be distinguished primarily by the length of time they persist. See Crowder, 1993a, esp. pp. 116–117.

8. Some of these feedback loops are essential for the process of *imagination*, where consciousness can re-create a sensory experience by using long-term memory to reactivate sensory neurons from an earlier stage that were originally involved in perception; these reentrant feedback loops further reduce the separateness of different kinds of memory. See Damasio, 1994, pp. 100–106. In addition, a description that truly tried to capture all aspects of this process would include connections to the emotional centers of the brain. The emotional impact of an experience, often connected with its relative novelty in relation to currently acti-

vated frameworks of memory, is an important factor in how well it is remembered. For a straightforward description of this process, see Kagan, 1994, p. 100.

9. A particular feature can probably be part of many different long-term memories. This would be the case if the feature is the basic unit of long-term memory. Different long-term memories may consist of different sets of connections between the same features. Thus long-term memories consist of massive connections between featural units. This idea seems to be supported by dreams, where features that are not usually connected combine to form new kinds of objects. See Fuster, 1995, pp. 97–99.

10. Although available to consciousness, such perceptual information has not been processed by higher stages of long-term memory. One example of how this component of experience might be isolated is as follows. In certain types of neural disorders called "associative agnosias," a person is able to perceive a sound or object, but unable to recognize it. Thus the person retains the perceptual component of an experience, but loses access to its long-term memory associations (its conceptual meaning). I realize that this is an attempt to distinguish *perception* from *cognition*, and that the nature of (and even the basis for) this distinction is still actively debated.

11. There is no simple boundary between feature extraction–perceptual binding and long-term memory. One major difference between these two functions is that in feature extraction–perceptual binding, the functions of the groups of neurons involved are at least to some extent established by evolution, whereas in long-term memory, they are established by experience. Moreover, the actual neural coding of these functions may well be different. The connections between different groups of neurons in long-term memory are historical as well as personal and idiosyncratic, with some categorizations influenced by culture.

12. This selection is one aspect of the process of *attention*, a subject not treated in detail in this book. For a comprehensive theoretical treatment of attention, see Baars, 1988, pp. 299–324, esp. p. 322; and Pashler, 1998.

13. This "filter" is metaphorical. As Niesser (1976: 79) points out, "There is no mechanism, process, or system that functions to reject . . . stimuli such that they would be perceived if it were to fail." Nonetheless, some aspects of incoming information are selected for consciousness, and many are not. (Probably it is particular groups of neurons that are selected by the environment—neurons that have the appropriate processing capability.) More recently, this has been described as a "matching process," with information that does *not* match stored categories being most likely to be selected for consciousness. See Baars, 1988, p. 49.

14. In one interesting current view, perceptual memories reside in the neural "hardware" where perceptual information is processed. Memory is defined as "facilitated pathways" of connections between neurons made when a particular situation occurs in the environment and reactivated when similar situations arise again. For a particularly compelling presentation of this view, see Rosenfield, 1988, esp. pp. 62–67, 76–80, 135. See also Fuster, 1995, pp. 35, 87–88; and Crowder, 1993b.

15. This is essentially another way of saying that consciousness is primarily "goal driven." For more on this, see Baars, 1988, pp. 225–245. See also Edelman, 1992, pp. 121–122. Edelman uses "value driven" to describe essentially the same thing.

16. The concept of three time levels of musical experience is introduced by Stockhausen (1989: 46–47, 93–95), although he makes no attempt to connect this idea to a particular model of memory or cognition. While my three levels were originally based on this idea, it will become clear that Stockhausen's experiential distinctions do not map quite exactly onto types of memory. I am indebted to Robert Gjerdingen (personal communication) for making this clear to me.

17. As explained in the preface, measurements of time and frequency or tempo are approximate unless otherwise stated.

18. The time scale represented in table 1.1 is not meant to be exhaustive. Some non-Western cultures have rituals and performances involving music that are many, many times longer than the longest time-length represented in this table.

19. This is even more true in some other (non-Western) cultures, where it is not uncommon for musical features to represent actual physical features of the environment in which a particular people finds itself. See Higgins, 1997, p. 91. A specific and very beautiful example of this is the Kaluli concept of *tok*, where the text and structure of song involves the evocation of features of a journey through a landscape. See Feld, 1982, pp. 150–156.

2

Echoic Memory and Early Processing

Echoic memory is the persistence of a large amount of auditory information for a very short time, usually on the order of 250 msec, and probably no longer than several seconds (see Crowder, 1993a: 120; Massaro and Loftus, 1996: 73–80). This information is believed to persist in a continuous form that is not yet encoded into any kind of discrete categories (Crowder, 1993a: 117–119). The concept of echoic memory reflects the fact that incoming auditory information persists long enough to be processed in the ways described below.[1]

Feature Extraction and Perceptual Binding: Perceptual Categorization

The processing of information persisting as echoic memory is called "feature extraction." An important aspect of this kind of processing (actually consisting of a number of different processes) is that the auditory information being processed gets organized in a very basic way. The input to these processes consists of impulses from an extremely large number of individual nerve cells in the ear. The information represented by these impulses persists briefly as echoic memory. The original auditory sensation consists of many separate trains of nerve impulses, each representing a particular frequency and amplitude that is present in the acoustical environment. Because these trains of impulses vary continuously and have no intrinsic relation to each other, any relation between the separate frequency and amplitude values they transduce must be reconstructed. When these nerve impulses have come from external acoustical stimuli that have particular features such as fixed or sliding pitch, noise content, or harmonic spectrum, and so on, each of these features is extracted by a group of neurons "tuned" to respond to that feature, although the nature of that "tuning" is probably rather flexible (Merzenich and deCharms, 1996; Weinberger, 1999). Many of these feature extractors may be established genetically;[2]

the particular features extracted represent aspects of sounds that the human auditory system has evolved or learned to categorize.

At this point, the information becomes categorical and is no longer a continuous
sensory representation, although there may be a "remainder" of continuous information that is not categorized.[3] This remainder may be available to consciousness,
although it may not interact with long-term memory; we can immediately hear more
than we can remember.

Features that happen at or near the same time or are related in other ways are then
thought to be correlated and bound into units (see von der Marlsburg, 1996). These
units are auditory events. For instance, when a number of frequencies that are whole-
number multiples of each other begin at the same time, a pitch event consisting of
overtones is perceived. This simultaneous auditory grouping binds the isolated
outputs from separate feature extractors into coherent auditory events. The purpose
of this process is to *reconstruct* discrete sound events in the world, which usually have
several correlated acoustical characteristics that happen simultaneously.

This binding of perceptual features is a basic form of association (see Fuster, 1995:
102; Edelman, 1989: 48; Edelman, 1992: 87–90). That is, when particular features
occur together, the groups of neurons that constitute their feature extractors are
thought to communicate with each other (Bharucha, 1999: 425–427).[4] These connected features become a representation of some particular kind of event: a perceptual category. Further occurrences of this kind of event will then be processed
through some of these same groups of neurons. A simplified example of perceptual
binding might be combining the change that indicates the beginning of a note with
its frequency and its tone color (each extracted by different specialized groups of
neurons) to produce the impression of a coherent note starting at a particular time
with a particular frequency and tone color. These note events are the auditory equivalent of visual objects, which are also formed from the binding of separate features
such as edges, shape, color, and texture. This formation of coherent auditory events
from separate acoustical features is a form of perceptual categorization. Categorization is a grouping together of things into a higher-level unit, and in this sense
the binding together of features into a single musical event makes that event a basic
auditory category.

The types of events that ensembles of neurons are tuned to respond to become
more complex as the nerves get farther from the ear and closer to the auditory cortex
(see Goldstein, 1989: 442; Barlow and Mollon, 1982: 300–302). They also become
determined less by immediate sensations and more by the past.

When two or more of these events are close enough together in time or pitch, or are sufficiently similar, the individual auditory events bond together to form a grouping on a still higher level. These groupings of events are called "primitive groupings" because at this stage of information processing, little memory or learned information is involved in their formation: it is an automatic function of early processing (see Bregman, 1990: 18–21, 38–44).[5] We shall consider such groupings in detail in chapter 3.

Thus grouping occurs on a number of levels of memory and perception. To keep the distinction between these levels clear, I shall use the term *pitch event* to refer to grouping at the level of event fusion, where single events are formed out of the fusion of individual vibrations, and shall reserve the term *grouping* for higher-level units consisting of several events.[6]

When events are themselves organized into groupings, these groupings can exhibit patterns that have (1) the melodic quality of pitch patterns, derived from changes in frequency or rate of vibration of different events; and (2) the rhythmic pattern that the events make in time. Both of these dimensions take place on a larger time scale than the formative fusion of individual events, although of course both consist of remembered strings of individual events that have been so formed.

The types of processing discussed above are said to take place at the "bottom" of the perceptual-cognitive system, and this basic and largely involuntary organization is therefore referred to as "bottom-up processing" (see figure 2.1). Bottom-up processing is also referred to as "data-driven processing"; it is based on sensory experience, as opposed to being memory driven. For instance, a sudden change in the frequency of a sound tells us that a new pitch has occurred; this bottom-up response does not have to be learned. The primary function of the kind of bottom-up processing described above is to partition our continuous auditory experience into manageable units for further processing (Bregman, 1990).

It has been established that even very young infants, unable to make higher-level learned groupings, are still able to make primitive groupings of acoustical events— just as they are able to see the shapes, outlines, and colors of visual objects without knowing what they are (see Trehub and Trainor, 1993; Fassbender, 1996: 76–80).[7] From an evolutionary point of view, this grouping mechanism makes sense, because sounds that are related in this way (i.e., close in time, or similar in pitch or quality) tend to come from single sources in the environment, and it is in any organism's survival interest to be able to accurately identify sound sources. Thus our auditory

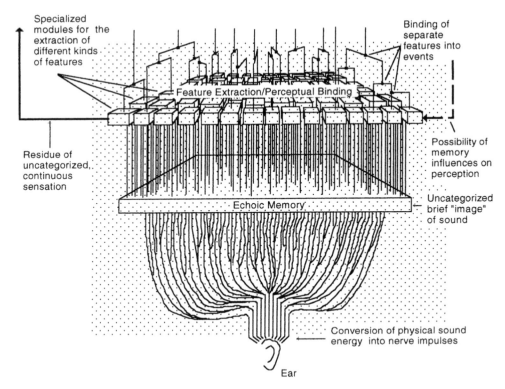

Figure 2.1
Echoic memory and early processing.

perception is optimized to integrate separate events that come from the same source into a single acoustical image of one source making several sounds (Bregman, 1990: 24–36). Again, note that this activity is *reconstructive.* At later stages in the chain, even contradictory groupings can be formed, based on higher-level learning and more complex perceptual forces over time.

Primitive melodic and rhythmic groupings contrast with learned *schema-driven groupings*, which require higher-level processing and interaction with long-term memory for their formation. This interaction is what happens in the processing of experience through long-term memory.[8] This type of processing is said to come from the "top" of the cognitive system (long-term memory), and is referred to as "top-down processing." Note that schema-driven grouping would not be possible without prior primitive grouping, the extraction of basic features that can then be compared with the contents of LTM. Schema-driven grouping will be discussed in later chapters.

Representation and Recognition

Echoic memory is an aspect of early sensory information processing by which a sensory impression persists long enough so that it can be encoded into basic features and bound together into events. According to several recent theories, what is formed at this point are basic perceptual representations of the world and the things in it.[9] These representations are thought to exist as "images," not necessarily specific visual images, but imagelike (i.e., perceptual—it is possible to have a sound or smell or taste image) abstractions that form a basic "picture" of the world.[10] The representations may also constitute a basic form in which many long-term memories are encoded. Existing prior to language and linguistic processing (perhaps also in animal species that do not use language), they may form a kind of prelinguistic syntax of mental representation. Some of these perceptual representations may be difficult to capture in verbal language.[11] Indeed, some of the meaning music conveys may take the form of such representations, which might explain why some aspects of musical meaning seem to resist concise verbal explanation. Memories of verbal language structures may be linked to perceptual representations in a later stage of processing. Language is here viewed as being built on top of this older, more direct form of representation, one that is "grounded" directly in perception (Harnad, 1993). All of which implies that at least some of our long-term memories (and thoughts) take a form that is not primarily linguistic.

Current experience causes the activation of perceptual representations in long-term memory.[12] The process of matching this long-term memory content to current perceptual experience is called "pattern recognition." Note that all of the processes described above, including the activation of the contents of long-term memory, occur very quickly.

Habituation: A Special Form of Recognition

We have seen that recognition involves an interaction between current experience and memory. When this interaction continually produces a perfect match, the phenomenon of *habituation* can occur.[13] When we completely "re-cognize" something, there is no longer any need to consciously process this information because it is already completely familiar to us, which usually causes this information to pass out of the focus of conscious awareness and become part of our perceptual and conceptual background. This means, not that the information is no longer being processed at all, but only that the memory activation it causes is no longer at a level that would place it in conscious awareness (Baars, 1988: 46–49). Aspects of our environment to which we have habituated move into the background of awareness, but are still very much a part of the unconscious context of ongoing experience.

Habituation is a result of the fact that when many types of neurons are stimulated repeatedly with an identical stimulus, their output of impulses does not remain constant, but instead decreases over time. This "adaptation response," found in every kind of organism with a nervous system (even very primitive ones), is the physiological basis of habituation (see Baars, 1988: 194; see also Rieke et al., 1997: 7–9; Davis and Egger, 1992: 237–241). The phenomenon of habituation is truly one of the places where memory and perception become indistinguishable.

Because habituation applies to aspects of experience that are fairly stable and constant or repetitive, aspects of the environment that are the most predictable or constant (and hence that match recent memory) will tend to move into the background, out of the focus of conscious awareness. For example, imagine sitting in a room with an air conditioner. When the air conditioner is turned on, we notice the sound that it makes because it is a change in the environment. After a short time, because it does not change, the sound of the air conditioner will pass out of our awareness and become part of our auditory background. If the air conditioner is turned off, we will again notice it, because the cessation of the sound it makes is another change in the environment. In music, patterns intended to function as background, such as accompaniments, are often more repetitive than patterns intended to function in the foreground. An accompaniment is, after all, a context for the more novel foreground events it accompanies. Thus habituation is one of the primary ways in which *attention* is structured: attention tends to move toward aspects of the environment that are not stable, constant, or predictable.[14]

Note that habituation is based on similarity to what is *already* in memory, and that this applies to *all* levels of memory (Baars, 1988: 192–193). Habituation can occur in relation to single extended events that do not change (habituation in relation to early processing); repetitive patterns of events (habituation in relation to short-term memory); and larger sequences of events that are similar to sequences that have occurred in the past (habituation in relation to long-term memory). Note that at this last, "higher" level of memory, the kinds of things that will be habituated into the background will be much more dependent on personal history, hence much more idiosyncratic. Habituation at each of these levels of memory is based on the match between current experience and memory content; it is hard to remain aware of that which we already know.

Brain Processes and Musical Time

There are limits placed on our perception of events at early points in the processing of acoustical information. It has been mentioned previously that regularly recurring acoustical vibrations that occur more rapidly than once every 50 msec fuse together into a continuous sensation called a "tone" or a "pitch." This is a result of the characteristics of the inner ear; there is a definite limit to our ability to resolve individual acoustical events, that is, to how many separate acoustical events we can process in a given amount of time. In the case of sound, this limit is slightly below 20 events per second. All of the senses have this type of limit, and hearing has the highest level of temporal acuity achieved by any of the senses; vision, for example, is considerably slower.

There are in fact three different time values associated with the process of converting physical sound waves into a perception within the nervous system (see figure 2.2):

1. The *window of simultaneity*, or the threshold time interval below which two audible clicks will seem to be simultaneous. This occurs when the clicks are closer together than 2 msec on average.[15] This value varies somewhat across individuals, and appears to increase slightly with age. In addition, the length of the window of simultaneity is different for different senses, with the interval for sound being the smallest. Two visual stimuli, for example, will still be perceived as simultaneous when separated by an interval as large as 30–40 msec.[16] Thus two events separated by 20 msec would be perceived as two separate events if they were acoustical, but as one event if they were visual. This means that the concept of (subjective) simultaneity itself is not absolute at all, but is *relative*, and depends on what sensory modality we are talking about.

2. The *threshold of order*, or the threshold below which two different events will be heard as separate (nonsimultaneous), but the time order in which they occur is not reliably identifiable (see Eddins and Green, 1995: 218–219). This occurs when the events are separated by a time interval of less than 25 msec (but more than 3 msec).[17] When separated by a time interval longer than this, however, two events

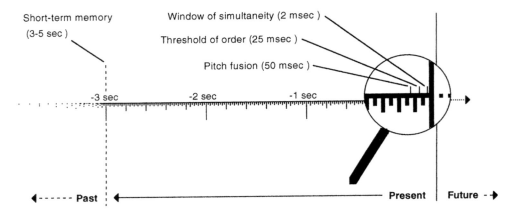

Figure 2.2
Brain processes and musical time.

will be heard as separate, and in the correct time order. The length of the threshold of order appears to be the same for different senses, implying that it is established in the higher centers of the brain, and not in the peripheral nerves of the different senses.

3. The *pitch fusion threshold*,[18] or the time interval below which *chains* of similar acoustical events (not just pairs of events) will fuse together to form a continuous sensation. This occurs when individual events of a chain are separated by less than 50 msec (1/20 sec). Note that the fusion threshold applies to long chains of very similar repeating events that form pitches, and not to isolated pairs of events, as the window of simultaneity does (see Barlow and Mollon, 1982: 244; Warren, 1993: 39). Rapidly repeating chains of similar events are processed differently than isolated pairs of events. For example, 100 clicks all separated by 2 msec (1/-500 sec) would not sound simultaneous (they would form a pitch with a frequency of 500 cps), whereas only two clicks separated by the same distance in time *would* sound simultaneous. Depending on frequency, it takes either more than a certain minimum number of vibrations or a minimum time length for a pitch to be heard.[19]

If we make a tape of regular, separate clicks and replay it, slowly increasing its speed, when we reach a rate of about 16 clicks per second (62.5 msec or 1/16 sec per click), they will begin to turn into a kind of grainy buzz. If we continue to increase the speed of the tape, when we reach 20 clicks per sec, the clicks fuse into a definite pitch. Below this rate, we refer to the "speed" of the clicks, and above this rate, to their "pitch," although in both cases what is changing is exactly the same—the *number of events per second*. Language reflects this change in the quality of experience: below this rate, we speak of "faster" and "slower," and above this rate, of "higher" and "lower." It is important to note that although the *only* thing that changes as we pass from below the 16 cps rate to above it is our own neural processing, the nature of our experience changes dramatically, as reflected in our use of distinctly different descriptive metaphors. At this time scale, the ear and auditory cortex switch over from functioning as an event pattern processor to functioning as a more holistic waveform processor.

Keep in mind that the window of simultaneity and pitch fusion threshold are established by processes occurring in the nerves in or near the ear, whereas the order threshold is established in the brain itself.[20] This is why the window of simultaneity and fusion thresholds can be different for different senses, whereas the order thresholds remain the same (Poppel, 1988: 8–40).

The musical time level referred to here as the "level of event fusion"—the level at which vibration events too fast to be heard individually in and of themselves are fused together to form actual audible events—is associated with echoic memory and early processing. We shall now look at how those events themselves group together to form groupings and phrases.

Notes

1. For a good thumbnail sketch and simplified diagram of the early processes in the auditory cortex, see Roederer, 1979, pp. 57–60. See also Handel, 1989, pp. 478–481; McAdams, 1993, p. 150.

2. As part of "phyletic" memory, these feature extractors have evolved over a long period of time and become tuned to biologically significant features of the environment. They appear to be innate, and not learned, and different for different species. This is the most basic kind of auditory categorical perception. For more on this, see Barlow and Mollon, 1982, pp. 300–302; Buser and Imbert, 1992, pp. 315–316.

3. While not completely understood at this time, it is probably the case that this perceptual "remainder" may be brought into the focus of conscious awareness (in figure 1.1, this possibility is represented by the heavy line connecting the feature extraction stage directly to short-term memory), which is related to the idea of nuance, treated in chapter 7. See McAdams, 1993, pp. 192–194. What is being presented here could be called an "early categorization" theory because the process of categorization is hypothesized as occurring early in the chain of auditory processes. There are also "late categorization" theories. See for instance McAdams, 1993, p. 156.

4. It is currently thought that features of a coherent event are bound together by synchronous electrical activity between the groups of neurons representing those features. See Singer, 1996, pp. 101–130; Crick, 1994, pp. 208–214. Feature extraction is a difficult concept to sustain "all the way up" with features simply becoming more and more complex. That is, it is unlikely that memory is organized in such a way that it converges on single feature-extracting neurons for very high-level features such as entire objects or scenes. For more about this "grandmother cell" idea, see Gazzaniga et al., 1998, pp. 167–169. Alternatively, complex memories may be represented by ensembles of relatively low-level feature extractors combined in different ways. For a discussion of the merits of various models, see Fotheringhame and Young, 1997, pp. 49–54.

5. Note that top-down (memory) factors, most notably, a previously established patterning of the same sounds that are currently occurring, may influence grouping. This is often referred to as "parallelism."

6. To some extent, the term *pitch event* corresponds to what would be referred to as a "note," although, as its name implies, "note" really describes a written symbol, not a sound. Nor, by any means, does a pitch event always correspond exactly to a note. See Gerdingen, 1988, for a classic article about the difficulties of the note concept in relation to non-Western music.

7. In fact, the hearing of infants is initially much better than their sight.

8. For an interesting discussion of the early history of the concept of this type of filter or selection process see Lachman, Lachman, and Butterfield, 1979, pp. 183–209.

9. I am well aware that the nature of the forms representations take in memory is a largely unsettled issue in cognitive psychology and philosophy of mind. See Barsalou, 1993; Harnad, 1993; Edelman, 1989, pp. 141–142; and Baars, 1988, p. 262. Some theorists consider perceptual representations to be a separate form of memory. See Schacter and Tulving, 1994, p. 26. For a discussion of some contemporary ideas about mental representation, see Gopnik and Meltzoff, 1997, pp. 49–72.

10. For a good discussion of ideas about the nature of perceptual "images," see Palmer, 1996, pp. 46–51.

11. There are documented cases of people who have never learned verbal language or conventional sign language because of congenital deafness, and who have nonetheless been relatively functional socially. Undoubtedly, these people have thoughts and images. See Schaller, 1991; and Donald, 1991.

12. A recent view (Rosenfield, 1988) is that this comparison takes place because the present is processed *through* long-term memory, that is, the neural connections previously established to process a particular kind of information are again used to process a similar situation in the present. See also McClelland, 1995, pp. 69–70; and Edelman, 1989, pp. 110–112.

13. This matching process is part of what is is meant by saying that perception is processed "through" long-term memory. The current incoming perception resonates with a representation already in memory by being processed by some of the same groups of neurons that comprise that representation. For an explication of a possible relation between this process and perceptual symbolic representations in long-term memory, see Barsalou, 1993, pp. 60–61.

14. Note that this is a *bottom-up* definition of attention. Attention can of course also be driven by *top-down* forces: we can also *choose* to focus on repetitive background events.

15. Poppel (1988) gives the window of simultaneity a value of 3–4 msec; this is very close to the value of 3 msec given by Hirsh (1961). Also see Eddins and Green, 1995, pp. 219–223. Note that this figure represents the amount of time needed to distinguish between the onsets of two sounds of known identity. It is also undoubtedly the case that order on this very short time scale is perceived "holistically." That is, different orders of events have a different overall quality, almost like a timbre, rather than being heard as two completely discrete events.

16. The visual system is slower to respond than the auditory because the photoreceptor nerves in the retina operate by a chemical mechanism inherently slower than the mechanical mechanism of the ear.

17. A different threshold of order based on the ability to *name* (identify) individual sounds in groupings of more than two is given by Warren (1999: 117–133) at 200 msec.

18. Note that the term *pitch fusion threshold* should not be confused with the term *fusion threshold*, which is sometimes used instead of the term *window of simultaneity*.

19. It has been established that below 1,000 cps, it takes a minimum of 3 *cycles* to create the sensation of pitch, whereas above this frequency, it requires that the pitch be present for some minimum *amount of time*, which gets longer with decreasing frequency (about 10 msec at 2,000 cps). See Buser and Imbert, 1992, pp. 59–60.

20. This has been established by clinical evidence indicating that brain injury increases the values of the order threshold, but not the window of simultaneity. See Poppel, 1988, pp. 20–21.

3

Grouping

To say that something in the world is "organized" is really just a way of saying that it lies within the limits of the processing capability of the human nervous system. The organization of our experience often correlates with the order of the physical world because the human nervous system has evolved to comprehend and survive in that world (Shepard, 1987). We shall now explore some of the ways in which sequences of sounds can be organized.

One of the main problems the auditory system has to solve is how to take the single continuous variation in air pressure present at each ear and, from this, form a representation of all the separate sound sources present. This is a truly remarkable achievement. We hear many levels of organized patterns in speech, music, and environmental sounds that are not obvious in the physical sound waves themselves (Bregman, 1993: 12–14). Rather than hearing completely isolated sounds or an undifferentiated continuum, we hear phonemes, words, sentences, melodies, rhythms, and phrases, all consisting of parts that seem related despite their taking place at different frequencies and at different times. We can also hear the wind blowing, a bird singing, an automobile engine starting, and someone speaking as four separate sounds, even if they are all occurring simultaneously. If this were not the case, all we would ever hear would be a single sound, consisting of the sum of all sounds present at a given moment. These levels of organization are the result of certain aspects of our own perception, cognition, and memory.

By *grouping*, I mean the natural tendency of the human nervous system to segment acoustical information from the outside world into *units*, whose components seem related forming some kind of *wholes*.[1] A grouping is to melodic, rhythmic, or formal organization what an object is to visual and spatial organization—a coherent entity within a set of boundaries. Grouping factors in early processing can favor segmentation or continuity—every musical event either develops a connection with the previous event or separates itself from it to some degree. Control of the relative segmentation or continuity of patterns is one of the primary ways music can be made to be dynamic and push forward in time.

Because sound is inherently temporal, the boundaries of auditory events are defined by various degrees of *change*. The primitive bottom-up grouping effects that help us construct auditory events seem to be remarkably consistent across different individuals, which suggests that they are not learned, but are innate, the result of evolution.[2] For instance, a change in pitch of a sound is an event that will be heard by all listeners, and we cannot by an effort of will not hear that it has happened. As a basic "chunking" mechanism, grouping forms sensations into units that can be stored and later remembered. Features or aspects of sounds that are *simultaneous* or nearly so can be grouped or fused into *events*, and events themselves can be grouped over time into event *sequences*.

Primitive and Learned Grouping

There are two very general ways in which grouping of events can occur. In addition to primitive grouping, there is *learned grouping*, sometimes referred to as "schema-driven grouping," formed top-down from memory factors, usually taking place on a larger time scale than primitive grouping.

Primitive grouping factors are primarily determined by the structure of the human nervous system itself, and the ways it has evolved to understand the world around us.[3] This chapter will concern itself primarily with primitive grouping effects.

Primitive grouping processes always function in the same way: we have little control over them (although we can sometimes reinterpret their output in the light of further memory-related processing). Basic features, such as frequency, amplitude, and boundaries where events begin and end, are detected in the earliest stage of processing, feature extraction, which extracts cues that can be recognized by higher-level processing (long-term memory). These basic features are bound into events by *simultaneous* grouping processes, and these events are then themselves grouped together over a longer time span by *sequential* grouping processes. In this book, we shall be primarily concerned with sequential grouping; when not otherwise qualified, "grouping" will refer to sequential grouping from now on.

Primitive grouping is considered a "bottom-up" process because it operates on the perceptual data at the input or "bottom" of the perceptual-cognitive system, which in this case is the ear. Bottom-up processing involves only the immediate present (echoic and short-term memory). This is in contrast to "top-down" processing that usually operates on the data *after* primative grouping has taken place, and involves long-term memory.

The grouping that is the result of top-down processing with long-term memory constitutes the second kind of grouping effects, called "learned" or "schema-driven grouping effects." Much higher-level structure in music is comprehended by means of top-down processing, whose results, because they are based on individual learning and musical culture, are more idiosyncratic than those of bottom-up processing. When top-down processing is involved, what listeners perceive is dependent to a large degree on their previous experience. This means that higher levels of the organization of music (relationships over longer time spans) are something that is reconstructed by listeners according to their experience, influenced along lines laid down by the musician who created it. In light of this, at least for music that has communication as its goal, what a musician does is to try to create structures that give listeners the cues they need to reconstruct the patterns the musician intends them to hear.

Learned grouping effects, which are comprehended using long-term memory categories and schemas, always operate within a realm *already known* to varying degrees. An example of this would be recognizing a particular musical pattern we have heard several minutes earlier as a unit because we have heard it before. All learned groupings are formed from features that were originally primitively grouped. This makes primitive grouping especially important when dealing with materials that are unfamiliar because it enables long-term memory schemas to be built up out of basic features.

Primitive Grouping

When some aspect of the acoustical environment changes sufficiently, a boundary is created. This boundary defines where a grouping begins or ends, and is the most basic kind of feature that is detected in the earliest stages of perception. Often referred to as "closure," the establishment of grouping boundaries is the quality that makes a grouping seem relatively self-contained and separate from other groupings. Closure is not necessarily absolute: Groupings may exhibit many degrees of closure. This is a basic way in which some groupings are related to others, forming higher level *groupings of groupings*. Partial closure is a very important force in developing hierarchical structure in music and language, and will be dealt with in detail later.

A number of factors are relevant to what kinds of groupings result in a given situation. Viewed in relation to the evolution of the nervous system, it is interesting to note that all of these factors tend to favor sounds that come from single sources. That is, the kinds of acoustical features and events the brain tends to group together are the kind that would be likely to come from a single source. This is part of the way in which the nervous system reconstructs acoustical images of a world that consists primarily of coherent sound sources. Regularity is an important factor in this: the nervous system tends to look for characteristics that coherent sound sources regularly possess. Thus a rapid change in loudness usually signals a new event: single sound sources in the environment tend to change amplitude slowly. Also, different components of coherent sound sources usually begin together: it is rare that separate sound sources in the environment begin to produce sounds at exactly the same time. From this, our primitive grouping mechanisms create the experience that if there is a rapid change in loudness, a new event has occurred, and that if several sounds in the environment start simultaneously, they are part of the same single event.

Basic sequential grouping principles manifest themselves in several different ways. Sounds may be grouped in either the melodic or the rhythmic dimension, and usually grouping forces are operative in both these dimensions at the same time (see Jones, 1993).[4] While both dimensions take place within the limits of short-term memory, the basic segmentation of the boundaries of individual musical events takes place before this, in the early processing stage of perception.

Although similarity groupings can be assigned to larger time relations, as they are at the formal level, this is the result of representation in long-term memory and does not happen in the same way as it does at the other two levels. It involves the past. Hence we shall consider the formal level later, in chapter 13. Figure 3.1 illustrates the relation between the three levels of grouping and the three kinds of memory defined previously, as well as the kinds of groupings formed. A dot indicates a single, pitched musical event, and grouping boundaries are indicated by the spaces between brackets.

Grouping and Short-Term Memory

A distinction should be made at this point between grouping principles and the limits of short-term memory. Remember that the formation of boundaries takes place in the early processing stage, *before* information persists as short-term

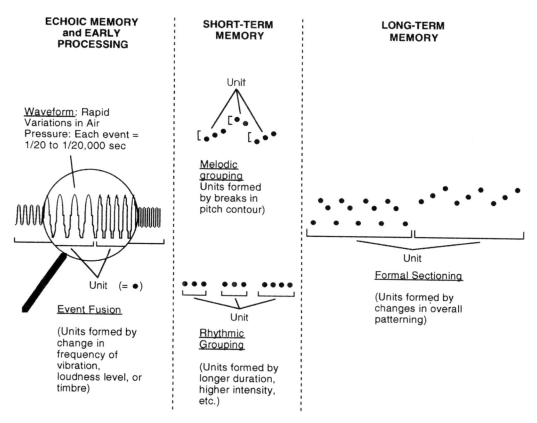

Figure 3.1
Levels of sequential grouping: Event fusion, melodic and rhythmic grouping, and formal sectioning. Note that pattern formation at each level requires comparison of events over increasing time spans. Event fusion requires comparison within 250 msec, melodic and rhythmic patterns require comparison across a time span of from 250 msec to 5 sec, and formal sections require comparisons across a time span of from 5 sec to as much as 1 hour. Also note that each individual unit at one level becomes a part of a unit at the next level up.

memory. This means that although a single grouping cannot exceed the time limit of short-term memory, grouping is *independent* of the structure of STM: *more than one* melodic or rhythmic grouping may exist within the time limit of STM. Thus, several groupings that have weak closure between them could cohere and form different parts of a higher level of grouping called a "phrase," and this phrase could still fit within the time and content limits of STM.

In addition to having a time limit, short-term memory also has a content limit of from five to nine (7 ± 2) *different elements*; seven on average.[5] The term *element* here refers to any of the basic elements in a sequence; each element may consist of more than one of the same item without necessarily increasing memory load. This is the size of the basic STM "chunk." Because "chunking" is a hierarchical process, an element in this sense may be a grouping that itself consists of five to nine elements. A musical phrase of STM length may then consist of several groupings of notes. The upper limit on how many events can comprise a phrase is probably about five groupings of five events each, or about twenty-five events, depending on how it is organized.

How the elements of a phrase are arranged can have a powerful effect on the "chunkability" and hence memorability of that phrase. For example, although we cannot quickly memorize and repeat the sequence of letters cbdacadcbadbcdab, if we rearrange the same letters as bacdbcadbaadbccd, the repetition of certain features creates boundaries, hence groupings, which make the new sequence easier to memorize and repeat. Not only are the letters "b" and "d" repeated at the start and finish of each grouping but the groupings are all the same size. All of this repetition *reduces* memory load and makes the pattern easier to remember. We no longer have to remember the pattern as a continuous series of completely separate items: it now has some clear boundaries within it. Although the number of letters is the same as in the first sequence, there are now only four elements, or "chunks" and the pattern is relatively easy to memorize. Because of this, this sequence could be said to be "more organized" than the first. Remember that items are maintained in short-term memory by rehearsal; when there is repetition present, each repeated occurrence of an element is somewhat like a rehearsal of its other occurrences. Even easier to memorize than the above example would be bacdbacdbacdbacd, where there is only one chunk repeated four times. In this case, the first grouping is literally a rehearsal of the others, and the association between them is very strong. Thus, in general, repetition greatly enhances chunkability, hence memorability. Repetitions of similar pitch or rhythmic groupings in music have the same effect as the repetition in the above sequences of letters. This repetition means that there is literally less to remember. This also demonstrates another principle: by no means do all distributions of the same events form the same groupings. Groupings are usually formed by the most organized possibility available at a given moment.

Grouping can take place on different levels. Musical notes, groupings, phrases, sections, movements, and pieces each define a different level of grouping, and each of these levels may use repetition for its organization to a different degree.

Note that although grouping boundaries are not formed by short-term memory, musical groupings are often created by composers so as to fit within the limitations of STM, thus giving their music a clearer and more memorable structure. The level of musical grouping which is most directly related to short-term memory is the *phrase*.

Groupings and Phrases

I shall refer to the smallest grouping of individual musical events in time (usually five events or fewer)—at the lowest level—as either a "melodic grouping" or a "rhythmic grouping."[6] The boundaries of *melodic* groupings are established by changes in relative pitch distance (interval), direction of motion, or both, whereas the boundaries of *rhythmic* groupings are established by changes in time interval between events, and accents. All of the above grouping factors are probably established in the early processing phase of perception (Edelman, Gall, and Cowan, 1988).

Melodic and rhythmic groupings usually consist of a small number of events (five or fewer) related by proximity or similarity and by continuity. Both melodic and rhythmic groupings usually take place at the same time and may conflict or agree about where grouping boundaries are (see figure 3.2). Because there may be different interpretations in cases of conflict between grouping principles, we should view them, not as absolute, but as *preferences* (Lerdahl and Jackendoff, 1983: 39–42). Thus, in situations where several grouping principles happen at the same time and conflict with each other, the grouping a particular person may hear on a particular occasion is not always completely predictable.

The next higher level of musical grouping, which represents a grouping *of* groupings, is called a "phrase." The difference between melodic and rhythmic groupings, on the one hand, and phrases, on the other, is that closure is usually established

Congruence of temporal proximity and melodic leap.

Conflict between temporal proximity and melodic leap. (Proximity dominates.)

Figure 3.2
Conflict of grouping forces.

more completely at the phrase level. Indeed, melodic and rhythmic groupings usually cohere into phrases because of the low degree of closure that is established at the lowest grouping level. Rather than causing a complete break into completely separate units, grouping boundaries provide the detailed features of the melodic and rhythmic contour of a phrase. This is the weakest form of closure, which might be described as "soft" closure. These boundaries can take the form of leaps in pitch interval, changes in duration, loudness, articulation, tone color, and so on. Roughly parallel phenomena can be found in the grouping of the units of language. A sentence consists of phrases, separated from other phrases by pauses, like musical phrases; each phrase consists of words, which are like melodic and rhythmic groupings; and each word consists of phonemes, which cohere like the individual notes of a grouping.

Melodic or rhythmic grouping boundaries are usually established by changes in one basic parameter, such as pitch contour or duration, whereas phrase boundaries, are usually reinforced by changes in *more than one* parameter. A phrase boundary, for instance, could be formed by a pause and by the last event of the phrase having a longer duration than any other event in the phrase (see figure 3.3).

Note that the distinction between grouping and phrase is not absolute. Thus a single grouping isolated by pauses could function as a phrase; it would simply be a single grouping, with no further internal closure. As mentioned before, phrases are the largest unit of musical material that can be accommodated by short-term memory. Because phrases are therefore also the largest units of musical experience that can be completely integrated in the present, a theme designed to function as a unit to be transformed is usually no longer than a phrase.

Musical phrases are also often linked to some variable of human physiology, such as how many events can be produced in a single breath on a wind instrument, or

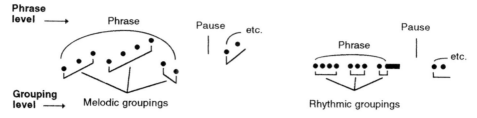

Figure 3.3
Melodic and rhythmic grouping.

in a single bowing movement of a stringed instrument. In this way, a musical structural rhythm is superimposed on a basic rhythm of human physiology. These are single coherent physical gestures, and it is worth noting that the action components of physical gestures are also "chunked." Thus memory limitations on the size of the units comprising coherent physical gestures are also related to the structure of short-term memory.

Any articulated structural unit of music larger than a phrase, such as a linked group of phrases, takes place on what I have called the "formal level." The distinction that separates the formal from the melodic and rhythmic level is the use of long-term memory. Note that in figure 1.1, the boundary between these two levels occurs at a time length somewhere between 8 and 16 sec, which corresponds to the length of the longest musical phrases. Our cognition of any units larger than this depends on reconstruction outside the time the events themselves occur. Of course, previously heard phrases do not completely disappear immediately. We can still have a sense of their similarity or difference with what we are currently hearing, and we may remember some striking features. Generally speaking, however, the farther away in time a phrase is, the more schematic our memory of it will be.

The nervous system functions to reconstruct representations of coherent sound sources in the environment: groupings and phrases are coherent auditory entities. We shall now examine some of the factors that help to establish that coherence.

Proximity

An aspect of grouping discovered by the Gestalt psychologists in the 1920s, the *principle of proximity* states that events close together in time (within the limits of short-term memory) will tend to be grouped together (see Goldstein, 1989: 403–406; Handel, 1989: 185–189; Bregman, 1990: 196–198).[7] Proximity is a very

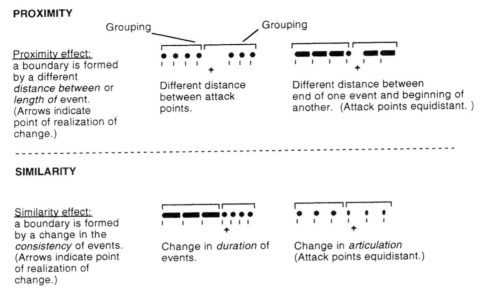

Figure 3.4
Temporal grouping.

powerful factor, an dca nof teno verr idel earne dpa tt erns. As the preceding phrase clearly demonstrates, in a conflict between primitive grouping by visual proximity and learned grouping by text, primitive grouping by proximity prevails.

In the ongoing flow of acoustical events, a slight difference in timing can form a temporal grouping boundary as well as a large difference can—it is the *change* in distance that is important. All other things being equal, an increase in time interval between the beginnings of two events in a sequence will establish a grouping boundary. This is the grouping principle of temporal proximity, which is a primary grouping force at the melodic and rhythmic level (see figure 3.4). Note that of all the primitive grouping factors, temporal proximity appears to have the strongest effects and can often prevail over other grouping factors (Lerdahl and Jackendoff, 1983: 47).

Similarity

Second factor in primitive grouping is the *principle of similarity*, which states that sounds perceived as being similar will tend to be grouped together. Similarity may be

SIMILARITY

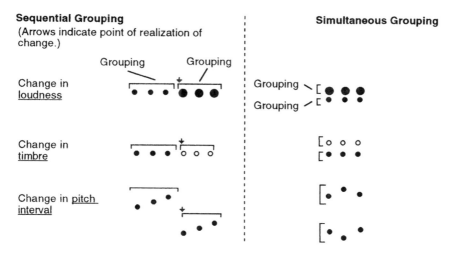

Figure 3.5
Acoustical grouping.

heard in any characteristic quality of a sound where what constitutes proximity is not clear, such as loudness, timbre, articulation, pitch interval, and duration.[8]

Similarity can create grouping in both vertical and horizontal dimensions of music. That is, similarity may act to form groupings of sounds that are *simultaneous*. Groupings that are the result of vertical segmentation are called "streams." From the point of view of biological adaptation, the similarity principle makes sense because sounds that are similar will usually tend to be coming from a single source.

Similarity can be perceived on several levels. At the event fusion level, the individual vibration events that fuse together to make up a single pitch event do so because they are sufficiently similar to each other. The single pitch that we hear is thus a higher-level grouping of events on a different time level. Multiple pitches also group in melodic space. Changes in the contour of pitch sequences will tend to cause melodic segmentation into separate groupings, and pitches that move in similar intervals will tend to group together (see figure 3.5). Larger changes in pitch range can cause the phenomenon of *melodic streaming*, (discussed in detail in chapter 11). Events similar in timbre, loudness, duration, and articulation may also be grouped. Although not melodic in the strictest sense, these grouping factors appear to involve processes much like those involved in melodic grouping.

Note that in figures 3.4 and 3.5, grouping preference rules are presented as being *temporal* or *acoustical* as well as involving proximity and similarity. That is, they may involve differences either in timing or in the acoustical qualities of the sounds. Acoustical grouping boundaries are grasped immediately with the occurrence of the changed event, whereas temporal grouping boundaries are grasped at a *slightly later time* from that of the changed event, a distinction indicated by the small arrows in figure 3.4. These arrows are in a slightly different place from the front edge of the second bracket which represents where the boundary is perceived to be located. In figure 3.5, on the other hand, the arrows and the space between the brackets are in the same place.[9] Thus temporal and acoustical grouping may use somewhat different processing mechanisms (Deliege, 1987: 356). It is worth noting that in some cases, two boundary positions may exist for the same pattern based on whether similarity or proximity is the deciding factor.

At the rhythmic level, events form groupings in time based on changes in degree of accent, and time interval between events. At the formal level, entire sequences of patterns of events can be similar to each other, and because of this, similarity can function as an organizing principle over large time lengths.

Orchestration in many orchestral music traditions is basically an application of the principle of similarity. Structural details meant to be heard as related and grouped together are orchestrated using the same instruments, and formal contrasts are delineated using changes of orchestration. Indeed, the concept of instrument is essentially one of similarity—an instrument is a sound source that produces a number of different sounds perceived as being somehow similar to each other and heard as coming from the same source. The traditional division of the European orchestra into "families" of instruments is a basic acoustical organization based on the similarity of the sounds produced by instruments of different size, but similar construction. In this way, the concept of an individual instrument is extended outward in range. This family organization is also reflected in the grouping together of these instruments in the graphic structure of the score and in the actual seating patterns of the orchestra's players. Thus similarity in all of its forms is a major factor in the establishment of higher-level formal groupings in much music.

Continuity

A third factor in primitive grouping, and another principle discovered by the Gestalt psychologists, is basically an extension of the principles of proximity and of simi-

Figure 3.6
Grouping by continuity. Melodic groupings (a, b, and c) cohere as long as motion continues in a similar direction in similar intervals.

larity. The *principle of continuity* states that when a series of events consistently (continuously) changes value in a particular direction in units of similar size, the events will tend to form groupings. In other words, consistent (continuous) movement in a particular direction tends to perpetuate itself in the same direction. This is an interesting extension of the idea of similarity: not only can events be similar to each other, so can *relations between* events. In music, this means we can have similarity in interval of motion. Thus a group of pitches will tend to form a melodic grouping if they move in the same direction in intervals of similar size (figure 3.6), as will a group of rhythmic events that are separated by a uniform time interval. Note that in music, complete continuity of pitch interval and direction of motion does not usually last for very long. Music does not usually just move in a continuous, scalar way. One possible reason for this, apart from memory-chunking considerations, is that extended, unsegmented continuity is simply not very interesting. Continuity is an important aspect of linearity (discussed in greater detail in chapter 13).

Higher-Level Grouping Factors

Other kinds of grouping factors operate on a larger time scale, hence at a higher level, than those shown thus far. Three are worth mentioning here.

Intensification, which occurs when several factors that could lead to a grouping boundary happen at the same time, usually operates at the phrase level or higher. Note that in figure 3.3, the end of one of the phrases is marked both by an event of longer duration and by a pause. This intensification is the result of two different grouping principles operating simultaneously, and creates a higher-level grouping boundary than either of the principles would alone. Intensification is usually the factor that differentiates phrases from melodic or rhythmic groupings. In general, the more grouping forces causing segmentation at a given point, the more likely a higher-level boundary will be created.

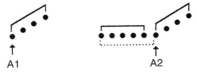

Figure 3.7
Grouping by parallelism. Event A2 would normally be heard as part of the series of similar
repeating events (as shown by the dotted line), but instead, because A1 has been previously
established as part of the upward-moving grouping, is likely to be heard as part of the four-
event grouping (as shown by the upper bracket).

A second higher-level grouping factor, *parallelism* often operates on whole groupings, rather than on event-to-event transitions, and usually involves long-term
memory. When a grouping of events is similar to a previous grouping of events,
grouping boundaries will often form in such a way as to emphasize that similarity.
In figure 3.7, the event marked "A2" would normally be grouped with other events
preceding it that are at the same pitch and rhythmically equidistant, indicated by
the dotted line bracket below it. In this case, however, A2 would probably be
grouped with the events that *follow* it because of parallelism with the pitch A1 in
the previous upward-moving grouping, indicated by the bracket above it. Parallelism is a higher-level similarity of *pattern*, not just of events. It is also an example
of how long-term memory can affect grouping. An interesting question arises in
relation to parallelism. When does a pattern *stop* being similar to another pattern?
This relates to the range of transformations and variation of materials that are possible in music. There is, of course, no simple answer to this question, although a
kind of long-term proximity effect may be one factor. That is, the closer together
two patterns appear in a piece of music, the easier it is to recognize their similarity, and hence the more different they may be and still be recognized as similar. On
the other hand, two patterns that are far apart in a piece of music must be very
similar for their similarity to be apparent (hence the concept of exact recapitulation). As they occur on larger and larger time scales, parallelism effects gradually
shade into the network of memory associations that operate all across a piece of
music (referred to below as "objective set").

A grouping boundary can also be established by the recurrence of a pitch central
to a tonality—a third higher-level grouping factor and one requiring long-term
memory to remember that the central pitch has occurred frequently, and in important places.

Set

Because they involve long-term memory, learned grouping effects operate at a "higher level" and take place further along in the nervous system than primitive grouping effects. It is worth noting that these primitive and learned grouping effects may sometimes be placed in conflict.

For our purposes, learned grouping effects can be subdivided into

(1) *objective set*, grouping effects established in and unique to a particular piece of music, which are learned during the course of listening to a particular piece, and which have to do with expectations unique to and established *during that piece*, such as recognizing a musical theme and its transformations; and

(2) *subjective set*, grouping effects that are part of a *style*, which are learned during the course of listening to *many* pieces, and which involve expectations established across many pieces that are *similar* in some way. Knowing that a particular kind of section is about to happen in a particular kind of piece would be an example of subjective set[10]. Making this kind of expectation possible is one of the functions of traditional musical forms. Traditions form frameworks within which deviations from stylistic norms can be appreciated and remembered. Traditions of this kind are one aspect of a musical culture.

Objective set relies on what is immediately (objectively) present within a piece to establish grouping, whereas subjective set uses longer-term (subjective) memory to compare basic style characteristics of that and other pieces (Tenny, 1988: 44). Both mental sets are essentially collections of expectations, with objective set shading into the larger time scale of subjective set. These expectations consist of semiactivated long-term memories that usually operate outside conscious awareness but have a direct effect on our ongoing perception. Depending as they do on long-term memory, objective and subjective set will tend to vary between different individuals. Both kinds of set are partly the result of the musical culture that particular listeners belong to.

Because learned grouping effects of the subjective type are unique to the syntax of a particular style, they will not be dealt with in detail in this book. On the other hand, because the human nervous system has the same characteristics everywhere, primitive grouping effects and some aspects of objective set should operate in a similar way in most forms of music. These grouping effects and their use in music are therefore a main subject of this book.

Notes

1. For a very extended discussion of auditory grouping and streaming research, see Bregman, 1990.

2. I am well aware of the controversial status of the term *innate*. I am using it here to mean an aspect of perception that does not seem to depend entirely on prior experience. No assumption is made about how this is achieved (e.g., inherited neural architectures, or an innate disposition "tuned by experience"). See Elman et al., 1998, pp. 1–46. In relation to infants' perception of Gestalt grouping factors, see Fassbender, 1996, pp. 73–74. For a description of research that seems to establish acoustical streaming as innate, see Mehler and Dupoux, 1994, pp. 68–69.

3. For a somewhat more detailed picture of how this early processing is broken down, see Roederer, 1979, pp. 57–60; Barlow and Mollon, 1982, p. 252.

4. Note, however, that there is some neurological evidence that these dimensions are processed separately and integrated at a fairly late stage in cognitive processing. See Peretz, 1993, pp. 216–223.

5. The term *element* here refers to the different kinds of events in a sequence; an element may be repeated without seriously increasing memory load. For example, the sequences abcd and abbcdd have the same number of constituent elements (four), but different numbers of actual items or events.

6. In traditional musical analysis, this lowest level of grouping is often termed a *motive* or *motif*, although the terms *cell* and *figure* have also been used. See Nattiez, 1990, p. 157.

7. Gestalt theory has undergone a great deal of reevaluation since its ideas were originally introduced in the 1920s. It is now thought that Gestalt phenomena are the result, not of a single, but of several perceptual or cognitive processes. For an overview of the status of Gestalt theory at present, see Hochberg, 1998.

8. It is not absolutely clear, however, when proximity ends and similarity begins. See Bregman, 1990, pp. 197–98.

9. There is a subtle distinction here between *where* the grouping boundary is perceived as being and *when* it is perceived as being there. It appears that temporal grouping effects are perceived at least somewhat retroactively, whereas acoustical effects are perceived at the point of the boundary itself. See Deliege, 1987.

10. The terms *objective set* and *subjective set* are from Tenny, 1988. Leonard Meyer uses the terms *intraopus* and *interopus* to mean roughly the same thing. See Meyer, 1989, pp. 24–30. Meyer also makes a number of more subtle distinctions in relation to these concepts. In fact this book is a very thorough presentation of Meyer's ideas about traditions of musical syntax.

4
Short-Term and Working Memory

It is clear that people consciously remember things in at least two different ways. There are memories that last only a few seconds before being forgotten, and there are memories that can still be recalled after a number of years.

The more durable memories, which may take as much as several months to form, involve our *long-term memory* (LTM). We also have another type of memory that is much more immediate but much less permanent, *short-term memory* (STM), our memory of the very recent past (see Anderson, 1990: 150–156; Barsalou, 1992: 95–103). It lasts 3–5 sec on average, although this depends somewhat on the relative novelty and complexity of the material to be remembered.

Short-term memory differs from long-term memory in that it does not cause permanent anatomical or chemical changes in the connections between neurons, as long-term memory is thought to do (Squire and Kandel, 1999: 131). A metaphor used by Karl Lashley, and later by Donald Hebb, to explain short-term memory was one of reverberation: a pattern of recirculating electrical energy that reverberates through reentrant loops of neural circuitry, sustaining the current pattern of activity (see Orbach, 1998: 25–31). Like actual acoustical reverberation, if new energy is not introduced into the process (in this case in the form of rehearsal), it soon fades out. The time limit of short-term memory is how long this circulating pattern of energy can be maintained *without* rehearsal. Note that the difference between echoic and short-term memory (in addition to time limit) is that the contents of STM are not primarily raw sensations, but activated categorized memories—this is true in both perception and remembering.

Short-term memory is a type of memory *process*, and in this sense there is probably more than one short-term memory. STM processes may exist at least for language, visual object recognition, spatial relations, nonlinguistic sounds, and physical movement (Jonides and Smith, 1997: 263–265). STM is referred to as unitary because all of these modalities have been shown to have roughly the same time and information capacity limitations.[1] Events in short-term memory persist *in a serial time order*, and STM is essential for integrating events over time. Indeed, it is our primary way of comprehending the time sequences of events in our experience.

Although our processing of experience may be cyclical and occur in some sort of discrete frames (Baars, 1988: 96–97, 115), our experience seems continuous. Short-term memory functions to smooth our experience out and make it seem continuous. Each frame persists for a time, fades, and is continuously related to others coming immediately after it while retaining its proper time order. At the same time, new memory and experiences are almost always fading in. In this way, separate "chunks" of experience are integrated into an ongoing, unified world. This allows us to make movements such as rapidly turning our head yet perceive the world around us as staying the same. Indeed, it is thought that short-term memory evolved along with the capacity for smooth sequences of movements (Edelman, 1987: 230–235). The construction of a smooth, continuous present probably depends as much on a capacity for smooth motion as it does on memory.

Information that comes to the focus of conscious awareness and short-term memory has at least two aspects: perception and long-term memory. Vivid current perceptual information persists after early processing and is overlaid with activated conceptual information from LTM.[2]

The process of semiactivated long-term memory becoming highly activated and coming into consciousness has been described as being metaphorically similar to the visual phenomenon of focus and peripheral vision (see Chafe, 1994: 53–54).[3] In this model, the peripheral part of consciousness consists of semiactivated memory associations fading *in* at a given time and information at the time limit of short-term memory fading *out* of consciousness, and *priming* new memory associations. The term *priming* here refers to the relatively low-level activation of further associations, which then have a higher probability of becoming fully activated. The central focus of conscious awareness would be the most highly activated part of STM. All of this activity together is often referred to as "working memory" (see figure 4.1).[4] The contents of working memory form an important part of the ongoing context of experience. Working memory is distinguished from short-term memory in that it consists of processes at various levels of activation, including the focus of conscious awareness, not just short-term storage. (STM is one of the components of working memory.)

Although much of the content of short-term memory is activated long-term memory, not all the long-term memory that a given experience evokes becomes fully

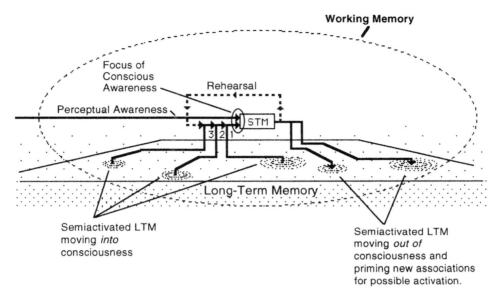

Working Memory

Focus of
Conscious
Awareness

Rehearsal

Perceptual Awareness

STM

3 2 1

Long-Term Memory

Semiactivated LTM
moving *into*
consciousness

Semiactivated LTM
moving *out of*
consciousness and
priming new associations
for possible activation.

Figure 4.1
Working memory.

activated and moves into consciousness. For example, I may have a feeling that the
section of a piece of music coming up next is in a higher pitch register, but I may not
remember anything else about it: I may remember only a single feature of it. This is
an example of *expectation*, a memory cued by present experience, but not fully conscious. With expectations, we can "feel" the future in the present. Because this imagination of the future is only semiactivated, however, it does not interfere with our
perception of the present: we hear it "out of the corner of our minds' ear."

Working memory thus consists of immediate perceptions and related activated
long-term memories, as well as contextual information that is semiactivated but not
in consciousness and information that has just been in consciousness. Because it
includes things both on the fringe and at the center of consciousness, working
memory is not entirely identical to consciousness.[5]

Limitations of Short-Term Memory

Much of the way we structure various forms of communication, and much of the
way we see the world, is a result of the limitations of short-term memory. Note that

in figures 1.1 and 4.1, short-term memory is depicted as being very small relative to long-term memory. From this, it should be obvious that STM is a real bottleneck in the information-processing capability of the memory system, both in its time limit and in its information capacity.[6] Indeed, compared to the information capacity of the sensory systems (visual, auditory, etc.), echoic memory, and long-term memory, the information capacity of short-term memory is very small.

The actual capacity of short-term memory has been measured in many different ways, and is said to be an average of seven *different* elements, plus or minus two (see Miller, 1956).[7] These elements are formed out of the raw materials of perception by the grouping processes previously described (see Baars, 1989: 37–39). Note that a pattern that fits within the time limits of STM can have repetition of elements, and hence have more actual events than seven, perhaps up to a limit of about 25 (Fraisse, 1982: 157). It is the number of *different* elements that must be remembered that is important.

The actual time limit of short-term memory can vary with the amount of information it is processing; it may occasionally reach as long as 10–12 sec, although its average is 3–5 sec. The implications for human communication are manifold. Three to five seconds is the average length of most sentences and musical phrases; within this length of time, recent experience is still available, in its original time order, as a highly activated memory. This memory can be sustained by rehearsal—by immediately recycling it back into the focus of conscious awareness. The focus of conscious awareness could be thought of as being at the "front edge" of STM (see figure 4.1). The focus of conscious awareness has an even smaller capacity than STM: three items at most. This is the cutting edge of experience as it is happening; it is what is in immediate awareness.

Because of the limited capacity of short-term memory, our acts of communication are not completely continuous, but are usually performed in pulsations of modulated energy whose length and information content do not exceed this capacity. Hence the existence of units of communication and thought such as verbal sentences and musical phrases.[8] A sentence or musical phrase cannot exceed the time limit of STM without losing its unified character and becoming unavailable to consciousness in its entirety. This means that strings of events that occur inside the time constraints of STM can have a kind of connectedness or temporal coherence. Events persisting as STM can all be immediately recalled as being connected together in the present and *in a particular time order* (Anderson, 1993: 27–29). Usually, when we hear the last word of a sentence, we still have a fairly good recollection of the first word. This is often important to meaning, as in the sentence "The shooting of the prime minister was upsetting to his wife and children, who had thought he was a better marksman." In this case, our interpretation of the meaning of the sentence changes at the end because we can compare it to the beginning. In the same way, if we are to be able to perceive the contour or pitch outline of a melodic phrase, we must in some sense be able to recollect all of the notes comprising it at the same time. This is the essence of short-term memory: the elements retained are all still highly activated and available; hence relations between them can be recalled directly. This is the meaning of "the present" (Fraisse, 1963). This present has fuzzy edges, as the focal metaphor of consciousness mentioned above implies. Events happening longer ago than the time limit of short-term memory, if they are remembered at all (and many of them are not) are remembered in a much more abstract and schematic way (discussed in chapter 9).[9]

Focus of Conscious Awareness

The capacity of short-term memory limits the number of elements that can be maintained in immediate memory through rehearsal. Although these rehearsed elements are in a relatively high state of activation and although they and their time order can be accessed immediately, they are not all present in consciousness at once (see figure 4.2).

Short-term memory is thus what is immediately *available* to conscious awareness at any given time. Only the focus of conscious awareness is completely conscious. The number of elements that can be simultaneously present in the focus of conscious awareness without going back over them (rehearsal) is about three at most.[10] Most of the time we probably have something more like one object of consciousness at a time. For example, when we are consciously remembering a phone number, we do not have all of its digits in the focus of our conscious awareness at the same time. Note that the contents of focal awareness may come from immediate perception, and from activated long-term memory (usually from both).

The number of elements in focal awareness may seem quite small, but only because we do not usually realize the extraordinary extent to which the coherence of our experience depends on memory.[11] Our sensory organs and thoughts are virtually always in motion, and we are constantly scanning the environment and holding previous scans in short-term memory. Figure-ground relationships are often rapidly changing as part of this motion. Only this motion and rehearsal allow us

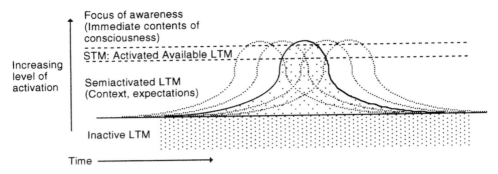

Figure 4.2
Levels of neural activation (after Fuster, 1995). This diagram represents successive states of mind as waves of neural activation, with each successive wave involving different groups of neurons and lasting about 100 msec. Degrees of unconsciousness are indicated by the density of the dot screen.

to feel we are processing more elements. Note that the idea of rehearsal in this sense may include many different forms of repetition. For instance, music uses limited repertoires of elements such as pitches and durations to form patterns. This naturally creates a considerable amount of internal repetition in those patterns, which constitutes a kind of implicit rehearsal that eases memory load. Moreover, because much of our environment remains stable most of the time, we can train our limited focus of awareness on just the changing aspects that need our attention at a given time.

Rehearsal

Information that has entered short-term memory does not last indefinitely, but quickly decays unless maintained by the process of *rehearsal*, which consists of repeating the contents of STM to keep them active (see Anderson, 1990: 151–154; Barsalou, 1992: 119–122). This is represented in figure 4.1 by a dotted line that leads from the "output" of STM back into its "input." Rehearsal is somewhat like the physical act of juggling in that it involves keeping a particular limited pattern of energy going, or it will be lost. For example, imagine hearing a melody or sentence of medium length where each note or word is separated from the one before it by 30 sec. Understanding a sequence of events presented in this way requires an entirely different type of memory processing than understanding a sequence of events presented in the normal way, where the events are in immediate succession. We might be able to remember and understand such a sequence, but only by continually rehearsing all of the events already heard (to keep them actively present as STM) and by adding each new event to the rehearsal cycle. In addition, this process would only work until we reached the STM limit of five to nine elements.

Rehearsal is necessary not only to maintain information temporarily as short-term memory, but to store that information more permanently in long-term memory. In intentional acts of memorization, this happens consciously. The longer the contents of STM are kept active, the more likely they are to persist as long-term memory, especially if the material to be remembered is already meaningful in some way.[12] In this way, what is already retained as long-term memory can influence the retention of new material: knowledge influences memorability.

Rehearsal can also happen less consciously. When something particularly striking occurs and strongly engages our attention, it reverberates in our awareness and we automatically replay it to ourselves. (Language reflects this when we refer to this kind of event as being "re-markable.") The persistence of this repetition depends on the degree of unexpectedness and the emotional significance of the event. Very unexpected events need to be recirculated for a longer time so that their significance can be ascertained. The notion of rehearsal can be extended to include various types of rumination, reflection, and obsession, all of which will cause a particular pattern of thoughts to be recirculated and extended in time, and hence more likely to be remembered later (J. Mandler, 1984: 111).

Another, more subtle form of rehearsal exists in the form of redundancy in messages. Indeed, *any* repetition of elements in a pattern of experience constitutes a kind of rehearsal, reduces memory load, and helps us to maintain an image of the immediate past. The reason we can process relatively complex patterns of information such as music and language is that there are usually many levels of repetition in their patterns. This is why repetition is essential in the construction of memorable patterns.

Chunking

It may seem paradoxical that the capacity of our consciousness is so limited, and yet we seem to be able to recollect fairly long sequences of events. How is this possible?

One way in which the limits of short-term memory can be stretched considerably is through *chunking*. Note that the number of different elements that can persist as STM simultaneously is on average seven. An element may, however, consist of more than one item. For instance, in order to remember the numbers 1776149220011984, we do not really have to remember sixteen numbers once we realize that these digits can be remembered as four dates. These groups of four numbers have been associated with each other so many times that these sixteen digits have actually become four elements. These elements are called "chunks," small groupings (from five to nine elements) frequently associated with each other and capable of forming higher-level units, which themselves become elements in memory (see Baars, 1988: 37). Chunking is the consolidation of small groups of associated memory elements. Just as a single number is a unit that is distinguished from all others by its unique visual features, the individual items in a chunk become its features. It is as though chunking helps memories to "coagulate" or solidify. This is especially true with repeated exposure to a particular experience. Experiences that cannot be easily chunked are more diffuse, and do not stabilize as easily in long-term memory. The grouping processes mentioned in the previous chapter are an important aid to chunking.

Any group of elements that can be associated with each other can become a chunk; associations are the glue that holds chunks together. A coherent musical unit such as a phrase is an example of a chunk. Chunking is one of the ways in which short- and long-term memory interact and work together. The association that forms a remembered chunk must be built up over time in LTM, but its effect is that it reduces the memory load in STM because long-term memories are not only formed one chunk at time; they are also *recalled* one chunk at a time. Thus even though chunks are LTM structures, their *size* is determined by STM.

Any time we can combine things in this way to make higher-level units (chunk them), we can reduce the number of elements and save memory space. Our decimal number system, for instance, is based on this idea. Rather than creating a new symbol for every number we might want to use, we use ten symbols hierarchically to create literally trillions of possible numbers. Another example of this is the limited number of elements in basic musical repertoires, such as scales, which can be arranged into an almost infinite number of melodies.

A remarkable fact about chunking (which is what makes it a vital memory extension technique) is that it may occur on multiple levels. That is, a chunk can itself become (through strengthening of associations) an element in a larger chunk.[13] In this way, chunking leads to the creation of structured hierarchies of associations.

Whole chunks at "lower" levels in the hierarchy become the elements of chunks at "higher" levels. Because we cannot process more than one chunk in short-term memory (awareness) at a time, the way we remember long time-ordered sequences of chunks is that the *last* element in each chunk can act as a recall cue for the *next* chunk (see Rubin, 1995: 25, 31, 181–183).[14] As a sequence is more thoroughly memorized and smaller chunks consolidated together, larger chunks are created. As higher-level chunks are created, larger parts of the sequence can be cued in this way. In cases where time order is important, this means that it is harder to start recall of elements from the middle of chunks at any level because we have access to sequences of long-term memories primarily at chunk boundaries. Indeed, it is very difficult to recall sequences of chunked memories in *any* sequence that is out of their original order.[15] For example, imagine memorizing a fairly lengthy text. Now imagine trying to recall every other line of this text very quickly, without remembering the lines in between, or imagine trying to recall the text backward. The reason these tasks would be very difficult is that long-term memory is reconstructive, and we cannot reconstruct the time order of a sequence without the proper recall cues from the chunk boundaries (although it is sometimes possible to forget a chunk, or even several, and then pick up recall at a later chunk boundary). This implies that the entire text itself is not stored in one temporal sequence, but in chunks, with a cue at the end of each chunk which "points" to the next chunk. The sequence *as a whole* does not exist in memory—only its elements (chunks) and their connections exist. The better learned the sequence is, the larger the chunks become, and hence the higher the structural level of important chunk boundaries. In general, chunk boundaries are very important points in memory.

The limit on the number of elements in a single chunk is the same as that on the number of elements in a short-term memory (7 ± 2); a chunk is one short-term memory. Because chunks can be telescoped by hierarchical rechunking, we could theoretically remember an average of seven chunks having an average of seven elements each. How far could this process of hierarchical compression extend? How many levels of memory could be established in this way? Taking the more conservative number, five ($7 - 2$), it has been suggested that this process may have its final limit at five levels. This would create a hierarchy of 5^5 elements, or about 3,000 items total, a number which seems to coincide with the number of elements in at least several kinds of basic vocabularies (Mandler, 1967).

Thus hierarchical organization of materials optimizes memory storage and retrieval. This has important implications for construction of long-term memories of sequential information such as music. Music that is constructed so as to have clear hierarchical structure is much easier for a listener to form a representation of in LTM.

Associations need not be only hierarchical, however. They may happen between any kind of long-term memories. In addition to creating structured hierarchies, association allows mobility between chunks in *different* hierarchical LTM structures. Indeed, we can move through many types of memories from whole different types of experiences. If it were not for this "free" associative mode of memory retrieval, we would be trapped inside of hierarchical sequences of reminding (or inside particular vocabularies) and thought would lack much of its fluidity. Note that patterns of associative reminding can be highly idiosyncratic, and hence are harder to study experimentally than hierarchical recall.

Short-term memory is associated with the level of melodic and rhythmic grouping, the level of our most immediate perception of patterns in music. In table 1.1, we see that it extends from 16 events per second to 1 event every 8 seconds. Events on this level are neither too fast to be perceived individually (as individual vibration events at the level of event fusion are) nor too far apart to be immediately related and require retrospective long-term memory to form relations between them (as do events at the formal level). Sequences of events at the melodic and rhythmic grouping level that fall within the limitations of short-term memory are perceived as being in the present and as forming various kinds of groupings and phrases that can be apprehended in their entirety. This is the level at which the "local" order of music is perceived.

Notes

1. For the classic article on the capacity of short-term memory, see Miller, 1956.

2. It is worth noting at this point that immediate perception itself does not always result in a high degree of neural activation. We can all think of many instances where we were "lost in thought" and were unaware of our perceptual experience for some time. During this time, perceptual experience was undoubtedly present, but with a very low degree of activation. Dramatic perceptual events such as very loud noises do seem to have a high priority for access to consciousness, and can cause us to move from internal thought to our immediate perceptual experience very quickly.

3. It should be mentioned that it is not yet clear exactly what constitutes activation, and that the concept of levels of activation is at this time still somewhat metaphorical. What is clear, however, is that individual neurons produce more electrical pulses or "spikes" at some times than at others, and that different areas of the brain are more electrically active at different times. See Nairne, 1996, pp. 101–104.

4. This is a description of what has been referred to as "extended working memory" because it includes memory activation at the periphery of consciousness. In this view, the boundaries of working memory are fuzzy; echoic memory, short-term memory, and long-term memory are seen as different *states* of a more unified memory system. The activation of STM would use the same neural hardware as LTM, but this activation would "fade" relatively quickly unless activation was maintained by rehearsal. See Logie, 1996, p. 38; Eagle, 1996, pp. 91–92; and Baars, 1997, pp. 42–48.

Working memory is usually described as having at least three parts (and probably more; see chapter 1, note 3): a visual short-term memory, an aural short-term memory (the part of working memory referred to in figure 4.1 and described in this chapter), and a "central executive." See Barsalou, 1992, pp. 92–115. The central executive is postulated as having the function of overseeing and maintaining plans or goals that shape the flow of current thought and perception. In this sense, the central executive forms a kind of bridge between short-term and long-term memory, connecting the constantly changing contents of short-term memory together over time into larger goal-oriented patterns, and maintaining the continuity of context and goals across momentary distractions and disruptions. (Note that maintenance of these contexts and goals does *not* seem to require explicit rehearsal.) It should be noted that, at this point, the central executive is a functional theoretical construct, probably necessary, but as yet neither clearly defined nor clearly understood. However, see Jonides, 1995, pp. 254–260.

5. Exactly what constitutes consciousness or awareness is a highly complex question that at present has no simple answer. For an idea of the complexity of the issues involved, and the variety of points of view, see Velmans, 1991, pp. 651–726. It is also not clear that consciousness is defined only by a higher level of neural activation. Consciousness probably also involves the activation of specific anatomical parts of the brain, such as the reticular formation and the thalamus. See Baars, 1997, pp. 27–31.

6. It may seem paradoxical that something as seemingly important as consciousness has such a limited capacity. One current theory has it that this is because consciousness can draw on many different types of memory and perceptual processing, and hence is a kind of "global work space" of the mind. In order to have this kind of flexibility, the capacity of short-term memory must be small. This kind of flexibility of processing is called on primarily in novel situations, where the more specialized and automated unconscious modes of processing may not be able to solve the problem. New situations require new combinations of cognitive processing. This is the primary reason why conscious attention is constantly being drawn to the novel aspects of situations. Unconscious processes, on the other hand, because they are probably highly specialized and relatively isolated from each other, can handle large amounts of information. See Baars, 1988, pp. 39–43.

7. More recent research has suggested that seven elements may represent short-term memory capacity *with rehearsal*, and that without any consciousness rehearsal, three or four elements may be a more typical value. See Baars, 1988, p. 37.

8. A sentence is actually a typographical unit; real speech is usually much more loosely organized. Recent linguistic thought has it that the primary unit of spoken language is not the sentence or clause, but the *intonation unit*, a vocal pitch contour that usually moves down at the end, the drop in pitch signaling a basic segmentation in language. This suggests that verbal language is segmented on the basis, not just of grammatical structure, but of what

amounts to musical closure. See Chafe, 1994, pp. 53–70, which has many interesting things to say about the focus of consciousness, and its relation to short-term memory.

9. It should be noted that the decay of short-term memory is not absolute but asymptotic—approaching but never reaching an absolute value—and that some small amount may still be activated after longer amounts of time.

10. This is established in a running memory span test, where subjects are continuously read words from a long list and asked at random to remember backwards over the list, making rehearsal impossible. This usually results in subjects being able to remember about three words. By contrast, where subjects are read a relatively short list of words and told to remember as many as they can, making rehearsal possible, they remember on average 5–9 words. See Cowan, 1995, pp. 98, 115.

11. For instance, for some remarkable examples of how little we actually see at a given time, see Grimes, 1996.

12. Thus the most effective form of rehearsal is, not simple repetition (learning by rote), but *elaborative* rehearsal, where the material rehearsed has some meaning in relation to something already in long-term memory. Referred to as "memory processing in depth," elaborative rehearsal creates new memories that can be "anchored" or associated to older ones. (Note however that rote learning does appear to aid in implicit *recognition*, but not in explicit *recall*.) See, for example, Jahnke and Nowaczyk, 1998, pp. 108–110.

13. One explanation of why this might happen is that although chunks themselves are processed serially (in a time order), once the elements in a chunk have become firmly associated, the entire chunk is processed in parallel, as a unit, with the time order of its elements relatively fixed. See Barsalou, 1992, pp. 96–97.

14. Although Rubin focuses on memory for verbal texts, his is one of the best studies dealing with the structure of large long-term memory sequences. Also note that serial cuing, while not the only way in which large memory sequences are held together, especially if they are very well learned, seems to be a primary mechanism by which large sequences are initially remembered. Well-known musical forms may also help to orient large long-term musical memories.

15. Recalling memories in a time order is called "serial recall": strings of associated elements are recalled in a specific order. Many aspects of music, especially music organized in a linear way, are recalled and recognized serially. There are also associations that occur in music across different time spans, where associated elements are not next to each other in time, such as recapitulations and recurrences of musical patterns in different parts of a piece. This aspect of association in music has been little studied to date.

5

Closure

We have already encountered the idea of closure in chapter 3, where the term *soft closure* was used to describe a basic articulation of musical patterns and did not imply finality, as the term *closure* usually does. In this chapter, closure will be discussed at levels higher than individual grouping boundaries, particularly at the phrase level. At this level, the term closure more closely matches its normal meaning. Closure of phrases has more of an effect of finality than the soft closure of grouping boundaries.

As with groupings, relations between phrases can imply continuity or separation. We have seen that the formation of phrases creates boundaries, points where things begin and end. These boundaries help phrases function as memory "chunks." Phrase boundaries are usually not absolute, and may establish various degrees of separateness between phrases. When phrases are related to some larger-scale pattern of musical motion, ending boundaries may have various degrees of finality (create more or less stasis) in relation to that motion. Beginning boundaries may be seen as a continuation of the material that preceded them or as starting something new, depending on their degree of difference from what preceded them. A particular phrase may feel incomplete and imply subsequent activity, or it may feel final and not imply that anything follows. These degrees of continuation or finality are referred to as "degrees of closure." Because it involves more than an immediate segmentation between events, closure involves short-term memory. Note that the use of terms such as *closure* or *boundary* to describe sequences of events is metaphorical and attempts to give a kind of physicality to abstract musical shapes.

We have seen that short-term memory imposes limitations on the size of musical units, and that musical structure is often tailored to these limitations. This has been described as the reason for the existence of phrases. In fact, the boundaries of phrases can be manipulated in interesting ways to form different degrees of connection between those phrases. Indeed, closure derives its power as a musical effect from the fact that short-term memory is limited to chunks, and the need to connect those chunks together. In this sense, exerting control over the strength of phrase boundaries represents a creative exploitation of the limitations of our own short-term memories. After all, if it were not for the limits of STM, there would be no need for any boundaries or any kind of "units" at all.

The phrase units of short-term memory are not frozen in time. Because the front edge of consciousness is always moving forward in time, the time limit of STM forms a continuously moving window. At a certain point, the boundary between two phrases will be part of what is inside this window. Like the events in the interior of a phrase, this boundary can be manipulated to emphasize either its continuous or its segmental aspects. The same factors that help individual events cohere into phrases can be used between phrases to create higher-level continuity or segmentation. The last event of one phrase and the first event of the next may have a relationship of varying degrees of proximity or similarity.

Closure on the phrase level is a characteristic of musical *motion*, not just of individual phrases, and may affect phrases insofar as they are elements of a larger overall musical pattern. This metaphorical motion provides continuity by tying phrases together, and makes them related on higher hierarchical levels, just as groupings tie individual events together and make them related on the lowest level. (We shall examine the idea of musical motion in greater detail in chapter 13.)

I have said that closure is not absolute, that there are degrees of closure. A phrase exhibits more or less closure when heard in relation to other phrases, which also exhibit more or less closure.

A higher degree of finality of closure usually defines the boundaries of larger-scale groupings of phrases. In other words, phrases that are incompletely closed will be followed by another phrase that is more completely closed. The incompletely closed phrases will create expectations of eventual closure, and a more completely closed phrase will then close not only itself, but the less completely closed phrases before it. In this way different degrees of closure articulating phrasing on different hierarchical levels can create a chain of ongoing expectations. Closure is a way of establishing chunk boundaries and of connecting chunks with varying degrees of strength.

The most definite musical expectations of closure are usually created by a tradition of rules for the use of learned patterns signifying that closure. These patterns form part of what can be called a musical "syntax." The recognition of patterns is a necessary condition for the establishment of syntax. Closure is one of the musical functions that can be established in this way. Through repetition in many different musical pieces, certain kinds of patterns can come to signify closure. It is important to realize that these patterns may be relatively arbitrary, and that their closural significance is established primarily through repeated use. The most complex musical hierarchies of closure are created within traditions of style with an established syntax, which create very specific gestures of closure, hence very specific expectations. Because these particular patterns of syntax are learned and style specific, I shall not deal with them in this book. I shall, however, speak of closure established in other ways.

One reason why many levels of hierarchy of musical groupings are possible is that music is multidimensional. Musical sound has many aspects—*parameters*—and closure may be established more or less completely in any of them. Partial closure is achieved by reaching closure in some parameters and by leaving others incomplete. This is one of the most important ways in which music can establish dynamic continuity and sustain our interest. Generally speaking, the *more* parameters that reach closure at a given point, the *higher* the structural level of closure achieved at that point. This means that, as a rule, the ending of an entire piece, for example, has many parameters reaching closure simultaneously, whereas the endings of lower-level structural units such as phrases and sections involve closure in fewer parameters, with more "loose ends." Because closure grows out of organized patterns of motion and expectation, patterns that lack these characteristics will end without implying closure—they will simply *stop*.

Saying that a pattern has "organized motion" means that we can process the pattern and develop expectations about where it is going. In a sequence without any recognizable directed pattern of motion, any element can be the last one—we have no basis for predicting. To establish closure, especially at higher levels, we must have some basis for predicting what we think will come next. Although our predictions may be wrong, the very fact that we can have expectations creates a tension that carries us through a sequence and makes closure possible. These expectations may be based either on primitive grouping tendencies, on learned patterns, or both.

The relation between predictability and closure also means that repetition is an important aspect of closure. Generally speaking, a repetition of a previously introduced musical pattern will seem more closural than a new pattern. European music of the classical period, for example, often uses recapitulation of previously introduced musical material at high-level closure points, such as final sections. The raga music of North India also uses repetition of a simple melodic pattern to achieve closure at the end of each rhythmic cycle (Wade, 1991: 173).

Much of our discussion of closure thus far is based on the idea of musical motion. We shall now take a closer look at how music can be said to be "in motion."

Intensity and Metaphors of Motion and Gravity

There are many factors that contribute to closure. The previously cited factors of proximity and similarity not only contribute to grouping formation, but to closure as well. Closure is of course also established by silence. All of the above are primitive mechanisms, and do not need to be established by musical syntax. There are other types of closure that are also non-syntactical, but which may not be learned. These forms of closure are probably examples of implicit memory, a type of memory that is learned without conscious effort (discussed in greater detail in chapter 6).

Still another factor that usually affects closure is *intensity*, here broadly defined as any change in a stimulus that causes an increase in neural activity (Tenny, 1988: 33–41). By this definition, *any* change in a sound—not just in its loudness—that causes increased neural activity makes the sound more intense.[1] This includes making the sound higher in pitch, harmonically more dissonant, brighter in tone color, faster in speed, or denser in temporal distribution. Notice that all of these changes also describe an *increase* in some physical aspect of sounds.[2] The metaphor of *mobility* is often applied to the idea of intensity in music. Points of higher intensity are said to be "in motion," and points of low intensity are said to be "at rest." In this metaphor, musical motion operates by continually oscillating between these two poles of tension and release. Under the complementary notion of *stability*, music is said to be "in motion" when its current structures are "unstable" (we expect them to move further). This instability is directly connected with intensity. Higher intensity or motion, which is unstable, leads to lower intensity or rest, which is stable. This, in turn, is related to the metaphor of *goal orientation*. Maximum points of stability can be thought of as "goals" in that the structure of the more intense music preceding them is determined by the possibility of eventual arrival at those points. Note that the metaphorical character of these descriptive concepts is a way of relating the abstract processes in music back to our basic physical experience of the world.

Thus *decreases* in intensity can establish closure. If we look at changes in intensity of the elements in a melodic, temporal, or formal grouping, we find that all other things being equal, a grouping feels more closed the more the intensity of its various musical parameters decreases at the end. If we think of musical phrases as gestures metaphorically related to actual physical gestures, we see that many types of physical gestures are cycles of energy that also move to reach their "lowest" point at their conclusion.

This tendency toward closure with dropping intensity may be learned, although probably not consciously. The idea of "falling" being associated with closure is also found in language, where falling is often a metaphor for reduction of activity, as in falling asleep, falling ill, or simply amount of activity falling off. The intonation (pitch) pattern at the end of declarative sentences in many languages is essentially a falling pattern. The more declarative and definite (or semantically closed) the content of the sentence, the clearer this pattern is. Falling voice pitch is a near universal indication of declarative linguistic closure (Cruttendon, 1986: 168–169).[3] A question, which is not semantically closed insofar as it is meant to be continued in an answer, is usually pitched higher than its surrounding linguistic context. It is incomplete—"suspended" above its more definite surroundings.[4] Also, speaking at a higher pitch, or "raising" the voice, indicates emotional tension or anger.

Returning to our argument, we can see that one of the most basic forms of closure is a drop in intensity. As a rule, tension is associated with higher values of parameters in a musical situation, and repose with lower values. This is of course a relative notion. There is no absolute meaning to "high" or "low"; these are usually established as particular limits within a piece. In European music, points of maximum tension are often referred to as "*climaxes*," (from Greek *klimax*, ladder) and points of minimum tension as "abatements," "resolutions," or "cadences" (from Latin *cadere*, to fall).

Duration can also establish closure: closural events in sequences in both language and music are often of longer duration (Chafe, 1994: 59–60). Indeed, all of the segmenting factors mentioned in chapter 3 can contribute to closure.

Linearity: A Metaphor of Causality

Linearity is a way of constructing music so that events in a sequence seem connected to and to grow out of each other. When a number of weakly closed phrases are connected to each other in such a way as to form a progression, we have a situation that can be described as "linear." One important factor in creating linearity is the *organization* of patterns of intensity, which gives musical motion a direction. The term *organization* again leads us back to the ideas of proximity, similarity, continuity, and the like.

One way of organizing patterns of intensity is by tying together groupings with incomplete closures, creating higher-level groupings, as described above. Music may have closures, but if the relative structural importance of successive closures is not progressive and hierarchical, there will be no linearity on higher levels. To establish a higher-level linear progression, one closure must lead to the next in succession; they must form a graduated series of intensities.

Another way of directing tension is to organize parametric values into patterns so that similar values are next to each other (proximate) and progress in a particular direction. Some examples would be a series of events of increasing loudness, rising pitch or brightening tone color. By the principle of continuity, we expect that once something begins to move in a particular direction, it will continue to move in that direction. (Continuity can be seen as a special case of similarity, where successive events display a similar *interval of motion*.) This expectation is what makes linear motion seem dynamic, because it ties events together into a progression, and makes later events seem to be the *result* of earlier ones (Hopkins, 1990: 4–14).

The simplest directed pattern is a *scale*, a pattern where parametric values change in a single direction in intervals of similar size. (Our sense of the term *scale* is more general than common usage, which restricts scale to the parameter of pitch.) As examples of the principle of continuity, scales lead us to expect that they will continue to move in the same direction: scalar motion creates expectations of continuity.

That scales are predictable puts them within the realm of expectations, norms, and schemas. We might think of a scale as the most general and abstract default schema for directed motion, against which all actual directed motion is compared. In this sense, all directed motions are only highly elaborated scales. Generally speaking, however, in linear music, only global average values of parameters move in simple scalar patterns. Scales in and of themselves are not very interesting: their motion is *too* predictable. Interest is generated by violating the expectation that motion will always continue in the same direction in intervals of similar size.

There are only two directions in which a parameter can change continuously: it can either increase or decrease. Directed linear motion is therefore always leading toward a maximum or a minimum point on some level—toward a climax or a resolution. These points are usually central and goal-like (syntactical closure is also often established at these points). It is worth noting that because arrival at these points usually involves reaching a limit of some sort, the direction of motion must then reverse itself or cease.

Interesting motion toward these points usually contains temporary shifts of direction and interval size that frustrate expectations. Also, as mentioned above, all parameters will generally not be directed in the same way at the same time.

Like closure, linear motion may or may not exist on many levels. For instance, small patterns may be strongly directed, but may not cumulatively lead anywhere on a larger time scale. On the other hand, comparatively static small patterns may be arranged so that, over a longer time, the order of the patterns themselves leads in a particular direction. (We shall return to the different levels of linearity in chapter 13.)

Not all patterns are linear, however. Nonlinear patterns include those whose parametric values do not change over time, but merely repeat; fluctuate between fixed values in no particular order; or are randomly chosen. Note that in all of these cases, the global average of parametric values does not consistently change or move in a particular direction over time. In these cases, the expectation of events does not relate to previous events in a linear way: it is either continually frustrated or always satisfied in the same way. In a sense, the difference between linear and nonlinear is the difference between an ongoing and developing set of expectations and a fixed set of static assumptions or conditions.

Repetition

Repeatedly returning to a particular pitch or pattern creates a closural effect. This is especially true of returning to the central pitch of a tonality, a form of tonal closure that involves the memory of other occurrences of that pitch. This memory does not appear to have to be consciously learned, and is an example of implicit memory (Dowling, 1993; Cuddy, 1993).

Repetition also acts to create closure on higher formal levels. Many traditional forms of European music are based on this idea, and use recapitulations of musical patterns at important closural points. This is often described with the metaphor of returning to a familiar and central place. The familiar is more closural than the unfamiliar.

All of which also bears on the memorability of music. Closure tends to divide music up into a number of hierarchical levels. Groupings on these different levels can be seen as *chunks*, the basic units of memory. Indeed, it is much easier to build up a representation in memory of music that exhibits clear groupings and closures than of music that does not (Bigand, 1993: 252–257). Because some aspects of memory appear to have a hierarchical structure (through chunking), music that is hierarchically organized (by multiple closure levels) tends to be retained in memory with maximum efficiency: it is actually reflecting an aspect of the nature of human memory.

It follows that music that does not exhibit clear patterns of closure is much more difficult to recollect: each detail must be remembered by itself, rather than as part of an organized memory chunk. Because it is unclear where the chunking boundaries are, it is hard to know how to break the patterns up to retain them as memory.

Music we have characterized as nonhierarchical and without clear patterns of closure essentially exists on the fringes of the capabilities of human memory.

The purpose of this type of music could legitimately be described as the "sabotage of memory." Often referred to as "existing in the present only," it provides either no memorable patterns or no basis for expectation, or both. This lack of memorabilty also tends to emphasize the qualities of individual acoustical events, rather than their relationship to each other as parts of larger patterns. Nonhierarchical music can of course be processed in conscious short-term memory, but does not easily form an image that can persist as long-term memory. Thus the approach to memory divides music into two very large categories (discussed at greater length in chapter 13).

Notes

1. The correspondence between an increase in stimulus intensity and an increase in neural activity, *rate coding*, is only one of the parameters of the neural code, and much remains to be discovered about how different aspects of the environment are coded by the nervous system. See Rieke et al., 1997, p. 7; for a listing of all of the parameters currently considered relevant, p. 38. See also Stein, and Meredith (1993), pp. x, 17. For an account of a possible origin of musical intensity patterns in the communication between mothers and infants, see Papousek, 1996, pp. 90–97.

2. The one seeming exception to this is duration: a *decrease* in duration constitutes an *increase* in intensity. That is, given two sequences of sounds with the same time intervals between sounds, the sequence with the shorter event durations will sound more intense (have

a higher tension value), than the same sequence with longer event durations. One possible reason for this is that both the onset and termination of a sound are changes in our auditory experience, and both constitute events. When the duration of a sound gets shorter, these two events move closer together, creating an increase in the frequency of events in a given amount of time, and hence an increase in intensity.

3. Although it seems clear that the closural quality of falling musical pitch patterns is related to speech patterns, it remains unclear whether the musical use of downward pitch movement is derived from its use in language or whether both usages appear together and stem from a deeper source, such as an image schema or even an innate predisposition, see Bolinger, 1978 p. 514. In either case, this form of closure does not seem to be learned consciously, and hence is an example of implicit memory. For a good, brief comparison of the use of pitch in music and language, see Bolinger, 1986, pp. 28–32; and Trehub and Trainor, 1993, pp. 293–294. The most complete argument I am aware of for the derivation of musical phrasing from speech is in Norton, 1984, pp. 65–71. Norton makes a case for the idea that the pitch dynamics of musical phrasing are derived from speech patterns. For an account of research with infants about these questions, see Fassbender, 1996, pp. 76–80.

It is important to realize that the phenomenon described in Western music as "falling pitch," although found in many musical cultures, is by no means always described with the metaphor of falling. Nor do all musical cultures describe musical pitch using the metaphor of physical height. Those of Indonesia and the Venda tribe in Africa, for example, describe pitch as "larger" and "smaller" rather than "lower" and "higher". On Vendan musical culture, see Blacking, 1995, p. 83. The metaphor of size describes the quality of pitch in relation to the size of the instrument that produces it: lower pitches *are* produced by larger instruments, and higher pitches are produced by smaller instruments. For a theoretical description of the relation between voice pitch and size, see Ohala, 1994, p. 330. Other metaphoric terms used to describe pitch relationships are "sharp" and "heavy" (used by the ancient Greeks), and "young" and "old" (used by the Suya of the Amazon basin). See Zbikowski, 1998, for a good introduction to the use of contemporary metaphor theory in relation to music.

4. This has been verified for 269 different languages. See Bolinger, 1989, p. 39. Bolinger has done exhaustive research on intonation patterns in spoken English, and his books are highly recommended for a thorough examination of the melodic aspects of this language.

6

Long-Term Memory

Patterns and relationships between events on a time scale larger than that of short-term memory must be handled by *long-term memory* (LTM). Relationships between events separated by more than an average of 3–5 sec are not perceived immediately, but only in retrospect: they are not automatically part of the conscious present, but must be *recollected*.[1] In listening to a whole piece of music, we are only able to consciously understand the relationship between different parts of the piece by having events come back into awareness from long-term memory, which is unconscious. Our long-term memories *need* to be unconscious: if they were all in our consciousness, there would be no room for the present.

Long-term memories are thought to be formed when repeated stimulation changes the strength of connections between simultaneously activated neurons (see Fuster, 1995: 25; McClelland, 1995).[2] When a group of neurons is originally activated to process an experience, that processing changes the strength of the connections between them (Squire and Kandel, 1999: 30–45), making it more likely that when a similar experience is encountered later, some of the same neurons will be involved in its processing. This explains what is meant by saying that new experience is processed "*through* long-term memory." The connections between groups of simultaneously activated neurons are called "associations" and exist on many levels of long-term memory. These levels extend all the way from the association of different features in the perception of objects and events to the long strings of associations that form our conceptual knowledge and autobiographical memories of experience. As mentioned previously, the basic unit of association is called a "chunk."

Association is a process whereby events that happen close together in time or seem similar form memories that are connected together.[3] This is the basic mechanism by which a chunk is formed. Association is a facilitated neural connection:

anything activating one of the associated memories may also activate the other memory. This process is referred to as *cuing*. One memory *cues* another memory with which it has formed an association. For example, hearing a particular passage in a piece of music may cause us to think of another passage about to happen. Associations can rapidly move through different parts of the brain as different groups of neurons become activated (see figure 4.2). Indeed, the cuing process usually causes a low level of activation of a considerable number of associated memories. Although many may not become fully activated (conscious), these semiactivated memories are said to be "primed" for further activation, which increases the likelihood of their becoming conscious. Primed associations form the *context* of currently activated memory and can shape our expectations. Not only can the recall of a particular memory prime its context for activation, but many of the component memories of that context can cue the recall of the memory itself. For example, looking at a cloud may make me think of Debussy's *Nuages*, and hearing that piece may make me think of clouds. There is therefore considerable redundancy built into the recall process, at least for memories with rich, active contexts.

There are three types of cuing: (1) *recollection*, where we intentionally try to cue a memory; (2) *reminding*, where an event in the environment automatically cues an associated memory of something else; and (3) *recognition*, where an event in the environment automatically acts as its own cue. Recognition and reminding are spontaneous processes that are going on constantly.

The real challenge of long-term memory is to retain the association between a specific cue and a specific memory over time. This usually works quite well, but the process can be derailed by irrelevant cues similar to the correct cue, which can produce various kinds of *interference* with recall.

The cuing process described above is an important mechanism by which larger long-term memories are retrieved. We have seen that memories are stored in chunks, which are quite limited in size, but that an element in a chunk may act as a cue for another chunk, connecting them together in an unfolding sequence of associations. A musical example of this would be building up a memory of a piece of music phrase by phrase, with each phrase constituting a chunk. In this way, even though the size of the basic chunks of memory is limited, larger units of memory may be created by making stable connections between chunks. This process may continue on multiple levels and in multiple directions of association so that memory representations of sequences or bodies of knowledge of considerable size may be built up.

The reconstruction of large-scale temporal patterns using long-term memory takes much more effort than pattern recognition in early processing and short-term memory, and usually involves repetition of experience. For instance, it may take dozens (or more) of repeated listenings to build up an accurate LTM representation of the patterns of order in a one-hour symphony. Whereas the contents of short-term memory are always immediately available to awareness, the contents of long-term memory must be cued and reconstructed and come at least partially back into awareness from the unconscious. This process is very dependent on how long-term memories are connected together by associations. On the other hand, the contents of short-term memory decay rapidly and are lost unless rehearsed, whereas material entered into long-term memory is thought to be retained for a long time, although it may not always remain easily accessible.

That long-term memories could be permanent may seem to be inconsistent with the idea of forgetting. It is believed, however, that what is lost in forgetting is, not the memories themselves, but the *associative connections* between them (Fuster, 1995: 11). These connections are what create the recall "paths" to a particular memory. For example, a performer who forgets a particular phrase in a piece of music may be unable to go on because the performer has lost the cue for the memory of the music that follows.

When a particular long-term memory is recalled or activated frequently, it develops many connections to other memories and hence its retrievability is great: its context is rich and many different things can cue its recall. On the other hand, when a particular long-term memory is no longer actively used, its connections with other more active memories become much weaker, and there are fewer associative pathways through which to cue its recall (Schacter, 1995: 25; McClelland, 1995: 69–73). It may however, still become activated by some specific part of its original context. Because it is dependent on a very specific cue, this type of memory is much harder to access. That it is still possible is proven by the fact that we can, under the right circumstances, revive even early childhood memories.

Long-term memory is not at all static. Unlike computer memory, which has fixed addresses with stable configurations of information in them, human LTM is highly dynamic (see Schank, 1982: 1, 23, 224–225; Edelman, 1989: 109–112, 211, 244; Edelman, 1992: 101–104).[4] This must be the case, or human beings could not adapt to a constantly changing environment. Therefore a model of memory as a stable record of experience is much too simple to capture the essence of the memory process: our memories constitute who we are, and who we are is always changing.[5]

The creation of long-term memories is often referred to as "coding," which implies a sort of translation into some new set of terms (a code) and which high- lights the fact that memory is not a direct representation of experience (Schvanevelt, 1992). Remembering is largely a process of *reconstruction*, rather than reproduc- tion, as we have seen in the many forms of information reduction (categorization) associated with perception and memory (chapter 1). The memory code can be described as a composite of features that are attended to. Because we know that the discrimination of many features is learned, it follows that our memories are based on, indeed largely constructed from, what we already know.

New long-term memories are thus encoded largely in terms that are already familiar: new memories are built up largely out of the elements of older memories (Edelman, 1989: 109–118). Even quite novel events are usually experienced as devi- ations within some kind of framework of preexisting knowledge. If we do not have such a framework within which to frame an experience (for example, hearing a complex piece of music in a style about which we know nothing), we are not likely to remember much about it. Another way of saying this is that everything is expe- rienced and remembered as part of a *context*. This context consists of both indi- vidual and shared cultural knowledge. In the case of music, our memories of music are constructed largely from other memories of aspects of music previously heard, and other knowledge and metaphorical experience connected with music in our minds. This implies that a person who has rarely or never listened to music would probably retain only the most general impression of the character of a particular piece.

Long-term memory forms a third level of musical experience, which I shall call the "formal level." This follows musical terminology, in which groupings or pat- terns larger than phrases are said to constitute aspects of "musical form." Memory theorists distinguish between two very general types of long-term memory, referred to as "implicit memory" and "explicit memory."[6]

Implicit Memory

The functioning of many of our cognitive processes is not available to conscious- ness. This includes *implicit memory*. Indeed, when we use it, we are generally not consciously aware that we are memorizing or recollecting anything at all. Implicit memory may actually constitute another memory system, anatomically distinct from that of explicit memory. It may also be an older memory system, one that evolved before the development of more conscious forms of memory (Reber, 1993: 7–8).

The contents of implicit memory are often impossible both to examine consciously and to describe easily in words. There appear to be several kinds of implicit memory phenomena.

Many implicit memories are memories of muscular acts ("motor" memories), which have no language component. Such memories are essentially the same as skills: knowledge of *how* to do things.[7] Playing the piano, knowing how to produce a clear tone on a wind instrument, and knowing how to read music are examples of implicit skill memory—one may know how to produce a clear tone on an instrument, but not be able to *tell* anyone else how to do it. The groups of neurons that process these memories are probably not connected to the groups of neurons that process language; implicit and explicit memory are thought to reside in different parts of the brain (Squire, 1994: 204). Indeed, the memory of well-learned physical skills may actually be stored in "lower" parts of the nervous system, closer to the actual muscles that execute them (Fuster, 1995: 169–173).

Some types of implicit memories are slowly formed, usually through laborious, repetitive practice, and are relatively inflexible. Unlike explicit memories, which can be compared and revised, implicit memories can only be slowly refined rather than radically changed (see Squire, 1994: 213–214; Eichenbaum, 1994: 152–154). For instance, once it is learned, a bad fingering for a passage on a musical instrument is very difficult to unlearn. Implicit memories are, however, quickly and automatically recallable, without conscious effort. In fact, conscious effort often impedes the use of implicit memory (Reber, 1993: 47).

Implicit skill memories are usually expressed through some sort of *performance*, rather than recollection. Although critical to any discussion of the performance of music, implicit skill memories will not be a primary focus in this book.[8]

Another type of implicit memory is manifested in the phenomenon referred to as *priming*. Priming is essentially the capability of previous experience to affect recall *without* any *conscious awareness* that this is taking place. It is an activation of unconscious context. This is a different kind of memory use than conscious recollection, and it takes place all of the time in the everyday phenomenon called *recognition*. We recognize objects, people, and their names automatically, without ever realizing that this use of knowledge is an act of memory. A musical example of priming would be feeling that there is something familiar about a musical phrase that is like one we have heard earlier in the same piece.

There is also evidence that certain other types of learning can take place without our conscious awareness. Our learning of certain types of syntactical information seems to be implicit. (Here I use "syntactical" in a broad sense, referring to any systematic aspect of a situation.) It seems we can learn rule systems of relations between elements without ever consciously trying to memorize them (see Reber, 1993).[9] We do this all the time when we produce new, grammatical sentences without having to remember the rules of grammar, many of which we may not consciously know anyway. This general type of memory can also relate to other kinds of systems, as when we realize that an object in a familiar room has been moved, without ever having consciously memorized the positions of objects in that room. This type of implicit memory appears to be important musically in the recognition of syntactical structures like tonality (treated in greater detail in chapter 11).

Certain kinds of emotional memories also appear to be implicit (LeDoux, 1996: 200–204). An emotional response to an immediate experience, while seeming to originate in the present moment, may actually be an unconscious reactivation of a previous emotional response to a similar situation.

It follows from all of the above that implicit memories may be the only types of memories we can have before we acquire language. Very young children would thus have almost exclusively implicit memories. It is also the primary type of memory used by most other organisms with nervous systems, which use memory all the time without being aware they are using it. What remains unclear, however, is how the transition is made from the prelinguistic to the linguistic stage of development (Mandler, 1992).

Explicit Memory

In addition to implicit memory, we possess *explicit memory* capabilities, which we use when we consciously memorize or recall information.

Explicit memory is of events or concepts. It is knowing that something is or was the case. The contents of explicit memory can generally be described in words, although the memories themselves may also consist of other types of information, such as images. Explicit memory is usually organized into spatial or temporal sequences or into knowledge hierarchies. Most implicit memories take much repetitive practice to establish but are then used automatically and quickly, whereas most explicit memories are established quickly, but take relatively slow conscious deliberation to use.

A further distinction, introduced by Endel Tulving, divides explicit memory into "episodic memory" and "semantic memory" (Tulving, 1972: 381–403; Tulving, 1983: 35).

Episodic Memory

Episodic memories are memories of specific experiences or events, each occurring in its own unique time sequence and place in the ongoing context of a person's life. This type of memory is sometimes referred to as "autobiographical memory," because it always involves the presence of the *self* (Brewer, 1986). This type of memory is always of things that happened *in the presence of the rememberer*. Much of our initial memory of a particular piece of music may be episodic, especially if we are hearing it for the first time.

Episodic memories are created very quickly. Time and especially place are the organizational principles of this type of memory, which means that, at least initially, episodic memories are recalled in a particular temporal or spatial order. Much of our everyday conscious remembering is of episodic memories, and it is such memories we are referring to when we speak of "our memories." The memory disorder commonly referred to as "amnesia" is usually a loss of episodic memories. Amnesiacs usually retain their general knowledge, but lose memories of personal situations related to the self.[10]

Episodic memories seem highly susceptible to distortion, especially with repeated recollection. That is, when we repeatedly recollect specific episodic memories, they are changed by the very process of recollection.[11] This may be because recalling an episodic memory is itself an episode that becomes remembered, and this copy of the memory replaces the original. There is, after all, no way to distinguish between a memory, and a memory of a memory. Rerembering an episodic memory might then be thought of as a kind of selective rehearsal, during which various details get amplified or suppressed, usually in relation to the value systems and schemas of the rememberer.

Episodic memories appear to interact dynamically with our values, models, categories, and so on, all of which have a bearing on *how we represent things to ourselves* (previously referred to as "coding"). What we "remember" thus interacts dynamically with what we know, feel, and want. Episodic memories are not constructed from scratch or entirely from experience, but at least partly from knowledge

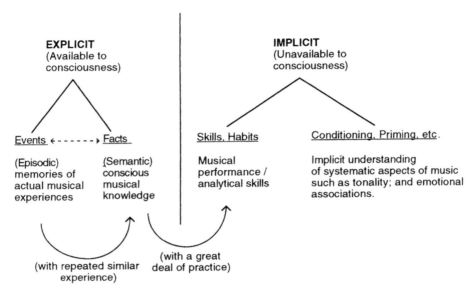

Figure 6.1
Types of long-term memory.

categories (*semantic memories*) already formed by many previous experiences (see D'Andrade, 1995: 189). This means that semantic and episodic memory are somewhat interdependent, as indicated by the dotted line in figure 6.1.

Our categories (as we first noted in chapter 1, and shall discuss at length in chapter 7), enable us to deal with the enormous amount of information in even the blandest experience, to stabilize or anchor our memories, and indeed to make sense of our experience at all. The details of episodic memories generally become integrated with our categories. Episodic memories are usually constructed within a framework of preexisting memory. These categories are thought to be formed around *prototypes*, or best examples of things (Lakoff, 1987). All of which means that our memories of the specific aspects of situations are often not very reliable, especially if they have been recalled repeatedly.

For example, say that on listening to a recording of a particular piece of music, I categorize a section in the piece as "loud" or "fast." If I listen to the piece again at a later time, it is possible and even likely that I will be surprised that the section is not as "loud" or "fast" as I remembered it to be. This will be especially likely if I have thought about the music between listenings, without actually hearing it again. The actual episodic memory of the experience has been "colored" by my categorization of it. Indeed, some theorists (e.g., Edelman, 1989: 109–118) would say that my memory of the experience *is* my categorization of it. In this way, an episodic memory is somewhat like a caricature of an experience, an example of how much the initial categorization (coding) of an experience shapes the memory of that experience.

The basic categorical units used in the construction of episodic memory are probably not very large. It is thought that these types of memories are stored as individual, relatively low-level features (see Schank, 1982: 90–91; Shapiro and Olton, 1994: 101; Fuster, 1995: 34). The features are then recombined in various patterns (chunks) to form specific episodic recollections. The same feature may well be incorporated in many different memories. Over time, these features may recombine in different ways, and even features from different episodes may combine. (This type of confabulation of features happens regularly in dreams.)

The need to have a more stable record of episodic aspects of things may be one of the reasons for developing systems of measurement, which are ways of objectifying aspects of things so that they may be stored in a nondynamic way *outside* a constantly evolving individual memory. Language itself may be viewed as having this same kind of stabilizing function, freeing human beings from the limitations of episodic (and short-term) memory (see Donald, 1991).

It is worth noting that all our knowledge memories were originally episodic memories; that is, all our memories were originally of experiences that occurred in particular spatial and temporal contexts.[12] As we accumulate many episodic memories or experiences that are similar, these similar episodes may cause interference with each other in memory. For example, if we do something every day, it may be very hard to remember the details of how we did it on a particular day. Over time, multiple episodic memories of similar experiences begin to lose their individuality, and form another type of long-term memory.

Semantic Memory

As memories of abstract concepts or categories of objects or events, *semantic memories* are not necessarily organized temporally or spatially, but are often organized hierarchically in levels of various kinds of abstract conceptual knowledge categories. Semantic memory is what we refer to when we speak of "knowing" as opposed to "remembering."[13]

Much of semantic memory is related to the abstract categories of language. Knowing that all birds have two legs is an example of a semantic memory.

Remembering that a particular bird landed in a tree outside my window at around 11:00 A.M. last Sunday morning, on the other hand, is an example of an episodic memory. Our knowledge of music—knowing the names of notes, recognizing particular chords, the sounds of particular instruments, and musical styles—would all constitute semantic memories, whereas a memory of a particular performance would be episodic.

Semantic memory is the primary type of memory involved in *recognition*. Semantic memories are often used implicitly, without our even being conscious of them. Much of our abstract categorical knowledge about the world is employed in the selection of sensory input, a recognition process that usually takes place outside conscious awareness.[14] This process is based on *identifying* the things around us by processing them through the appropriate semantic memory categories. Semantic memory can thus be either explicit or implicit. With continued, regular use, concepts in semantic memory are evoked automatically, and hence become implicit. Trying to recollect what the capital of Idaho is would be an explicit use of semantic memory, whereas immediately recognizing and naming an apple would be an implicit use. That some explicitly learned knowledge can with practice come to be so well learned it can be used implicitly is represented by the rightmost curved arrow at the bottom of figure 6.1.

Most of our experiences involve both episodic and semantic memory, and the two interact in many ways. Our (semantic) categories are built up from particular (episodic) experiences, and our particular (episodic) experiences are of things that usually fit into our (semantic) categories. The relation between particular experiences and generalized categories is of course different for each person; the illustration or prototype of a category is to some extent personal because the particular episodic memories which are related to each semantic category are different for each person. In addition, the formation of semantic memories is not a static process; we continue to elaborate and refine our semantic memory categories, and to create new categories all our lives.

Although eventually the details of episodic memories of similar experiences are lost, an abstract *schema* derived from commonalties running through all the experiences remains. This schema is a more general type of semantic memory category. Whereas knowledge categories deal with particular types of objects or single events, schemas are like metacategories: they are categorizations of entire types of situations.

It appears that most of our episodic memories undergo this evolution into semantic memories over time. That is, most of our particular experiences eventually merge into general categories and lose their specific details. Unlike the formation of episodic memories, which seems to be a rapid capturing process, the formation of semantic memories is a result of a slow accumulation.

Many of our particular experiences thus gradually become generalized into our (semantic) knowledge base. This type of generalizing function is a fundamental aspect of human thought. We shall now look at ways these generalizations might be structured.

Notes

1. This statement applies to the *recollection* mode of long-term memory, not to its *recognition* mode, which is unconscious: the past is always in some sense affecting our perception of the present. Note in this regard Minsky, 1985, p. 247: "For although words are merely catalysts for starting mental processes, so, too are real things: *we can't sense what they really are, only what they remind us of*" (emphasis added). See also Fuster, 1995, pp. 12–16, 35, 106, 113–114, 293, esp. p. 253; and Edelman, 1989, p. 105. For how memory might be used to handle perceptually novel situations, see Barsalou, 1993, p. 60.

As I see it, novelty of an experience is determined by the level of associations at which it can be processed. An altogether novel experience, for example, might not have many higher-level associations, but would still consist of perceptual features that could be processed by already existing neural circuits. That is to say, although there is probably no such thing as a *perceptually* uncategorized experience, there are undoubtedly *conceptually* uncategorizable experiences. For more on this, see chapter 7.

2. It is now established that synaptic *growth* is also part of the memory process: although the number of neurons probably remains constant, new synaptic connections between previously unconnected neurons can grow in response to experience. See Abel et al., 1995.

3. This is the long-term potentiation referred to in chapter 1. See Fuster, 1995, pp. 23–36; and Swain et al., 1995. Note that associations can form between "mental" as well as perceptual events.

4. An important difference between human and computer memory is that human memory is *content addressable*, or associative. Thus it now seems that many of the memory metaphors derived from the structure of serial computers are misleading.

5. A unique experiment, which provides a striking demonstration of this idea, is chronicled in Linton, 1982, pp. 77–91.

6. Terminology in this area of research is not standardized at this time. Other pairs of terms which are more or less comparable to the *explicit* versus *implicit* distinction are *declarative* versus *procedural* and *memory* versus *habit*. For a brief history of the development of these terms, see Eichenbaum, 1994, pp. 174–178. For a discussion of musical aspects of explicit ("declarative") and implicit ("procedural") memory, see Brinner, 1995, pp. 27–45.

7. The term *implicit memory* has recently replaced the older term *procedural memory* because there are memory phenomena other than skill (procedure) that are implicit. These would include various types of nonassociative learning, classical conditioning, emotional

memory, and priming. What all types of memory referred to as "implicit" share is their lack of availability to consciousness. See Squire, 1994, pp. 203–215, esp. p. 205.

8. Note that explicit and implicit (or procedural) memory are not mutually exclusive: they can overlap. This is especially clear in musical traditions where explicit notation systems have been developed to encode part of what was previously oral knowledge. See Brinner, 1995, p. 34.

9. Reber's work seems to indicate that people can learn certain kinds of rule systems without ever being conscious of trying to learn them at all. This may have implications for phenomena such as the ability to perceive the tonality of music of other cultures.

10. What is described here is called "retrograde amnesia." Loss of the ability to form new memories is called "anterograde amnesia." There are of course other types of memory disorders that do affect various aspects of semantic memories. For a state-of-the-art book-length study of all of the things that can go "wrong" with long-term memory, see Schacter, 1995.

11. Some interesting research into the fallibility of episodic memories can be found in Jacoby et al., 1989, pp. 391–422; Wells and Murray, 1984, pp. 155–170; and Neisser, 1986, pp. 69–83.

12. Note that this is even true when acquiring general knowledge from a book such as a dictionary or encyclopedia—this experience is still initially remembered as occurring at a particular time and place. In addition, this general knowledge might not be remembered as knowledge unless it was memorized in repeated episodes (sometimes referred to as "studying").

13. The distinction between these two types of memory is represented in our legal system by the distinction between eyewitness (episodic) and expert (semantic) testimony.

14. I am aware that the process of filtration of perceptual input is a complicated issue. It seems clear, however, that novelty plays an important part in directing attention, and in creating memorability. It also seems clear that in a larger sense, attention is directed by schemas and values, which are often goal directed. For an interesting discussion of the role that values play in cognition, see Dreyfuss, 1992, pp. 260–280. See also Edelman, 1989, pp. 197–207, and Edelman, 1992, pp. 120–121. For an in-depth discussion of some of these issues, see Cowan, 1995, pp. 137–199.

7
Categories

If they are to survive, all organisms must reduce the huge amount of information that comes in from the outside world, deciding which information is relevant to their survival. One of the primary mechanisms through which this is accomplished is *categorization*. A central mechanism of perception and semantic memory, categorization may be the primary basis of memory (see Edelman, 1987: 240–270; Edelman, 1989: 110–112).[1] It is here defined as the ability (1) to group features together and thereby differentiate objects, events, or qualities; and (2) to see some of these as equivalent, and associate and remember them together in a *category*.[2] Different categories are distinguished through the creation of boundaries between categories. The physiological correlate of a category may be a coordination of groups of neurons in different neural maps in the brain (Edelman, 1987: 240–270). Categories form the connection between perception and thought, creating a concise form in which experience can be coded and retained. This conciseness is important because of chunking considerations mentioned previously. Categories are the primary terms in which many types of memories are stored and recalled.[3]

The consideration of a number of different things as being in some sense the same (in the same category) has the biologically adaptive function of eliciting the same response in similar situations—to quickly provide the appropriate response to a situation without having to consider each new situation in all of its detail. Categorization is not a uniquely human ability. Many organisms categorize aspects of their environments in order to quickly produce the appropriate response to situations, especially dangerous ones. Note that this implies that at least some kinds of categorization involve *implicit* memory—that is, we may form some categories without our conscious knowledge that this is taking place.

Categorization is essential for survival. This ability comes at a cost, however: whereas discrimination and memory *between* categories is very acute, discrimination and memory for distinctions *within* categories is usually poor, although not completely nonexistent (Harnad, 1987: 535). The ability to generalize allows fast responses and greatly reduces memory load, but at the cost of the ability to remember much of the fine detail of experience. Essentially, the level of detail of an experience that we are able to remember is largely based on the level of detail of our categories. What we remember often consists of our categories, colored by our experience. Many kinds of "experts" are simply people who through a great deal of practice, have developed fine-grained category structures. For example, take the way in which we see and remember color categories. Almost anyone can distinguish between the colors red and green (a between-category distinction). Without special training, however, most of us cannot accurately reidentify a particular shade of red (a within-category distinction) reliably at a later time. Again, from the evolutionary point of view, this allows us to attend to aspects of the world that promote survival, while suppressing unnecessary detail and conserving memory. Because categories function at several levels of perception and thought, at this point it is important to distinguish between *perceptual* categories and *conceptual* categories (see Edelman, 1992: esp. 124–125).[4]

Perceptual Categories

Bottom-up distinctions, some of which are built in to our perceptual systems (Barsalou, 1992: 22–24), *perceptual categories* operate directly on our sensory input at the earliest stages of perception, previously described as feature extraction. Basic features such as a sound's pitch and loudness are perceived at the most primitive level of auditory categorization, which combines the stimulation from separate auditory nerves into features.

The next level of perceptual categorization is the binding together of different features that have already been extracted. At this stage of perception, individual features are bound together to form unified entities, often based on invariances in the environment. Thus features such as edges, areas of color, surface texture, and other visual properties that remain essentially the same when viewed from different angles are combined to produce the visual impression of an object. Certain features such as the acoustical resonance and timing characteristics of a particular musical instrument would be examples of auditory invariances.

Perceptual categorization is the process by which our nervous systems automatically divide the world into discrete "things".[5] Individual objects and events are perceptual categories in this sense, because categorization is a way of grouping things together, and perceptual categorization groups individual features together into unified objects and events. Perceptual categorization functions to create boundaries in our perception of the world, and boundaries help create units for memory. Indeed, in this very basic sense, the edges of a visual object, or the beginning and ending of a pitch are category boundaries. That we recognize a musical event as being separate from its background is a kind of rudimentary perceptual categorization. In this sense a single musical event is a perceptual category. The previously mentioned principles of proximity, similarity and continuity are some of the operating principles of perceptual categorization.

Perceptual categorization is also the process that unifies our different and changing views of an object into a constant "thing." That we perceive the sounds of a musical instrument or a person's voice as coming from the *same source* across multiple events and despite changes of pitch, timbre, and timing is an example of this kind of perceptual categorization. This is a higher level of perceptual categorization where multiple events are categorized as coming from a single source. Thus perceptual categorization is a basis for the *constancy* of objects as they are perceived.

Basic to the idea of a perceptual category is the idea that, given a continuous range of values of some stimulus, we will tend to perceive only a limited number of discrete categories within that range. A classic example of this is the color spectrum of visible light. We know that the visible spectrum is a continuum of frequencies of light energy, and yet when presented with the full spectrum of these frequencies, as in a rainbow, we do not see a continuum—a smooth or continuous change of color—but a small number of color categories (bands) with fuzzy edges that shade into each other. This particular categorization is neither learned nor related to language distinctions about colors (Hardin, 1988). Rather, it is built into the structure of our mechanisms of vision. The division of continuous auditory experience into the three levels (event fusion, melodic and rhythmic, and formal) described in chapter 1 is another example of a broad type of categorization that is not learned.

Conceptual Categories

Whereas perceptual categories operate primarily to segment patterns of energy that immediately impinge on our senses, *conceptual categories* operate to *identify* and *generalize* (relate through long-term memory) the perceptual units established by perceptual categorization. Conceptual categorization operates on information within the brain (memory) in relation to its sensory input. Unlike perceptual categorization, conceptual categorization can be the result of a conscious act. Where perceptual categorization deals with single objects or events, conceptual categorization links together memories of objects and events that have occurred at different times (Edelman, 1989: 207–209). The connections between the components of a conceptual category, rather than being established on the basis of simultaneity or spatial contiguity, as in much perceptual categorization, are established in relation to an organism's memory and values; conceptual categories can thus be idiosyncratic—they can vary, depending on individual history. Conceptual categories always involve the past. Note that conceptual categories are not necessarily equivalent to, or dependent on, language.[6] They can exist prior to language, although many conceptual categories may be related to words in a language.

Conceptual categorization groups the separate objects or events of perceptual categorization into higher-level categories, which consist of abstractions of memories of many objects or events that are somehow related.[7] The process I have called "identification" is essentially "re-cognition" of category membership. Conceptual categories are memory-driven ways of dividing up experience. As part of the structure of long-term semantic memory, they help form the context for experience. The ability to conceptually categorize an area of experience can enhance memory. The activation of conceptual categories in long-term memory can help to encode experience in remembered units. Learning to recognize types of objects and events, such as cars, birds, or pitch intervals (as opposed to merely discriminating their individual presence, as in perceptual categorization) is a primary aspect of conceptual categorization, although it is probably the case that not all conceptual categories are established just on the basis of experience (Hirschfeld and Gelman, 1994). Whereas conceptual categories may become connected to words in a language, many concepts themselves are prelinguistic (see Harnad, 1993).[8] They are a kind of generalized perceptual abstraction.

That they are largely learned and assume a variety of structures are defining characteristics of conceptual categories.[9] Common to many conceptual categories is a graded structure, in which some items are considered "better" or more representative members—more "prototypical"—of a category than others. In the category of bird, for example, a robin is considered more prototypical than a pelican (within the European culture, at least). In the category of musical interval, an interval of a perfect fifth perfectly in tune could be considered (by a trained listener) more prototypical than an interval on the border between a perfect fifth and a minor sixth.

Due to the phenomenon of chunking, many conceptual categories are arranged in multileveled memory structures called "hierarchies," whose different levels often correspond to different amounts of detail and abstraction. There is usually a particular level of detail at the "middle" of the hierarchy that is the most accessible and the most frequently used. Called the "basic level" of categorization, it serves as the entry level to the hierarchy. It is the level at which we most easily categorize the world, indeed, the level at which our conceptual grasp of the world is grounded (Lakoff, 1987: 31–40). Midway between the highly abstract and the extremely detailed, it is also often the first level at which children learn words for things. An example of a basic level category would be *dog*, rather than *mammal* (which is more general and abstract) or *German shepherd* (which is more specific). Thus in music, a basic level categorical unit would be a *phrase*, rather than a *note* or a *section* (Zbikowski, 1991: 88), the level at which we most easily immediately grasp (chunk) musical structure. Another aspect of basic level categories is that they are the result of our physical interactions with the world. A musical phrase, for example, often represents one coherent physical gesture, such as a single breath, or a single movement of a bow. Because the physical capacities of human beings (as well as the capacity of short-term memory) are similar in many different places and times, the phrase level of grouping is found in many different kinds of music. As has been mentioned previously, this physical coherence also gives phrases a coherence in memory. We shall see later that basic level phenomena play a role in our structured memories of music.

Certainly perceptual and conceptual categories interact in many ways. Most conceptual categories must be built up from perceptual categories. Because they involve individual long-term memory, however, the higher-level conceptual categories can have a much more idiosyncratic structure. Conceptual categories are represented differently in different individuals, and even in a single individual, depending on how they are used (Barsalou, 1993: 70–72).

Categories and Nuance

Several important aspects of music, notably, pitch, rhythm, and form display categorical effects. As we have seen, categorical structure tends to emphasize differences *between* categories (at category boundaries) and to suppress them *within* categories.

From an evolutionary (adaptive) point of view, it is easy to imagine why it would be more important to discriminate the "borderline cases" than those clearly at the center of a category, especially if the border was between safe and unsafe situations.[10]

Categorization operates at several different levels in music. Individuals (and cultures) develop categories for musical intervals, for the position of pitches in a musical scale, for the position of a beat within a metrical unit, and for the recognition of patterns on the formal level. Essentially, what this means is that we recognize individual pitch intervals and beats and patterns as examples of certain categories despite local variations in their values.[11] No musician plays a particular note at exactly the same frequency every time. Nonetheless, trained listeners are able to hear a particular interval, say, a perfect fifth, *despite* these variations. We are also able to recognize a type of musical pattern, even if its fine details are not exactly the same every time it occurs. These types of musical categories are primarily conceptual and learned, which means that the categories into which musical phenomena are placed may be different in different cultures. Also, the size of this type of conceptual category may be refined (made smaller) with practice (see Gibson, 1953; Murphy and Lassaline, 1997: 122–126). This type of categorical refinement is an aspect of many kinds of expertise involving sensory qualities.

Nuance is the variation that takes place inside of the boundaries of a musical category (see Raffman, 1993). Musical nuance in this sense includes a range of different phenomena. Melodic nuances include the subtle bending of pitches, vibrato, and small variations in intonation (see figure 7.1). Rhythmic nuances include the rushing and dragging of beats and groups of beats, as well as small variations in overall tempo. Formal nuances can include repetitions of a pattern so subtle it is unclear whether anything about the pattern has actually been changed.[12]

Nuances are variations that we can notice on some level, but that do not affect our basic sense of which category we are hearing at a given time. They are represented at the level of echoic memory, and are then usually lost in the later conceptual categorization processes. In other words, nuances may be present at the beginning of perceptual categorization, but are absent at the level of conceptual categorization. They can be noticed, however, because they may be brought directly into perceptual awareness, bypassing the category structure of long-term memory.[13] Thus, as we have seen before, we can experience more than we can remember. Although not remembered, nuances contribute to the subtle ongoing "feel" of the music, and often carry important emotional information.[14] Nuances in this sense

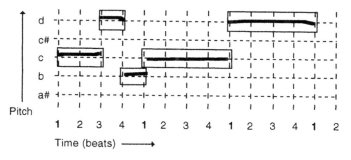

Figure 7.1
Musical categories and nuance. A sequence of performed nuanced pitch events is mapped against notated pitch and beat categories. The dotted lines represent the most central or prototypical values of the categories, and the rectangles represent category boundaries.

are like colorations or shades within a basic category, and have been referred to as constituting the "expressive aspects" of music.

This gives rise to a distinction between *structure* and *expression* (Clarke, 1987b). Musical *structure* consists of patterns of events that constitute a musical *syntax*, a sequence of patterns compared over time for similarities and differences. For a syntax to function within the limits of short-term memory, the musical elements of the syntax must be reduced to a relatively small number of discrete categories. These are usually stabilized in a musical culture in the form of tuning systems, metrical systems, and the like, which form the basic vocabulary of categories a culture uses to create musical patterns. Musical *expression*, on the other hand, consists of the varying nuances that exist within these categories.[15] The relative importance of structure versus expression can vary across different musical cultures.

The patterns of rhythm, melodies, and so on that we are able to remember from music consist of sequences of musical categories. Each occurrence of a category, however, is shaded in a particular way by its nuances, which constitute the expressive aspects of the music. Unlike categories, which are discrete, expressive nuances are *continuous* variations in the pitch or rhythm of a musical event.

Nuance and Implicit Memory

An important aspect of nuances is that, under normal circumstances, they cannot be easily remembered by listeners (see Raffman, 1993: 83–91).[16] Because category structure is a basic feature of explicit long-term memory, nuanced information, which bypasses this type of memory, is difficult to remember: it is "ineffable." This is probably the major reason why recordings, which freeze the details of particular musical performances, can be listened to many times and continue to seem vital and interesting.

That nuances are *continuous* and not discrete seems to contradict previous statements about categorical perception. In some sense, perceptible nuances must exist outside the mechanism of conceptual categorization. It may be that nuances are a kind of "remainder" left over after perceptual categorization (Clarke, 1987a: 22). In figure 1.1, a possible path for the perception of nuances is indicated by the thick line labeled "perceptual awareness" running from the feature extraction/perceptual binding stage directly to short-term memory. This path represents the possibility of bringing our perceptual experience directly into awareness *without* an abstract conceptual aspect (although it is more typical to have experiences with both perceptual and conceptual aspects). It may explain how nuances can be perceived but not consciously remembered: the path bypasses the formation of long-term memory. Each nuance is unique, hence not easily rehearsable. Nuances can therefore be part of our ongoing experience of the music, but not necessarily part of our explicit memory of it (nuances may in fact evoke implicit emotional memories).[17]

The above ideas have some bearing on the concept of written musical notation. Generally speaking, when a standardized written musical notation is used, it is primarily a description of general pitch and time categories, or what has been referred to above as "syntax." This syntax constitutes the *structure* of the piece—its musical patterns and the relations between them. The very fact that this structure *can* be represented in notation makes it a kind of explicit memory. We might say that the structure of a notated piece consists of aspects that remain the same between different performances. Nuances, which in a very real sense make the music "come alive," cannot usually be captured in notation, which normally represents only the basic syntax of musical categories.[18]

One result of this is that nuanced performance cannot really be taught through written texts or notation. This is because the performance of many kinds of nuance may involve skill memory that is primarily *implicit*: if they are there at all, notational indications of nuances are *unquantified signs*. After all, because of the subtlety and variation of nuance, if nuances *could* be captured in notation, it would take almost an infinite number of symbols to do it. Thus nuances are generally taught, not through notated examples, but through live performance examples. One of the hallmarks of implicit skill knowledge is that usually it cannot be taught through symbolic description: it must be *demonstrated.*

Indeed, maintaining traditions of expressive nuance is one of the primary functions of music teachers. Although many of the technical aspects of playing an instrument (such as fingering) can be learned by reading explicit texts and through practice, it takes a teacher who can play interpretative examples to teach students how to form their own nuanced interpretations.[19] Recordings of other musicians can also act as teachers in this sense. From this point of view, all musical traditions are, to some extent, "oral" traditions.

The term *interpretation* as used above refers to what might be called "management of nuances," which is of course what distinguishes different performances of the same notated music. In addition to carrying emotional information, interpretation is critical to making aspects of the music such as phrasing clear. Expressive nuances can function in the service of elucidating structure.

Nuances are provided by the musician at the time of performance: they differ with each performance, and even with each rendering of the same category of event within a single performance. A particular musician will not play the same notated pitch at exactly the same frequency each time it occurs. In other words, every performance, even of notated music, is to some extent an *improvisation* at the nuance level. It is worth noting again that if we did not categorize musical materials rather broadly, if instead we heard every nuance as completely different, the profusion of categories would immediately overload our memory capacities, and we would not be able to remember much of the music at all. Organized patterns emerge in the music precisely because of categorization because the patterns are patterns of instances of categories.

Not all music has the presentation of categorical patterns as its goal, however. In some types of music, such as some free improvised music, the distinction between structure and expression starts to break down.[20] This music emphasizes nuance by producing uncategorizable events that cannot easily be assembled into a syntax, such as continuously sliding pitches, nonpulsed rhythmic patterns, unpitched noises, and so on. It takes an altogether different stance toward memory from that of music seeking to establish clear and rememberable structure.

Different types of musical instruments make different types of nuance possible. Whereas wind and string instruments can produce both temporal and pitch nuances, acoustic keyboard instruments, because their tuning is fixed, can produce only temporal, loudness, and some timbral nuances. We shall consider the exact nature of particular types of nuances in detail in relation to pitch, rhythm, and form in chapters 11, 12, and 13, respectively.

In summary, we gradually build up explicit memories of structured patterns of general categories such as pitch and rhythm, while forgetting the minute variations within these categories, although these variations contribute much to our ongoing emotional involvement with the music. As we form a mental representation of a piece of music, each subsequent performance is brought to life by different unrememberable nuances. As mentioned earlier, this is even true for recordings. We shall now consider how the categorization process operates on levels higher than that of the single event.

Notes

1. The ability to categorize may be inherent in the response characteristics of some types of neural networks. See Elman et al., 1998, p. 53.

2. Here we should distinguish between *categories* and *concepts*. This is no easy task, as these words have been used in a number of different ways, including both words being used to mean exactly the same thing. In this book, *concept* is understood to mean the linking of a perceptual category with a conceptual category. This grows out of an ability to generalize across different perceptual experiences (categorization) and to form a general representation in memory that is separate from and endures beyond individual perceptual experiences themselves (see Edelman, 1989: 140–146). Grounded directly in perceptual experience, the concept is believed to be a fundamental unit of thought. A concept is a single generalized mental entity, whereas a conceptual category consists of examples of that concept. Category membership is not absolute, which tends to give most categories a graded or "fuzzy" structure. It is not necessary that *every* member of a category be stored as a separate representation; an abstracted *prototype*, or best example of the category may alone be stored and new experiences compared with that prototype to establish degree of category membership. Generally speaking, however, the more dissimilar the members of a category are from each other, the more likely they will be stored as individual examples. For an elaborated, in-depth review of ideas about concepts and categories, see Barsalou, 1992, pp. 153–177; and Smith and Samuelson, 1997, pp. 181–195. It should also be emphasized that although the development of language requires concepts, the development of concepts does not require language. Note that the above implies categorization may take place without higher-level consciousness, and therefore may be an example of *implicit* memory. See Goschke, 1997, pp. 247–318, esp. pp. 309–310. For a book-length treatment of this topic, see Weiskrantz, 1988.

3. Of course, new categories *can* be formed, often by modifying aspects of categories that already exist. This means that, at least for adults, new knowledge is usually established by extension of existing categories. This process of extension is often metaphorical. See Holyoak and Thagard, 1995.

4. There are other pairs of terms used to describe the same thing, such as "sensory perception categories" and "generic knowledge categories"; see Medin and Barsalou, 1987, pp. 455–471. In addition, perceptual and conceptual categories may be viewed, not as an opposition, but as endpoints on a continuum; see Goldstone and Barsalou, 1998, esp. pp. 168–170.

5. It is important to note that how the nervous system partitions the environment is not determined entirely by that environment, which is by no means an unambiguous place. Values and culture play an important part in determining how categorization proceeds. This is especially important at the conceptual level of categorization. See Edelman, 1987, pp. 26–32, 244–259.

6. It is clear that some organisms that do not possess language nonetheless have considerable categorizing ability. See for example, Pierce, 1988. Note that the idea that human concepts are relatively independent of language is part of a particular theoretical position, and that there are many different ideas about the relation between conceptualization and language. For an overview see Pederson and Nuyts, 1997.

7. Note that I have used the general concept of "relatedness," rather than similarity. Similarity is a complex issue because at the conceptual level, it is related to values, which specify what the relevant variables of similarity are. See Barsalou, 1992, pp. 25, 171–174; Edelman, 1989, p. 99. For a good discussion of issues about similarity, see Hahn and Chater, 1998.

8. Although at this point no one knows for sure how concepts become connected to language, Harnad has an interesting three-stage model of how perceptual and conceptual categorizations take place. See also Barsalou, 1993; Edelman, 1989, pp. 265–268.

9. For an overview of different kinds of structure of conceptual categories, see Barsalou, 1992, pp. 15–51; for a book-length discussion of the variety of conceptual category structure, see Lakoff, 1987.

10. "Categorical perception" in Clarke's definition (1987a: p. 22), "functions so as to separate essential structural units or events from non-structural information; in other words it separates the invariants of a perceptual context from the uncontrolled variations or perceptual 'noise' that inevitably accompany them."

11. The exact location of category boundaries is not absolute, but is generally somewhat contextual. Category size can also be refined with learning. It is also possible that different kinds of categories may be encoded in different ways. Much more research needs to be done on categorical phenomena in relation to musical sounds. See McAdams, 1993, pp. 189–191. This article also has a good summary of ideas about the nature of possible types of memory representations for sounds.

12. This sense of the term *nuance* does not appear in Diana Raffman's discussion (1993); it is essentially my own metaphorical extension of *nuance* to include types of phenomena she does not discuss. I believe that in certain types of music, the categorization of entire musical phrases can be dealt with in a nuanced way, that is, one that causes interference effects and makes memorization difficult. See Deliege, 1996.

13. This "bypassing" is probably metaphorical. That is, the neural activity caused by nuances may take place in the same groups of neurons that represent our conceptual categories for

the events being experienced, but this momentary activity does not cause any permanent changes in the connections between those neurons. Hence the nuances are experienced but unremembered: they bypass the process of LTM *formation*. See Globus, 1995, pp. 24, 40, 56, 66, where the process described above is referred to as the "tuning of neurons." See also Pashler, 1998, pp. 328, 353, where this process is referred to as "stabilization."

14. See Keil and Feld, 1994. This article presents some ideas about the importance of nuance in various kinds of music. The authors use the term *participatory discrepancies* to describe phenomena that occur between different simultaneous parts in musical ensembles in a way similar to what I refer to as "nuance." Thus nuances exist between different parts in an ensemble as well as within a single part. For a listing of some characteristics of expressive performance, see Sloboda and Davidson, 1996, p. 173.

15. Note that some aspects of the distinction between expression and structure do not hold on the formal level because the function of nuance at that level may be the *confusion of structure itself*. (More will be said about this in chapter 13.)

16. Note that this statement applies primarily to the experience of the listeners; the experience of the performer is somewhat different. See note 17.

17. One might ask the question: if nuances are unrememberable, how do performers ever learn to produce them? Because the performance of nuance involves skill, at least some performative nuances must be implicit memories. Like most implicit skill memories, they must be built up slowly over time. Performers usually do this in the form of either group or individual *practicing*. Listeners rarely practice listening to anything like the degree that performers practice performing, hence their memories of heard nuances are rarely established to anything like the same degree as those of performers. Because they function as *expression*, nuances can carry emotional information in music. See Brinner, 1995, p. 34: "While the basic 'correctness' or acceptability of a performance may depend on the proper application or execution of procedures within declarative (explicit) frameworks, *feeling and emotional charge are the unquantifiables that distinguish one performance from another qualitatively*." (Italics added.) Although there has been little research in this area, it is believed that emotional memory may be primarily implicit. For more about the implicit nature of emotional memory, see LeDoux, 1996, esp. pp. 55–64, 201–204; Tobias, Kihlstrom, and Schacter, 1992, esp. pp. 69–70.

18. There are some types of musical notation, such as "swing lightly" and "rubato," that attempt to capture nuances. Certain jazz arrangements also use slanted lines to indicate pitch inflections, such as "falling off" of a certain pitch. I would maintain that because correct performance of these notated nuances depends on a tradition of implicit background knowledge, they do not really contradict my statements about notation. See, for example, Progler, 1995, p. 21.

19. This is just as true in musical cultures that do not use notation as in those which do. It is just that in cultures not using notation, what we are calling "technical aspects" is transmitted by example, too. The larger issue involved here is what constitutes musical *competency*, which of course varies greatly across musical cultures. For an outline of some of the characteristics that may comprise musical competency, see Brinner, 1995, pp. 40–43.

20. For a description and analysis of some of the motivations and performance practices of free improvised music, see Corbett, 1995. For a discussion of these issues in relation to other contemporary music practices, see Clarke, 1987b, pp. 215–221. The tendency to subvert syntax by producing uncategorizable events is evident in some traditional ethnic musics as well. See Cohen and Katz, 1997, esp. p. 36.

8

Schemas: Frameworks for Experience and Memory

In addition to categorizing objects and single events, we generalize and categorize entire physical situations and temporal sequences of events. When a number of different situations occurring at different times seem to have aspects in common, they are eventually averaged together into an abstract memory framework. This is the process of formation of semantic memory, which has been described previously. Built up out of the commonalities shared by different experiences, these frameworks are referred to as "schemas". Like conceptual categories, schemas are thought to be central structures of semantic memory.[1]

The distinction between categories and schemas is of course not absolute. Schemas are a sort of metacategory; indeed, the elements or "slots" of which a schema is composed are categories.[2] Both schemas and categories are sets of long-term memory associations. Schemas are larger sets of associations. The internal structure of schemas and categories may be somewhat different. Categories are usually arranged hierarchically in levels, whereas schemas may be organized purely in terms of the structure of the situation (spatial or temporal) they represent (Mandler, 1979).

Schemas are organized sets of memories about sequences of events or physical scenes and their temporal and spatial characteristics, which are built up as we notice regularities in the environment. When we encounter similar situations repeatedly, we do not remember every detail of each encounter. As with categories, this would require enormous amounts of memory and would be very wasteful. Rather, we form an abstract model of the situation, based on the invariant aspects our repeated encounters have in common.[3]

Schemas function as norms or sets of ideas about how things *usually* are, and allow us to move through situations without having to repeatedly consciously evaluate every detail and its meaning: they operate unconsciously to contextualize current experience. They are an important part of the semiactivated memory contexts mentioned in chapter 1. The operation of schematic memory contexts during perception is what makes the world seem familiar. Extremely rapid processing through schematic connections between groups of neurons and neural maps is thought to be an important aspect of the selection of the perceptual information that enters short-term memory. Schemas provide frameworks within which to evaluate novelty and thereby guide attention (Bregman, 1990: 398–399).

Schemas are large patterns of generalized associations in memory that determine how whole situations are processed. Our initial scanning of a situation reveals features that then cause particular higher-level schematic connections to be selected. In this sense, situations are processed *through* schemas. Selecting the correct schema to process a situation is the basis for the process of *understanding*. This happens very quickly—usually within milliseconds of our seeing or hearing something and usually outside our conscious awareness: we deal quite well with many types of situations without ever consciously thinking about how to do it. Note that the term *understanding* metaphorically refers to a process that takes place "underneath" the conscious mind—in the unconscious.

If most of the details of a situation fit reasonably well with a schema, our attention immediately moves to the details that do not—to the novel details that stand out against a background of the familiar. (This is a point at which "direct awareness" in figure 1.1 might be activated.) If many of the details of the situation do not fit with the currently evoked schema, a search for a new schema—known as a "double take"—will usually cause us to focus consciousness on the unusual details of the situation.

Thus schemas are large networks of memories with potential associative connections. When particular scenes or events in the environment trigger our expectations, some of these memory networks become semiactivated; these semiactivated memories may enter our peripheral consciousness as a "feeling" of what is about to happen. Schemas in the form of musical patterns and styles are largely responsible for our feelings of expectation while listening to a piece of music. This feeling usually stays on the fringes of the focus of consciousness. In some instances, however, we may see or hear what we expect, rather than what is "really" there.[4] While our expectations usually do not intrude into our conscious present as hallucinations, the very possibility of hallucinations reminds us that a sizable part of our experience of the outside world does not come directly from that world (Dennett, 1991: 3–18).

Schemas may be of physical scenes or of temporal event sequences. Because music consists of acoustical event sequences, we shall be primarily concerned with temporal schemas.

Schematic Organization

Schemas are based on what similar situations have in common; because no two situations are ever exactly alike, schemas must be somewhat flexible: their elements, that is, the categories of objects, single events, actions within a scene or event, are variable within certain limits. This flexibility makes a schema somewhat like an equation, with abstract variables that can be filled in with different values. These variables, in turn, are like "slots" into which various particular features can be fitted, provided they do not violate the basic nature of the schema. This flexibility is one of the things that make schemas so useful, because they can be adapted to many different situations.

An example of a temporal schema would be eating in a restaurant (Schank and Abelson, 1977: 42, 153). This schema would have a relatively stable sequence of events, such as ordering, eating, and paying the bill, as its components. Note that in order to correctly deal with the restaurant schema, not only do we have to be familiar with the temporal organization of the schema itself, but we have to recognize instances of categories (slots) relevant to the schema. This means that we must recognize instances of the categories of table, chair, waiter/waitress, cash register, and so on, and that we must know what to do in response to these instances. All of these have a role in the schema, and all of these can differ considerably in detail, and still evoke the restaurant schema.

A musical example of a schema slot would be the category of the downbeat in music that is organized metrically. The organization of musical time into repeating cycles of meter works in a schematic way (see Chap. 11). The downbeat is a very important type of category in metrical structure. It is a beat that marks the beginning of a metrical cycle, and functions to maintain the cyclical grouping standard of meter. The downbeat is like a schema slot, in that many different kinds of musical events may occupy the downbeat position in the measure and still function as downbeats. The category of downbeat actually has a graded structure, with some types of events being more prototypical or better examples of the downbeat than others. (More will be said about the schematic nature of meter in chapter 12.)

The categories that comprise a schema may also have "default values" (Barsalou, 1992: 160). Details of a situation that are not noticed as unusual quickly drop out of awareness and their slots are assigned default values in memory. Default values fill in typical or average instances in memory for variables not attended to at a particular time—creating a kind of generic reality. In our memories of things that have taken place outside, for instance, the sky is usually there, although we may not have looked at it at all. The sky slot may therefore have a default value. Based on the category prototype effects mentioned earlier, schema default values are probably responsible for many episodic memory distortions. When recalling a particular episode, we often do not remember which parts of the experience we were actually paying attention to, therefore we do not know which parts of the memory may be our own default values and which parts "really" happened. We have filled in the unattended-to parts of the memory with our own previously established prototypical values. In this way, different generations of memories can get conflated. In the very long term, this probably causes the details of episodic memories to slowly drift in the direction of default values (J. Mandler, 1984: 104–105): our memories slowly modify themselves to become more and more like the most prototypical instances of our own categories and schemas. Because our categories and schemas themselves are evolving or being updated based on new experiences and expectation failures, this means that subsequent experience can actually modify our older memories (see Linton, 1982).

Schemas and Normalcy

We are most likely to notice and remember things when they *do not fit exactly* within our schemas, and these novel episodic memories will tend to be connected by association with a relevant schema. This means that noticing and remembering are most likely to take place when our expectations *fail* (see Schank, 1982).[5] A waitress in a gorilla suit, for example, would not be a part of our restaurant schema, and would be immediately noticed as being unusual, as would a loud, dissonant chord in the middle of a piece of music that was quiet and consonant. We would tend to remember these types of events, and would also tend to be reminded of these episodes when something in a later situation evoked the same schema.

From the perspective of biological adaptation, when our expectations fail is when we most need a specific (episodic) memory of another failure of the same expectation to help us figure out what to do. That is, we notice and remember things when expectations fail because these types of situations could eventually require that a schema be modified, or in more extreme circumstances, that a new schema be formed. If a particular set of expectations fails a number of times, the schema for that particular situation will need to be updated. Hence specific episodic memories representing the failure of particular expectations (schemas) are connected to those expectations by association: they are available to remind us at the relevant moment when we might need to consider updating a schema (Schank, 1982: 37–40).

All of our schemas taken together form a kind of averaged model of how the world usually is, a kind of generic reality. Without this complex of frameworks, the world would be always strange and unfamiliar, and we would spend all of our time trying to figure out where we were and what was going on. Most of the time, this model works so well that we do not need to pay much attention to many details of our lives. When something deviates sufficiently from the normal, it receives our attention; it is remembered and this memory is associated with the relevant schema in memory.

Because they are part of semantic memory, different levels of schemas may be hierarchically arranged, moving from schemas about generalized aspects of reality to very specific schemas about particular kinds of objects or events (remember, however, that the internal organization of a particular schema is usually based on the organization of the scene or event it represents). For instance, in addition to the previously mentioned restaurant schema, we might have more general schemas about dinners, food, or eating in general, and we might have more detailed schemas about which kinds of food are served in which kinds of restaurants. The actual restaurant schema itself, however, would derive its time sequence from the sequence in which the events typically happen. In relation to a particular piece of music, we might have more general schemas about the large-scale organization of a piece or its musical style, and we might have more detailed schemas about the local arrangement of sections, particular types of patterns in those sections, and so forth.

The disadvantage of a generalized, schema-driven recognition system is that over time, because they are always undergoing the process of being slowly generalized, particular episodic memories of experiences that are similar and fit the same schemas tend to become confused. That is, when we have any type of experience repeatedly, we have great difficulty remembering the details of any particular occurrence, unless they are fairly unusual. This is referred to as an "interference effect" and is based on the idea that similar memories interfere with each other. Interference effects are a direct result of the limits of categorization: we simply cannot retain all of the minute differences between different but very similar experiences. Music that uses repeated, highly similar patterns is designed to produce this effect.

Because a schema has been defined here as a higher-level categorization of experience, and because categories create boundaries, an interesting question arises. What constitutes the boundaries of a temporal schema? One answer to this question that has been proposed is that schemas are bounded by the achievement of goals (Schank, 1982: 86–98). This means that schemas are groups of memories organized around particular goals, and that once a particular goal is achieved (or discarded, for that matter), a new set of expectations directed toward a new goal goes into effect. This is a kind of high-level grouping of real-life experience. Certainly, in real life, these schemas and goals are nested, and there can be a number of both short- and long-term goals in operation at the same time. In linear, goal-directed music, which is far less complex than real life, there may still be a number of hierarchical levels of goals operating at a particular time. It is often the case in such music that the arrival at a goal of some sort signals the end of a section—in essence, a temporal category boundary. (More will be said about this in chapter 13.)

Schemas and Music

With regard to our mental representation of a piece of music, all of the foregoing has several implications. First of all, on first hearing a piece, we do not remember all or even most of its details. What we remember is a rather abstract "gist" of what went on (see Schank, 1990: 170–176).[6] This gist might consist of defaults, based on our ideas of what is normal (schemas) for this type of work. This generalized semantic memory model might be peppered with more vivid and specific episodic memory fragments of details that in some way did not fit our expectations and were somehow remarkable, and hence were remembered. As we listen to the piece repeatedly, we build up a more and more detailed model of specific events in it, although it takes many listenings before we literally know in detail what is coming next throughout the entire piece. In the early stages of listening, our fragmented episodic memories may be quite different from what is actually in the piece—indeed, they may tend to be more like other fragments of similar music which we already remember. A comparison of the actual piece with what we remember, especially if made after a considerable time, may be startling in the depth of its "errors." As we build up our mental representation through repeated listening, it slowly becomes more "accurate," that is, in closer conformance with the original. If we listen repeatedly to the extent that we learn to know exactly what is coming next at any point, we might say that we have exhausted the piece because our mental representation is practically equivalent to the piece itself, and we do not notice what we already know. This generally takes a very large number of repetitions, however, because of the difficulty of remembering nuances. (This argument is being made in relation to a fixed performance such as a recording because live performance nuances would always produce many microsurprises.)

Compositional strategies can have profound influence on the process described above, making it anywhere from relatively easy to very difficult to form a complete schematic (mental) representation of a piece. Examples of ways to make pieces difficult to represent schematically would be 1) building a piece with virtually no repetition so that schemas would be difficult to form (it would be hard to develop a gist); 2) building a piece so that there appears to be only one repeating schema with variations so slight that comparisons of pattern differences are very difficult because of memory interference effects or; 3) building a piece out of indefinite and uncategorizable events such as indistinct pitches, slides, noises, etc. These compositional strategies will be discussed further in the chapter on musical form.

Schemas as Musical Frameworks

Schemas in music generate expectations about the kinds and order of musical events; they serve as frameworks for memory, increase chunkability, and help us form representations in long-term memory. There is a kind of reciprocal relation between schemas and some kinds of musical experience. While we derive schemas from musical experiences, we can also construct musical experiences so that they will be easier to schematize. On the highest level, this would include many kinds of relatively stable musical forms or genres, such as symphony, raga, jazz improvisation on chord changes, and variations. Indeed, the classical version of the European form known as "variations" is an almost perfect model of how a schema works: basic musical material is introduced in the first section, then varied in different ways in subsequent sections, usually retaining some recognizable relation to the original, prototype section. Other examples of obviously schematically based music are structured improvisational styles such as mainstream jazz and North Indian raga, where understanding the improvisation requires constant comparison with a schematic archetype. These styles are purposely constructed so that we can have relatively stable expectations (subjective set) about the general type of events which will happen. Also, particular styles, cultures, or historical periods of music structure our expectations schematically on a very general level.

On a lower level, systematic and categorical aspects of music that relate to details of the music within particular pieces, such as tuning systems, metrical organization, scales of duration, and organization of instrumental sounds into families of instruments, would also qualify as schemas. (We shall examine each of these in detail in later subsections dealing with particular musical parameters.) We also develop expectations within a particular piece, based on previous events in that piece (objective set). This would have to do with the nature of the actual patterns encountered in that piece. All such musical schemas serve as frameworks for our expectations: they allow us to have some idea of "where we are" and possibly "where we are going" in the music (see Francès, 1988: 188).

Schemas and Musical Culture

Most of our discussion has involved the representation of music in the mind of the individual listener. There are, however, aspects of the mental representation of music that may be shared among many minds (D'Andrade, 1995: 122–149). Schemas are memory structures created by generalizations made across seemingly similar situations in the environment. When musical concepts and practices seem related in different situations, involving different musicians, schemas may emerge that represent these relations. When a number of individuals develop such schemas in a particular place and time, the result could be referred to as a "musical culture," a shared repertoire of musical concepts (not all of them necessarily explicit) and practices among different individuals.

A musical culture, by this definition, would consist of music-related schemas—evolving concepts and practices—that were shared by a group of people. These shared concepts and practices would form a context for the perception and understanding of music,[7] and would consist of many levels, from concepts about what constitutes an example of music at all, or the circumstances under which it occurs, all the way down to details about what constitutes a well-formed phrase.[8] Note that even though many musical schemas are part of a shared musical culture, a particular person still learns them through repeated individual experiences, including musical study. By no means do all the schemas that form a musical culture exist in the form of explicit knowledge.

Speculations about Schemas and Perception

I would speculate that the schemas of musical culture might affect perception in the following way. The perceptual-conceptual distinction made in relation to categories can also be made in relation to figure-ground relationships. That is, figures (objects and events) can emerge *perceptually* from backgrounds in experience because of boundaries such as visual edges and acoustical event onsets. There are often many different objects and events available to perception at one time, however, and all of them cannot be in the focus of conscious awareness at that time (remember that the capacity of the focus of conscious awareness is very small). As we have seen, one function of schemas is to guide our attention. From all of the possible objects and events in our perception at any given moment, we tend to foreground the most perceptually *and conceptually* novel or important to us (Cowan, 1995: 140–142). Musicians usually try to design perceptual foreground-background relationships, using the kind of bottom-up effects described earlier so that listeners can reconstruct their organization of the music. Within complex acoustical textures, however, there are still a number of possible perceptual foreground-background relationships. This means that the experiences of different listeners will not necessarily be the same, although most of the time, basic sequential units such as phrases are similar across listeners.

For instance, a professional cellist listening to a Brahms symphony very likely has a different experience (perhaps with the cello parts more foregrounded) from that of an amateur oboist, who has a different experience from that of a listener who listens primarily to Beethoven. This listener has a different experience from that of another, who listens primarily to popular music, who has a different experience from that of a third, who listens primarily to North Indian music, and so on and so forth. Each of these listeners could be said to be part of a different musical culture to increasing degrees. Hence each of these listeners hears the music through a different repertoire of schemas, concepts, and experiences. One of the major differences between these different listeners' experiences lies in *what is foregrounded*: what features stand out and immediately emerge in the experience. Although it is certainly true that in some sense, the acoustical stimulus is "the same" for different simultaneous listeners, because there is much more information than awareness can handle at any given time, the perceptions of the respective listeners are selective and partly driven by their repertoires of schemas. This would be especially true in the case of experienced listeners. Inexperienced listeners would tend to have a more "bottom-up" perspective, that was more directly dependent on perceptually novel features in the music, such as unusually loud moments, large shifts in timbre, and so forth. Because activation of long-term memory is an important component of perception and understanding, it is clear that a listener with a larger repertoire of schemas in memory usually finds more information in a given piece of music (which says nothing, of course, about the *value* of that experience to that listener). This might in part account for different levels of detail in the experience of different listeners and for many of the differences in an individual listener's experiences of the "same" music.[9]

Notes

1. Other terms which are used to describe somewhat similar types of mental structure are "frames" (Barsalou, 1992; Minsky, 1985) and "scripts" (Schank, 1982). All of these terms are used to describe large groupings of memory associations that, when activated, can form contexts for particular types of experiences. Much of the use of schemas involves semiactivated memory contexts; that is, schemas are usually not used explicitly. The idea of semiactivated schematic contexts of expectation is an example of implicit memory use. It is quite possible that schemas have no symbolic existence as such in the brain and, like categories, are really networks of facilitated pathways or established connections (associations) between networks of groups of neurons, see Edelman, 1989.

2. Some authors use these terms differently, calling some instances of what I am calling categories schemas. See, for example, Anderson, 1990, pp. 137–143.

3. Belief in the probability that the future will be similar to the past affects how we talk about the future. That the probable future will be "like" the past generates the probability concept of "likelihood"—we say that it is "likely" that something will happen.

4. In one such instance, called the "phonemic restoration illusion," a phoneme in a word is replaced with a burst of noise, and experimental subjects report hearing the missing phoneme "behind" the noise, even though it is not there at all. See McAdams, 1993. An excellent example of this can be heard on tracks 11, 13, and 15 on the CD accompanying Warren, 1999.

5. This description of a situation likely to produce an episodic memory is similar to a description of a situation likely to produce an emotional response. The connections between memory and emotion are not dealt with in this book, although there are clearly connections between the two. See G. Mandler, 1984; Scherer and Ekman, 1984, pp. 295–297. See also Kagan, 1994, pp. 92–101. Kagan makes the important point that it is *discrepancy*, rather than novelty per se, that stimulates emotional response. This highlights the importance of a framework (schema) within which expectations can be violated.

6. It is not clear at this time exactly what would constitute a musical gist. Certainly we have some kind of reduced representation of the music that we have previously heard in a piece, but what form does this take? In language, the gist consists of the general semantic meaning

of a passage, but music does not have semantic meaning in the same way that language does. See Kraut, 1992. Analytical tools that posit the existence of some sort of musical "deep structure," such as Schenker's (1969) analysis and Lehrdahl and Jackendoff's (1983) generative grammar, are attempts to explain more abstract types of representations of music. It is not yet clear that such theories are able to represent the perspective of the listener, especially at high structural levels. For discussion of these ideas, see Cook, 1994; and Dibben, 1994. For some very preliminary ideas about types of gists that could conceivably apply to both language and music, see Barsalou, 1993, pp. 66–68; Bigand, 1993, pp. 253–271.

7. Exactly how and to what extent culture affects perception and understanding is a large and difficult question, requiring a great deal more research. (See the end of this chapter for some speculation on this.) Certainly, musical training and the concepts it introduces alter experience. See Smith, 1997, and De Bellis, 1995. Also, there seem to be some aspects of music that are shared across cultures. See Harwood, 1976; Carterette and Kendall, 1999, p. 780. For a discussion of this, see Walker et al., 1996. For an investigation of the shifting nature of perceptual foregrounding in musical experience, see Berger, 1997.

8. It is also the case that many cultures do not have one general concept of music, per se, although all cultures have concepts for various types of activities that we (in the West) would call "music." Like many other types of concepts mentioned in an earlier chapter, the concept of music can be graded, having central examples, but gradually shading off into other types of human activity, just as other types of activity can shade off into what we call "music." See Nattiez, 1990, pp. 58–60.

9. Steven Feld tells a story about a cross-cultural muscial perspective in which some Kaluli people from Papua, New Guinea are listening to the music of the American jazz trumpeter Miles Davis. This story gives a small glimpse into the perceptions of another musical culture. See Keil and Feld, 1994, pp. 141–143. For an example of an experiment in cross-cultural musical perception, and its relation to musical cultural schemas, see Hopkins, 1982.

9

Metaphor

An interesting aspect of associative memory is that we can be reminded of some things by others in totally different areas of experience. This happens when aspects of what we are currently experiencing or thinking are somehow correlated to aspects of some other thing in long-term memory.[1] This is a much more common feature of thought than we might initially think (Lakoff and Johnson, 1980). Although no two situations are absolutely identical, we can still make generalizations that function across different situations. Imagine, for example, learning as a child to use the word "close" both to describe closing your eyes and closing a door. The relation between these two uses of the word "close" requires making a connection between two different types of experience. This way of experiencing one thing in terms of another is referred to as "metaphor."

Note that this definition of metaphor is not just limited to literature, and indeed *does not necessarily imply the use of language.* Metaphors not couched in natural language are referred to as "nonpropositional metaphors." That is, either or both the experience that cues the reminding, and the memory of which one is reminded, while they may or may not be describable in language, do not necessarily originally occur as statements in language. They may be connections between any kinds of experiences or memories, such as those of sounds, images, and smells, and some of the memories may be implicit, taking the form of the basic perceptual representations mentioned earlier.

Metaphor is therefore a relationship between two memory structures. This is true even when we create a metaphor from "direct" experience because our understanding of that experience still comes from long-term memory. More precisely, a metaphor is a relationship between two categories or two schemas. This relationship has been referred to as a "mapping" of one category or schema onto another (see Lakoff, 1987: 270–278).[2] For example, if we say, "a melody is a path," we are mapping the image schema of a path onto the more abstract concept of a melody. Both paths and melodies proceed step by step, and both have a direction, with twists and turns in them. Note, however, that not all of the details of either term in this metaphor map onto the other. Melodies, for example, do not have anything corresponding to grass growing on them, and paths do not have accompaniments.

Image Schemas

Recent theory has suggested that metaphorical mappings are not arbitrary, but are grounded in fundamental embodied cognitive structures generalized from recurring physical experiences, especially the experience of our own bodies. These cognitive structures have been referred to as "image schemas."[3] Image-schemas are thought to be derived from commonalities in different experiences that seem related; as such, they are believed to form a basis for our conceptual systems, indeed to connect our perceptual experience and concepts. Image schemas represent the most stable constancies and structures we all share as human beings, derived from dynamic patterns of interaction with our environment. They may be thought of as a kind of perceptual abstraction. A perceptual abstraction in this sense associates a number of different perceptual experiences into a schema (Barsalou, 1993).

The actual cognitive form that image schemas are thought to take is somewhere between concrete, specific visual images and abstract concepts. That is, image schemas are often derived from types of situations that we can visually imagine, but that are more abstract than any particular image. Our understanding of an image schema such as "up" and "down," for example, is not purely linguistic and involves mental imagery of some sort, although it is not necessarily imagery of specific things. This is why it may often be difficult to explain the meaning of image schemas using only words. (Try to imagine explaining the meaning of up and down without using some sort of visual images or physical gestures referring to our own bodies.) Although image schemas are not so abstract that we cannot form any kind of image in relation to them, the image we do form may have components that are not strictly visual.[4] This is another way in which image schemas are different from either visual images or abstract concepts—they can have a kinesthetic component and represent muscular sensations in relation to particular experiences; they can have a particular physical "feel" to them. This suggests that image schemas are at least in part implicit knowledge; hence our understanding of them is often metaphorical.

Although we cannot directly describe our implicit knowledge, it can sometimes be associated with other explicit knowledge we have through metaphor. Indeed, I believe that music itself can be one form of metaphor that may express image schematic implicit knowledge (see Blacking, 1995: 239–242).[5]

Unlike language, image schemas do not consist of arbitrary symbols having little intrinsic relation to what they represent. Rather, image schemas are thought to be directly grounded in perceptual experience (Harnad, 1993); they are nonarbitrary in that they represent experience by drawing directly from perceptual categories. It is believed that very young infants develop image schemas as their first representations of the world (see Mandler, 1992; Edelman, 1989: 140–148; Edelman, 1992: 108–110). The original function of image schemas may be to connect motor sequences together to begin the formation of a coherent picture of the physical world. For instance, out of activities such as falling down, watching other things fall down, lifting things, and watching other things rise, a generalized image schema of up and down could emerge. Some of these representations may later determine the structure of language. That is, language, as it develops, might structure itself along the lines of preverbal preconceptual structures like image schemas. Image schemas may therefore serve as a bridge between experience and conceptualization.

Among the rudimentary human experiences generalized into image-schematic form are those of up and down, of spatial centeredness, of one event being linked to another through some sort of causal connection, of moving along a path toward a goal, and of containment or "inside" and "outside" (Johnson, 1987). All of these image schemas require some sort of imaginary "space" in order to make sense, but they need not consist of specific (detailed) concrete images. So basic are they to our idea of how the world works that they are used not only literally but also metaphorically to represent many other, more abstract types of ideas. We use image schemas many times every day without thinking about it at all (this is of course a property of schemas in general).

For example, when we say, "taxes have gone up," we are using a metaphor that refers to our gravity-based experience of spatial orientation. To make it comprehensible, a very abstract and nonphysical concept, a change in taxes, has been referred to in terms of a basic spatial experience that everyone shares and understands, namely, that a pile of things gets physically higher as the number of things in it gets larger. In fact, this type of metaphorical usage of language is very common, and constitutes a major way we understand many different abstract ideas.[6]

Note that the example of an image schema that I have given refers to operations in physical space. This is true of many image schemas. It is as though our conceptual "space" is built on a prior model of physical space, and forces tend to operate in the same way in both kinds of space. To understand abstract concepts, we must refer to them metaphorically in terms of something more concrete (Lakoff and Johnson, 1980: 56–59). An interesting finding that has recently emerged in relation to the above is that a part of the brain known to be central in establishing the sense of spatial position in many mammals (the hippocampus) also appears to play an important part in establishing long-term memories in human beings.[7] It is possible that this is another example of an evolutionary phenomenon observed in other cognitive areas—an organism's ability to adapt old specialized information processing systems to new purposes.[8] This may explain why we frequently use spatial and physical metaphors to understand more complex abstract concepts. Thus systems of conceptual metaphors can emerge out of preconceptual image schemas, and different kinds of conceptual spaces can be metaphorically structured by referring back to the same image schema.

Image Schemas and Music

All of the particular image schematic metaphors mentioned above occur not only in language but in music as well.[9] Image schematic metaphors are based on recurring aspects of our relation with the world, and the experiences that generate music come from that same world. In other words, we create and understand music using some of the same tools we use to understand the world because music is a part of that world. We have seen that image schemas come into play in understanding abstract ideas, and one aspect of the meaning of music is certainly the projection of abstract ideas.[10]

The particular types of image schemas that I refer to in this book and that are the source of some metaphors used to understand music include up and down, centrality, linkage, causation, tension, pathways leading to a goal, and containment. In later chapters, I shall discuss the actual concrete musical features described with each of these types of metaphors.

Although many cultures use metaphor to understand abstract musical functions, not all of these particular metaphors are universally used in all cultures to explain music. Some exist cross-culturally, and some do not. Different cultures often use different metaphors to describe similar experiences.

The Kaluli of Papua, New Guinea, for example, talk about the singing of melody using a highly developed system of metaphors based on waterfalls. This system, while based on less abstract images than some of our Western metaphors for music, still uses the notion of up and down in relation to pitch (Feld, 1982: 252). In this book, unless specifically stated otherwise, I shall use metaphors that are standard in Western descriptions of music.

As we briefly consider the metaphors based on each of the above-mentioned types of image schema and its possible relation to musical structure, it is important to avoid a kind of "reification," wherein these concepts are described as being in the music itself, rather than a set of conceptual tools we can use to try to understand music. Understanding possible metaphorical connections between music and experience can help us not only understand music, but also *create* it. Note that the discussion below concerns how certain image schematic metaphors are used to describe music in Western terms. Its purpose is to show how a particular system of image schematic metaphors are used by a particular culture to help listeners (and musicians) "imagine" musical structure. Other cultures may use other image schematic metaphors to describe the same musical phenomena.

"Up" and "Down": Music and Gravity

As physical beings, we cannot escape the influence of gravity. Indeed, the origin of the words "up" and "down" is gravity; without it (as in outer space), there is no up and down. Our orientation to the world is based on the fact that up is *not the same* as down, that is to say, moving down is very different from moving up. Generally, of course, moving down is easier than moving up, and things that move are likely to come to rest later in time at a lower point than where they started; they are said to "run down." This is the basis of a metaphorical relation between downward movement and cessation of activity (as in "broken-down" or "shutdown").

In music, up and down are frequently used to describe motion in pitch "space": positions in pitch space are said to be "higher" or "lower." And indeed music often operates as though this were literally the case even though there is *nothing concrete* that is literally getting higher or lower.[11]

There are many kinds of characteristic musical patterns that rise and fall back to the "ground."[12] Indeed, one means of developing closure or finality is to move some aspect (parameter) of the music, in a downward direction, thus causing that parameter to come to rest at a "lower" value than where it was previously. This type of closure pattern can be found in music of many cultures and time periods, although it is not always described using the metaphor of up and down (see chapter 5, note 3).

The system of gravity metaphors is a pervasive one, used to describe many different kinds of things in the world. In general, increases in energy are thought of as "rises," and decreases, as "falls".

A related idea is that of musical *tension* (from Latin *tensus*, stretch). Generally, the "higher" the levels of particular musical parameters are in relation to other points in a piece, the "more tension" they are said to have. This tension is then said to be "resolved" by a "lowering" of these parametric values. (We shall have more to say about musical tension in chapter 13.)

Centrality in Music

Another image schema that grows directly out of our embodied human experience is the idea of *centrality*. Each of us is physically at the center of the world as we see it. This is the basis for the idea of *point* of view. When we transfer the idea of centrality to outside of ourselves, we create the possibility of moving away from and toward a central location (Johnson, 1987: 124–125). That is, we may be closer to or farther from a central location, in the same way that objects may be closer to or farther from us. This generates the idea that there are some places outside ourselves that are more central than others. Much of the architectural organization of social space grows out of this metaphor. Think of all of the various types of political and social "centers" that a city has.

In music, various kinds of metaphorical centrality are often used as an important structural principle. Just as we use concrete physical central locations or landmarks to create spatial frameworks to orient ourselves and remember our locations in physical space, so we metaphorically use "central locations" to orient ourselves in musical space. Physical centrality is based on the ideas that some places are somehow *more important* than others, and that because of this we *return* to these places *again and again*. These kinds of places are often marked or emphasized in some way. Musical centrality is based on these ideas as well. Because music is a temporal medium, musical centrality is often developed through repetition. Metaphors of musical centrality can refer to "central pitches," "central beats" in metrical structure, "central landmark events" in a piece, and so on—all of which gain their centrality by being repeated at different times, and by being made to seem different or marked in some way.

Motion-Linkage-Causation

Other important related metaphors in music have to do with the idea of musical *motion*. The idea that there is such a thing as musical motion is metaphorical because actual physical motion only occurs when *physical objects* move through space. In music, the tones or rhythms said to be "in motion" are separate *events*, not objects, and any motion they may seem to have can only be in their *perceived connections* with each other (Scruton, 1997: 49–52).

As we have seen, connections between musical events are based on proximity and similarity. These effects allow us to identify subsequent events with each other, and to create the metaphorical idea that these events constitute a "thing" that is "moving." This is somewhat like visual stroboscopic "motion," perceived when separate lights near each other are turned on and off in sequence and appear to be one light that is moving (Gjerdingen, 1994). Proximities and similarities between successive events are seen metaphorically as making them more or less tightly "linked," forming progressions that "move" in a particular "direction." Events that are not as strongly linked or connected are seen as forming the boundaries of self-contained units that are more or less "closed." The concept of "interval" as it applies to relations between pitches is a type of linkage metaphor.

Because motion involves change, the strongest musical motion is created by progressive change in one or more parameters. For example, although music that consists of identical repeating events can certainly be heard as "moving forward in time," it has no directed parametric motion, and is in this sense static. Its energy is only moving forward in time, not in a consistent *musical* direction toward any particular musical goal. Repetition is not progressive, and hence does not constitute "musical motion" in the sense in which I am using the expression here. Thus, for musical motion to exist, there must be graduated parametric change, such as pitches that get successively "higher" or "lower."

All of this is related to a metaphor of musical *causation*. That is to say, musical events are seen as "leading to," or "causing" successive events that are close to and similar to them. This is, of course, all metaphorical because musical events do not actually cause each other in the way that other kinds of physical events do (although they can *imply* each other). It is interesting to note that causation is also an important factor in the construction of linear verbal narrative; sequences of narrative events are also often linked by chains of causation.

Thus we have a system of metaphors related in the following way. Similar successive musical events changing in some parameters in similar intervals give rise to the idea of "motion," wherein these separate events are seen as more or less "connected" or "linked" in a way that implies the earlier ones have moved toward and "caused" the later ones. All of this can be established with many different degrees of strength.

The metaphor of musical motion implies a complementary metaphor—the *lack* of musical motion, or "rest." Rest in music is very closely related to the idea of gravity mentioned above—that is, parametrical "low" points are often also points of "rest." In addition, sequences of events that do not have a consistent "directional motion" are often described as having a "static" quality. (The particular ways these metaphors are implemented in various aspects of music will be explored in later chapters.)

Linearity: Paths and Goals

The metaphor of musical motion leading toward a "goal" brings up another type of image schematic metaphor, also derived from our basic physical experience, that of a "path" (Johnson, 1987: 113–117). An important part of the basic structure of the physical motions of our lives is the simple act of getting from point A to point B. Much of attaining many types of goals in our lives involves this very basic type of physical motion. Many kinds of progressive mental activities are also referred to metaphorically as having this type of "motion." Arguments, for example, are often metaphorically thought of as journeys that have a "line," parts that "follow" each other, from which we can get "sidetracked," and so on (Lakoff and Johnson, 1980: 90).

One definition of the boundary of a temporal schema, the point where one schema ends and another begins, is based on goals. When a particular goal is reached, we are at the end of a schema or path, and subsequent actions, in pursuit of another goal, will be part of a new schema (Schank, 1982: 95–97). We also use metaphors such as "getting somewhere" or "things not being there yet" to structure many kinds of conceptual "problem spaces" as though they involved passage through physical space toward a goal. Like the other image schemas we have examined, the pursuit of goals is an experience so fundamental it is probably shared by human beings of many times and cultures.

The idea of a goal normally implies that the present is somehow structured by an idea of how the future will or should be. As stated above, in music, one of the ways directedness toward goals is metaphorically represented is by similarity of motion, namely, that in successive events at least some musical parameters will change by the *same amount*, in the *same "direction."*[13] The strongest motion is created by continuation and similarity of pitch interval; therefore small intervals tend to create the strongest motion. In relation to the path metaphor, note a small pitch interval is referred to in Western music as a "step." When a musical parameter changes perceptibly by the same relatively small amount several times in a row, it creates an expectation that subsequent changes will follow the same pattern. When these similar changes result in the reaching of a limit of some sort or a preestablished goal pattern, a goal has been arrived at. This type of musical motion is referred to as "linear" (see Kramer, 1988: 20–25).

Of course a pattern of continuous change of musical parameters in equal increments is not very interesting. Indeed, even though most interesting music sets up patterns of expectation using at least some consistent change, it deviates enough from this pattern (putting the "goal" in question) to reduce its predictability, thus maintain our attention. Linearity can operate on a number of hierarchical levels in music (and will be discussed in greater detail in chapter 13).

Containment: Inside and Outside

Another image schema that structures much of our conceptualization of experience is *containment*, thought to be based on the experience of our bodies having an inside and an outside. This experience is extended in metaphors that describe many types of events and feelings as having an "inside" and an "outside." Think of being *"in* a war," *"in* love," or *"out of* touch." None of these states has anything like a real inside or outside, but our metaphors use the containment image schema to make them clear. The general metaphor at work here is "states are containers" (Johnson, 1987: 30–40).

Metaphors based on the containment image schema usually imply a "boundary" between the inside and outside of something. Saying that a person is "on edge," for example, implies a sort of emotional boundary. Expressions like "out of it" imply that normal consciousness has some sort of boundary "around" it.

Metaphors based on the containment image schema are used in the description of music any time a boundary is implied. Saying that a particular note is "in" a

particular phrase, for example, implies that the phrase has boundaries at its beginning and ending points. The interior of the phrase is "between" these boundaries.
Indeed the idea of "closure" itself is a containment metaphor. Containment
metaphors can be applied to musical "units" of many sizes. A particular pattern
can occur "in" a particular section or even "in" a particular piece of music; a
musician can improvise "outside" of the metrical structure of a piece, or play "out"
of tune.[14]

Another metaphorical type of boundary is involved in the concepts of *surface*
and *depth*. This metaphor, used in certain kinds of Western musical analysis,
implies that certain kinds of music contain "deep" structures that are not
immediately obvious from listening to the "surface" of the music (see Fink,
1999).

Metaphorical Extension

An interesting process discovered in the history of language is *metaphorical extension*, a process by which concrete literal meanings evolve into metaphorical meanings. Metaphorical meanings of words or phrases are not static, but evolve, with
new extensions to the metaphor developing over time.[15] Most of the metaphors
described in this chapter evolved gradually out of earlier, more literal meanings.
Recent etymological research has discovered that this extension is not arbitrary, but
systematic (though not always predictable; see Sweetser, 1990). That is to say, the
extension of a metaphor is like the creation of metaphor itself; it is a mapping of
features from one schema to another.

A similar process can take place in music. Certain types of metaphorical patterns
in one parameter are metaphorically extended into another.[16] This extension is part
of the historical development of musical style.

For example, "descending" gestures of closure in melodic patterns ("lowering"
of pitch) can be extended to "descending" gestures of closure in other parameters, such as loudness or timbre (Hopkins, 1990), to serve different aesthetic
needs.

This extension combined with the idea that new secondary parameters may also
be created by metaphorical extension demonstrates one of the ways in which music
evolves. The metaphor of "up" and "down," for example, might be extended by
finding new things to have "more" or "less" of. Thus there are always new possibilities for new types of progressions.

Other Metaphorical Possibilities

The foregoing has dealt with physical image schemas we can use metaphorically in understanding and creating music. Undoubtedly, there are other types of metaphors not covered in this book that can also help us do both. One broad type of metaphor that immediately comes to mind is social. Clearly, social relations between individuals or between individuals and society can be a basis for musical structure (see, for example, Leppert and McClary, 1987), principally through particular types of relations between different simultaneous parts in the music, rather than through specific parametric changes. This is one way in which social metaphors in music would differ from physical ones. In fact as of this writing, the analysis of music in social terms is a growing field.

Notes

1. This relation between the terms of a metaphor has been described as an "experiential correlation." See Lakoff and Johnson, 1980, pp. 147–155.

  Experiential correlations are associative, but they are not necessarily the same as similarity between the terms of a metaphor (see Johnson, 1997). For example, when a person sings, some pitches have points of resonance that feel higher in the body than other pitches. There is a correlation between these pitches and a feeling of height in the body (von Bekesy, 1970). This is one possible source for the metaphor of musical pitch being referred to as *higher* and *lower*. This metaphor has been applied to all sorts of sounds produced by sources other than the voice. Note that there is no objective similarity to physical height—sounds only have the quality of height when experienced by humans, and indeed not all cultures use this metaphor. So the use of physical height as the source domain for the metaphor of pitch height is not based on similarity between the quality of higher pitch and physical height (especially for a listener). Rather it consists of inferences based on correlations between two different bodily experiences.

2. In fact, metaphor can involve whole systems of concepts or schemas. The field of metaphor studies is a complex and evolving part of cognitive linguistics, which I make no claim to cover in any complete way. The view presented here grows out of an approach to metaphor referred to as "cognitive semantics." For a taste of the complexity of current discussion in this area, see Johnson, 1997.

3. Note that image schemas are thought to be a kind of mediating level of cognitive processing between perceptual images and concepts. As such, they would constitute a basis for concepts, largely grounded in bodily experience. This intermediate status means that they also have continuous, or analog aspects. Note that some authors refer to image schemas as preconceptual (e.g., Lakoff, 1987: 267) and some refer to them as conceptual (e.g., Gärdenfors, 2000: 164). For an extended discussion of image schemas and their relation to metaphor, see Johnson, 1987; for a discussion of image schemas in relation to music, see Zbikowski, 1998.

4. Most of the published discussions of image schemas use abstract visual diagrams, which certainly demonstrates that the content of image schemas cannot be completely described in language. See, for example, Mandler, 1992; Johnson, 1987, pp. 112–126; Talmy, 1988, pp. 49–100; Brugman, 1983.

5. I would interpret Blacking's idea of a human "biogrammar" as a reference to something like implicit image schematic knowledge. Blacking, however, regards this sort of knowledge as biologically innate. See also Jackendoff, 1987, pp. 236–239.

6. An example of this is presented in a classic paper by Brugman, 1983. Brugman examines over one hundred different metaphorical extensions of the word "over." To do so, she has to use many abstract visual diagrams as well as text, thus demonstrating that the meanings of this image schema are more than merely linguistic.

7. In a recent formulation of this idea, the hippocampus stores *relational* information, which includes many types of configurations of memory besides spatial ones. See, for example, Shapiro and Olton, 1994, pp. 97–98; Lynch and Granger, 1994, p. 78. When words have both a spatial and a temporal usage, for example; "go ahead," the spatial meaning usually precedes the temporal one both in the historical development of the meaning of the words, and in developmental language use in individuals. See Sweetser, 1990, pp. 9, 18.

8. The technical term for such adaptation is *encephalization*. See Lynch and Granger, 1994, p. 78

9. Although not covered in this book, for an interesting account of possible metaphorical sources of the *emotional* meaning of music in line with other ideas presented here, see Kivy, 1989, pp. 71–94.

10. Musical meaning is a complex issue, and I do not claim to be giving it an exhaustive treatment here. I am however interested in how music is related to the world, and I believe that image schemas may be one type of abstract reference by which music is connected to that world.

11. The physical experience of gravity is the source of a number of metaphors involving "up" and "down," "higher" and "lower." For the best article on this idea I have read thus far, see Tolaas, 1991, pp. 203–218. See also Mandler, 1992, p. 597; Gibbs, 1994, pp. 412–413. The difference between "up" and "down" in music and its relation to closure are clearly referred to in a number of different works. See, for example, Krumhansel, 1990, pp. 160–162; Meyer, 1989, p. 209; Narmour, 1990, p. 362; Francès, 1988, pp. 165–166; Kivy, 1989, p. 55; Trehub and Trainor, 1993, pp. 287–288, 294.

12. Music shares this form of closure with the pitch of spoken language. In the context of this chapter, what is most interesting is that both music and speech are described by metaphors using the *physical* term *down*.

13. Musical goals can also be created through syntactical means. Any pattern placed in a closural position and repeated often enough can come to have the quality of closure (discussed in greater detail in chapter 13).

14. For a description of how the containment metaphor is applied in certain kinds of musical analysis, see Saslaw, 1996.

15. For an example of words and metaphors describing sensory meanings shifting over time, see Classen, 1993, pp. 50–76. Metaphorical extension is one of the primary ways new ideas

are created and understood. Given that many types of thinking are memory based, metaphor provides a mechanism whereby the kinds of "leaps of thought" that characterize creative thought and learning can occur. For a discussion of how metaphor is used in the *under-standing* of new ideas, see Petrie and Oshlag, 1993, pp. 579–584. For a discussion of how metaphor figures in the *creation* of new ideas, see Holyoak and Thagard, 1995, esp. pp. 216–225. Note that these authors use the term *analogy* as a somewhat more general term, which includes metaphor.

16. Probably the most obvious example of this in Western music history is the twentieth-century musical style known as "serialism," in which a principle of pitch organization developed in a previous style (known as "twelve-tone music") was metaphorically extended to other parameters of music such as duration, timbre, and loudness.

II

Some Musical Concepts

10

Event Fusion

The variation of air pressure that constitutes the acoustic waveform as it comes into the ear is continuous; it doesn't necessarily have any clear separate "parts." All of the different frequency components that make up all the different sounds that are being heard are represented by one physical position of the eardrum at any given instant in time. The time level of event fusion is the point at which trains of vibrations from the air are perceptually categorized according to their frequency and loudness. Individual fibers in the inner ear are "tuned" to respond to a relatively narrow range of frequencies; the rate of nerve impulses produced by a given neuron is proportional to the amplitude of incoming sound at that frequency (Moore, 1997: 37). Thus a basic analysis is performed on incoming sound in terms of frequency and loudness. The results of this analysis persist briefly as echoic memory, during which time more global features are extracted, that is, higher-level features are derived from detected correlations in activity over larger numbers of individual neurons.

Although we shall primarily consider events that have the quality of pitch because many types of musical events are pitched, much of the processing just described also occurs for many types of *non*pitched sounds. Hence I have called this the "level of *event* fusion," rather than "*pitch* fusion."

Two concepts are particularly useful in discussing the level of event fusion: pitched event and interval. A *pitched event*, the smallest unit of organization in the melodic dimension, consists of a number of acoustical vibrations similar to each other that happen fast enough to fuse into a unified perception of pitch. Any type of sound that has enough repetition in its internal structure to sound "higher" or "lower" fits this definition. Pitch can be a matter of degree. The amount of repetition in the micro structure of sounds forms a continuum from purely pitched sounds to noise. Noises in this sense are sounds with very little repetition in their microstructure. The sounds of traditional string, wind, and keyboard instruments tend to cluster near the pitch end of this continuum; the sounds of many percussion instruments, nearer the noise end.

An *interval* is the melodic "distance" between two pitches, successive or simultaneous, one of which is heard as "higher," and the other as "lower;" This is referred to as a difference in "pitch height." Intervals may be of different sizes. In general, small intervals will be referred to as "steps," and larger intervals, as "leaps."

Pitched Events

I shall use the term *pitch* to indicate the quality of "highness" or "lowness," and the term *event* to indicate change in that or another given parameter. When the parameter of pitch changes over time, we have melody—this is a very general definition. Pitch is related to the frequency of mechanical vibrations. Human beings hear pitch when the eardrum is struck by regular mechanical vibrations at a rate of between 20 per second and 20,000 per second.[1] Each of the individual vibrations that constitute a pitch is referred to as a *cycle*, and the frequency of pitches are measured in *cycles per second* (cps).

Figure 10.1 reproduces part of table 1.1, a chart of the three time levels of musical experience. In this version, a new column labeled "Pitch" has been added in boldface which gives the musical note names that correspond to the "Events per second" and "Seconds per event" columns from the original chart. Also included are approximate representations of these pitches in Western music notation.

In addition, a new area, labeled the "Threshold of event fusion," has been highlighted at the bottom of the chart. This represents the transition range where, as the number of acoustical vibration events increases in a given amount of time, they become unresolvable as individual events and begin to be processed differently. This is a gradual process that takes place over the range of the fusion threshold (roughly 5–20 events per second). The fastest rate at which sequences of more than two nonidentical events can occur in music and retain the time order of each event is about five events per second (200 msec per event) (Warren, 1999). The time order of pitches that occur at this rate in melodic patterns is clear and identifiable. As the rate of events gets faster, the order of individual events becomes harder to identify accurately. At a rate of 10 events per second (100 msec per event), particular melodic patterns are no longer clearly identifiable, although they can still be discriminated as being somehow different from each other. At this point, melodic patterns are perceived "holistically" and are processed more like waveforms than like melodies

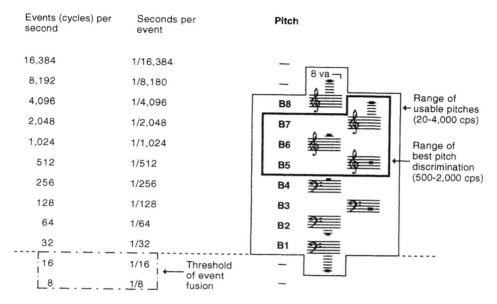

Figure 10.1
Time and pitch.

(Warren, 1993). (In this example, a waveform would be formed out of fully formed events, rather than simple vibrations—the point is that any kind of pattern of events that occur at this rate begins to fuse into a whole.) At a rate of 20 events per second (50 msec per event), the pattern of events for all practical purposes *is* a waveform, and its individual events fuse together to form a single higher-level event. What happens over the range of the fusion threshold is that the ear and brain gradually change from acting as an event pattern processor to acting as a waveform processor (see Warren, 1993).[2] What is referred to as a "rhythmic pattern of events" at tempos *below* the fusion threshold (at the time level of melodic and rhythmic grouping) becomes a *timbre* or tone color *above* it (at the time level of event fusion). Tone color then is the quality of the microrhythm of events that are too fast for us to perceive individually.

   Two areas are further indicated within the total compass of the time level of Event Fusion. First is the *range of best pitch discrimination*. This is the range of pitches (500–2,000 cps) within which the discrimination of different frequency values (the "just noticeable difference" between frequencies) is most acute. Within this range, we can discriminate frequency differences of about 0.3 percent (see Barlow and

Mollon, 1982: 315).[3] Surrounding the range of best pitch discrimination, the *range of usable pitches* is the range of frequencies (20–4,000 cps) within which clearly recognizable musical pitch intervals can be constructed (Semal and Demany, 1990). It contains the pitch ranges of all musical instruments with the exception of synthesizers, which can generate any frequency.[4]

Outside the range of usable pitches, sounds do not have a precise enough pitch to form musical intervals. This is particularly true in the range above 4,000–5,000 cps, where as sound frequency moves toward the upper limit of hearing, it is increasingly heard as "brighter" rather than "higher." Below 20 cps, we begin to hear a kind of buzz, which as it gets lower in frequency, becomes very "grainy" and eventually disintegrates into a rapid chain of separate impulses.

As long as vibrations repeat fast enough, and at a constant rate and are similar to each other in waveform, we hear a single pitch. The opposite of this, a sound with no internal repetitive structure at all is called "white noise," an undefined rushing sound that consists of a completely randomly varying waveform and that has no pitch content at all. (This sound is similar to the sound that a television makes when tuned to an empty channel.) Most sounds fall somewhere between these two extremes, and many sounds actually change their pitch or noise content while occurring. Words, for instance, may begin with a consonant sound (noise) and move to a vowel sound (pitch). The sounds of many musical instruments also begin with a short burst of noise and then stabilize into a recognizable pitch.

Generally, the more noise content a sound has (the less repetitive its waveform is), the less it sounds like it has a definite pitch. Noises have far fewer degrees of "higher" and "lower" than pitched sounds. This is because the ear, like much of the nervous system, is a repetition processor. Probably we are less able to discriminate noises because, in the initial stages of processing, we simply have far fewer feature extractors to deal with this type of sound. Most of the kinds of sounds the ear has evolved to deal with (e.g., speech and animal sounds) have a significant amount of pitch content.

The idea of regular repetition of a waveform is central to the sensation of pitch, and the idea of similarity of successive cycles of vibration is essential to the coherence of a pitch event as a unit. A pitched event is a grouping of separate, rapid mechanical vibrations that occur at a faster time interval than the lowest rate of pitch fusion mentioned earlier. The fusion of individual vibrations into a pitch is the most basic level of auditory grouping we can experience. Note that we are not equipped to resolve the individual vibrations that constitute a pitched event, we can only hear the qualities of pitch and tone color that represents their frequency and pattern of recurrence. Like other kinds of groupings, however, pitch fusion is established by similarity and proximity (the successive vibrations are of the same waveform and are in immediate succession). Indeed, if any dissimilarity or change of proximity occurs on this basic level, a grouping boundary is formed, and we have a new pitch event.

Pitch Discrimination and Memory

The total number of different frequencies that a human being can discriminate is large. Research suggests that a person can perceive at least 1,400 different frequencies under laboratory conditions (Handel, 1989: 268). The tuning system of Western European music makes use of about ninety different pitches, and this is a fairly typical number for tuning systems in general. The large difference between these numbers has to do with a correspondingly large difference in performance on two different tasks. The number of different frequencies that a person can distinguish is measured in a *discrimination task*, where a person is asked to compare sounds at two frequencies in immediate succession, and to rate them as being the same or different. The frequencies of the two sounds are brought closer together until the smallest difference that a person can hear is reached. Beyond this point, the two sounds, while still differing in frequency, will sound the same. This establishes what is known in psychology as a "just noticeable difference," a basic frequency resolution figure. (Just noticeable differences also exist for touch, vision, etc.) The just noticeable difference establishes the smallest perceptible distance between two values of a stimulus (the boundary between two perceptual categories) that still seem different *in immediate succession*. Because this type of task requires only an immediate comparison between two events, it uses only echoic memory, which for a very short amount of time can maintain a high-resolution representation of the two pitch events. Both of the pitches can remain in echoic memory for this short amount of time.

Performance is quite different on an *identification task*, where a person has to identify a particular pitch, saying whether it is the same as or different from another pitch, in a sequence longer than two tones. Comparison of a very small interval between two immediately *adjacent* tones is one thing; comparison of this same interval with one or more other tones *intervening* is a great deal more difficult because it involves memory to a much greater extent (Deutsch, 1999: 391). It happens on the time scale of short-term memory: it is no longer a comparison between the lingering image of the pitches themselves, but between their conceptual categories. Because this comparison involves short-term memory, the number of different elements that can be identified in this way is much smaller than on a dis-crimination task, and the smallest interval or distance between pitches that can be discriminated in this way is many times larger. This is because, with other pitches intervening, direct comparison is impossible, and events that are similar in pitch can be confused as identical. The identification task is far more like perceiving melodic patterns in music and requires far more memory because the pitch being identified has to be compared to *all* the discriminable pitches within short-term memory. The high-resolution representation of frequency and loudness that persists briefly as echoic memory is then encoded categorically based on (learned) long-term memory categories. At this point of categorization, small variations in the frequency of the sound (nuances) may be discarded. To make the comparisons necessary to identify a pitch in relation to learned LTM categories, the repertoire of pitches must be within the limits of STM (5–9 elements). (More will be said about this in chapter 11.)

Thus the size of immediate *perceptual* categories of pitch interval (the just notice-able difference) and the size of learned *conceptual* categories of pitch interval (the interval categories of a tuning system) are very different from each other. Short-term memory places limits on how many pitched elements (conceptual categories of pitch interval) we can use to build differentiated patterns such as melodies if we want these elements to be perceptibly different and individually re-presentable in memory. Moreover, small variations in the frequency of pitch elements (nuances), such as would naturally occur in performance, can be experienced, but are usually lost to the long-term memory of the listener. The trick is to have as many pitch elements as possible, without mistaking any for any other. Like language and other forms of communication, we must therefore use a limited ensemble of ele-ments (categories) and form many kinds of patterns by repeating some of them. Small variations in these elements must not interfere with the perception of a par-ticular event as an example of one of the elements. In other words, we must be able to perceive these elements categorically. Here we see why category structure is useful, making it possible to have a variety of patterns that can be compared and remembered.

Interval

Melodies operate through the successive "rising and falling motion" of pitches. This motion is metaphorical: there is nothing physical that literally rises and falls. One way to control literal rising and falling in the physical world is through stairways, consisting of steps. In most musical cultures, the continuum of possible musical pitches is divided into discrete units. In Western European music the smallest of these pitch intervals are metaphorically also called "steps." Just as physical steps must be neither too large nor too small to be manageable, so a musical step (although varying within limits in different cultures) is a pitch interval that is neither too large nor too small. That is, steps are basic units of musical motion that are small enough so that adjacent steps will be heard as closely related, yet large enough to be easily differentiated from each other. The size limits on steps are established by basic characteristics of the human nervous system, which has evolved over time to hear as related sounds that tend to come from single sources (Bregman, 1990: 39–40). (This phenomenon, referred to as "streaming," will be considered in detail in chapter 11.) In the natural environment, sounds originating from the same source tend to be fairly similar in pitch range, and tend not to make large leaps. For example, if a tape of a single speaking voice is edited so that a large leap in pitch is created inside a single word, it will sound as though a second voice has appeared: as a single sound source, a voice generally does not make leaps of this kind. Throughout the world, steps are by far the most frequently used musical interval size (Dowling and Harwood, 1986: 155).

A *leap* is an interval larger than a step; because of its more dissimilar pitch relationship, it usually forms a grouping boundary. The boundary between a step and a leap is somewhat contextual (Narmour, 1990: 76–78).

Interval is a metaphorical way to conceptualize a kind of "link" between two pitch events. Pitches in similar ranges are thought of as being more strongly linked than pitches in dissimilar ranges: steplike intervals form stronger similarity links than leaplike intervals. It is for this reason that a melodic leap often forms a grouping boundary. These links can also have different sizes *within* the basic categories of leaps and steps, which form the basis of a tuning system for a particular kind of music. Each of these intervals is said to have a different quality. In Western music, intervals are named after the number of keys on the span of a keyboard instrument: seconds, thirds, fourths, fifths, and so on.

Intervals are the primary features recognized in familiar melodies: as long as the interval sequence is maintained, the actual pitches at which a melody occurs can be shifted up or down (*transposed*) by a considerable amount, and the melody will still be recognizable to a listener. For example, a song like "Happy Birthday" will be sung by different people starting on different pitches, but the melody will be recognizable from its interval sequence and scale schema.

The Octave: A Special Interval

If we sound two identical pitches (in unison) simultaneously and gradually move one of the pitches higher while leaving the other stationary, we pass through a variety of pitch intervals. The smaller intervals fall into the category of steps. As the intervals are made larger, they enter the category of leaps. As the interval continues to get larger still, something interesting happens. Suddenly, a point is reached where, instead of sounding farther and farther away from the stationary pitch, the second pitch seems to blend into the first. It is almost as though there were no longer two different pitches.

This point is reached when the frequency ratio of the two pitches is $2:1$.[5] This interval is referred to as an "octave" because in Western European music, it occurs on the eighth step of the scale. The octave appears to have a special status in human perception. Two pitches that are an octave apart, although different and separated by a fairly large interval, also seem to be *somehow the same*. Indeed, in many musical systems, pitches an octave apart are given the same name. Thus, although there are eighty-eight keys on the piano, representing eighty-eight different pitches, there are only twelve pitch *names*, and these twelve pitch categories repeat every octave, just as the visual pattern of white and black keys on the piano repeats every twelve keys. Different octaves of the same pitch category are indicated by numbers (e.g., C1, C2, C3; see figure 10.2). This quality of *identity* ("sameness") that the different octaves of a particular pitch possess means that the concept of similarity in relation to pitch has two aspects: the actual distance between the pitches, and the pitch name. Thus two pitches may be similar in either of two ways: they may be similar in actual pitch *location*, as C and C-sharp are, or the may have the same *name*, as C1 and C2 do. These two characteristics of musical pitch are usually referred to as "pitch height" and "chroma," respectively (Dowling and Harwood, 1986: 107–108). *Pitch height* is simply the distance or interval between two pitches. *Chroma* is a scale position category, represented by the note name. All pitches with note name C, although they may be in different octaves (and hence different in pitch height), share the quality of "C-ness" or C chroma. Two pitches an octave apart

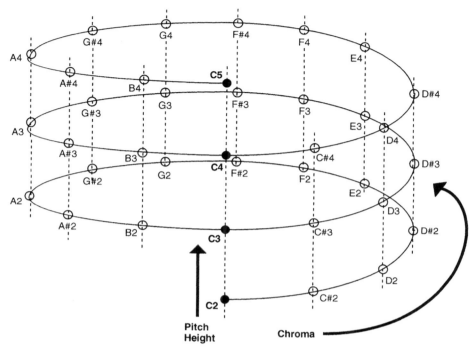

Figure 10.2
Pitch height and chroma (after Shepard, 1982).

have the same name, chroma, and scale position category because this repeats every octave, but a different pitch height. Thus two pitches can be different in pitch height, but still be identical in chroma, for example, C1 and C3. Or they can have different chromas (note or pitch category names) but be very similar in pitch height, for example, C2 and C-sharp 2. These two types of relations between pitches are often represented by a spiral (see figure 10.2) because the pitches continually move upward in pitch height, but also arrive back at the chroma at the octave of each pitch.[6]

The position of a particular pitch category in a tuning system is independent of pitch height. There are twelve chromas (pitch categories) represented on the keyboard of the piano, whereas there are eighty-eight relations of pitch height. Pitch interval categories are learned (they can be different in different cultures) and tend to be identified much better by trained musicians than by untrained individuals.

The octave is a special interval in two other ways: it is the basic generative interval of *virtually all* the tuning systems in the world (Dowling and Harwood, 1986: 92–95), and the only interval that is the same size in virtually all of the tuning systems of the musics of the world. Because of its basic feeling of identity, almost all tuning systems are constructed as divisions of the octave. And because the octave is the point at which the sequencing of intervals of the tuning system start over again, tuning systems and scales can often be completely specified by being notated within a single octave.

Another interesting fact about the octave is that the more we increase the size of an interval above an octave, the weaker its identity becomes: the less the interval has any specific interval quality other than being a very large leap (Deutsch, 1999: 399–400). This means that the octave is a kind of critical range within which we can discern individual intervals clearly, and beyond which our ability to discern intervals declines (see Dowling and Harwood, 1986: 155–156).[7] This may help explain the almost universal use of the octave as a generative interval.

In this chapter, we have been concerned with the basic perception of pitch and the concept of interval. In the next, we shall look at systems of long-term memory categories that govern the relations between multiple intervals.

Notes

1. Actually, our sense of *precise* pitch only extends to a frequency of 4,000–5,000 cycles per second (cps), the upper limit of the range of pitches produced by most musical instruments. Also, the upper frequency limit of hearing declines with age, from 16,000 cps for a middle-aged person to as low as 8,000 cps for a person aged 85.

2. At still higher frequencies, the ear is best described as a "spectrum analyzer." See Sethares, 1998: 15–17.

3. Note that the just noticeable difference is not the same as the *critical band*, the smallest distance at which two different *simultaneous* frequencies can be clearly distinguished, which is much larger. See Sethares, 1998, pp. 41–43.

4. The lowest note on the 88-note piano is A1, with a frequency of 27.5 cps, and the highest is C8, with a frequency of 4,186 cps.

5. In reality, the interval heard as an octave is a frequency ratio of slightly more than 2:1 (about 2.009:1 on the average for Western music in the midrange of hearing, and as much as 2.035:1 in some Javenese orchestral music), but this is not important for the explanation given here. See Carterette and Kendall, 1999, p. 740; Dowling and Harwood, 1986, p. 102. Note also that this explanation applies to sounds with a relatively *harmonic* frequency content (having components whose frequencies are related as whole numbers, 1, 2, 3, 4, etc.), as many musical instruments do. Nonharmonic sounds usually do not have clear pitch content,

and hence the octave is not necessarily an important interval in scales composed of these types of sounds. See Sethares, 1998, pp. 1–3. This book also contains a CD with examples of scales derived from nonharmonic sounds.

6. Note that above the range of usable pitches (i.e., above 4,000 cps), pitched events still have pitch height, but no longer have chroma.

7. Dowling and Harwood's chart, p. 155, shows the decreasing use of pitch intervals with increasing size.

11
Melody

Once acoustical vibrations are fused into events, they may be organized on a higher level into sequences. One aspect of these sequences is *melody*, defined here as any sequence of acoustical events that contains recognizable patterns of contour ("highness" and "lowness") in the time dimension with perceptible pitchlike intervals between successive events.[1] These events do not have to be pure pitches: they may be any kind of sounds that can be recognizably organized into a relationship of "higher" and "lower," and that sound similar enough to form a unified horizontal sequence. By this definition, melodies can be constructed from colored noise, non-harmonic spectra, or samples.

Besides pitch and interval, introduced in the previous chapter, there are a number of other concepts useful when talking about organization at the melodic level in relation to memory and expectation. A *tuning system* is an abstract generative system of intervals that defines basic interval categories and specifies details such as the size of the smallest allowable musical interval. The intervals of a tuning system are usually subdivisions of an octave. A *scale* is a subset of the elements of a tuning system. Whereas a tuning system can have any number of elements, the number of pitches in a scale is usually adjusted to fit the limitations of short-term memory. A scale may or may not have a centrally important pitch.

A *melodic grouping* consists of several pitched events that are perceived as a unit because of similarity of interval and direction of melodic motion.[2] When their component pitches are sufficiently far apart in pitch range, melodic groupings break apart and form separate "streams." A *stream* is coherent grouping of pitched events that separates itself from other such groupings by virtue of its distance from them in pitch space and the speed at which its events happen. We can only attend closely to one stream of events at a time. A *phrase* is a group of melodic groupings. Often separated from other phrases by silent pauses, a phrase is the largest melodic unit that can fit within the limits of short-term memory.

Contour is the metaphorical shape or outline of a melody created by the motion pattern of intervals. A contour consists of different-sized intervals: "steps," "leaps," and "edges" or turning points where melodic motion reverses direction. A contour need not always consist of discrete note events, but may be continuous or sliding.

A *tonality* is a way of using a musical scale so that it seems to have a central pitch.[3] By using the central pitch frequently and at important structural points as established by other factors, such as metrical accent and duration, these factors all help to create the expectation of return to this pitch. Although schematic in that it structures our expectations about what pitches will occur when, tonality is more general than a *melodic schema*, an archetypal melodic contour that can be elaborated on to form many different melodies. I think that melodic schemas are related to spatial image schemas, that is, they are metaphorically related to very basic ideas about our human relationship to physical space. A melodic schema is also a form of temporal schema because it roughly specifies an actual time order in which pitches occur. Let us consider each of these concepts in greater detail.

A Basic Melodic Category Structure: Tuning System

The first, and most general, set of constraints by which materials at the melodic level are organized, a *tuning system* determines the size of the interval categories to be used in a particular musical culture.[4] As previously mentioned, a tuning system virtually always consists of intervals that are divisions of the octave. A set of learned conceptual categories, it is the most general framework of organization for pitch and is often standardized for a whole musical culture.[5] It is a basic carving up of musical pitch space, and determines the size of the intervals used. This is its primary purpose—to establish standards of interval size for a given musical culture. Thus when we hear music of another culture with a different tuning system, we tend to hear it initially as an "out of tune" version of our own tuning system, translating the new pitches to positions inside the interval categories of our own tuning system. The actual pitches of the foreign tuning system are then heard as pitch nuances, rather than a new set of interval categories.[6]

Of all of the constraints placed on melodic materials, the tuning system appears to be the most resistant to change. The present tuning system of European music has been in general use for over 250 years. One of the reasons why it is so resistant to change is that the tuning system is often built into the actual physical structure of musical instruments, in the positions of frets on fretted string instruments, the fixed tuning of the strings of keyboard instruments, the placement of holes and keys on wind instruments, the lengths of tubing on brass instruments, the size of gongs and bells, and so on. These standardized physical limitations on the structure of musical instruments make it much easier for musicians to play "in tune" and much harder to play very far outside of the intervals of the tuning system.

A question arises in relation to the concept of "out-of-tuneness": how can we hear a particular interval as being "out of tune" if the way we hear interval is categorical? There are two answers to this question. The first is that most cases of "out-of-tuneness" arise *between* at least two different instruments that are playing the same or octave pitches. When two instruments play two somewhat different frequencies that are still within the same pitch category, they interact acoustically to produce a kind of pulsating roughness that is quite noticeable. In this instance, we might say that there are two conflicting concepts of where the center of the pitch category is.

When only one instrument playing a single line of music is involved, we can also perceive an interval as out of tune provided one of its pitches is close to a category boundary (see "Scales, Categories, and Nuance" below). Remember that discrimination is most acute near category boundaries. This would represent the limit of how out of tune an interval could be and still represent a particular interval category—a maximum of "out-of-tuneness." Within-category interval distinctions are not impossible to hear in the immediate present, just much more difficult to *remember* than between-category distinctions. Moreover, because our category discrimination is more acute as we approach category boundaries, a pitch close to the boundary tends to stand out as less representative of that category. In general, however, pitch discrepancies are less noticeable when played by a single instrument, where there is no other sounding frame of reference to compare them to.

As a rule, all of the pitches or intervals of a tuning system are considered equal—no pitch is more important or central than any other. In other words, tuning systems are usually not hierarchically organized: they define the intervals between the pitches, but in no particular order.[7] The tuning system contains *all* the interval categories used in the music of a particular culture, serving as a basic list of pitch resources from which actual music may be built, although as we shall soon see, these resources are usually not all used at one time.

Some tuning systems divide the octave into intervals of perceptually equal size. The control of the size of interval is called "tempering," and hence tuning systems consisting of intervals of equal size are called "equal temperaments." In such tuning systems, a pattern of melodic intervals (contour) can be exactly repeated starting at a different pitch from the original pattern—a type of melodic variation known as "transposition." Identical transposition is not possible unless all the basic intervals of a tuning system are of equal size. Otherwise, the size of the intervals would change with transposition.

Tuning systems in general use vary from as few as five to as many as twenty-four or more pitches within the octave, and experimental microtonal tuning systems may use many more than this.[8] As previously mentioned, the tuning system used in Western Europe for the last 250 years has twelve equally spaced pitches and is called "twelve-tone equal temperament."

It is worth noting that tuning systems can vary in the strictness with which their intervals are maintained (see Arom et al., 1997; Levy, 1982; Keefe, Burns, and Phong, 1991). Although many tuning systems consist of interval categories that have a stable center and boundaries, this does not appear to be universal. Some musics use interval categories more loosely than others. Nor is the size of particular pitch intervals within a tuning system necessarily exactly the same across a musical culture.

In Indonesian Gamelan music, for example, there is considerable variation from orchestra to orchestra in the actual size of the intervals that the instruments produce, although the pitches within a particular orchestra remain fixed. This makes it hard to find single prototypical examples of each interval category in the overall tuning system of the culture. These interval categories have boundaries, but less clear centers. (Note that this is a more complex type of graded category structure, as mentioned in chapter 7.) Nevertheless, there are still limits within which actual intervals are allowable, and these fall into categories that are consistent across the musical culture. In other words, it is still quite possible for a particular pitch event to be "out of tune." Each particular orchestra is heard as being in a particular subtle "dialect" of the tuning system.

The abstract nature of the tuning system is indicated by the fact that when it is notated (if it is notated at all) it is notated as a series of "pure pitches," with no duration values or other parametric qualities of any kind. Although a notated tuning system has to be presented as if "beginning" on a particular pitch, it is usually thought of as a series of intervals with neither beginning nor end.

The development of a tuning system does not necessarily precede the development of less abstract aspects of melodic organization. That is to say, tuning systems and scales are often derived from actual music (Butler and Brown, 1994: 194–195). The tuning system may be preserved in notation, or it may be maintained in a traditional practice of building instruments to certain traditional specifications. It may also be transmitted in an oral tradition of listening and mimicry. In general, the more a culture depends on standardized, manufactured instruments with fixed tuning, the more it needs to have its tuning system specified in some sort of notation.

Note that not all of the notes of the tuning system are necessarily used at one time. Although there are exceptions, the basic tuning system of a music generally contains more elements than are used in any one piece. This brings us to the second, more specific set of constraints on pitches that are used in music.

Melodic Category Structure: Scales

The pitch resources of a tuning system are usually divided into subsets referred to here as "scales" (from Latin *scala*, staircase or ladder; see figure 11.1). Like the tuning system, scales represent a set of categorical constraints that produce consistency (redundancy) in the use of materials at the melodic level. Scales are not necessarily used in their pure abstract form in music, but represent an abstraction of melodic possibilities, like the tuning system from which they are drawn. And like the tuning system, when they are represented in notation, they have no parametric values other than that of pitch. Unlike the tuning system, however, particular scales often have metaphorical cultural associations with other types of experience.[9] For example, the Hindu word "*raga,*" which represents a scale plus rules for melodic motion and ornamentation, can be translated as "that which colors the mind." Particular ragas are associated with particular times of day, and with particular

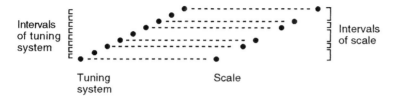

Figure 11.1
Tuning system and scale.

emotions. Another example is the minor scale, which in European music is often said to be "darker" than the major scale, and to represent tragic emotion.

Whereas the basic kinds of intervals of a tuning system are often all equal, a scale does not usually consist of intervals that are all the same size. The inequalities of interval in a scale serve an important dynamic function by introducing asymmetries into the intervals of the scale. These asymmetries act as orientation points so that we can know "where" we are in the scale (Krumhansel, 1990: 16–18). In a scale that is totally balanced, consisting of entirely equal intervals, it is much more difficult to "get our bearings." Constructing scales with different-sized intervals gives different parts of the scale their own character, and can help establish the centrality of a particular pitch. Moreover, using different intervals at different points in a scale increases the variety of intervals that can be produced by different combinations of pitches within that scale.

A scale normally has a central pitch called the "tonic pitch" of the scale and usually notated as being the bottom note of the scale (the pitch it "starts" on). When the scale is used in such a way that the tonic note is referred back to at important structural points, we are dealing with the phenomenon of tonality. (Note that all of the above descriptions of a scale are couched in terms of spatial metaphors.)

Scales and Short-Term Memory

Although tuning systems represent the total pitch resources available in a given music and may have many elements, scales exist to bring these resources within the capabilities of short-term memory (Dowling, 1978) so that the repetition in patterns can function like rehearsal and enhance memory (Deutsch, 1999: 398). The function of a tuning system is to generate intervals of a perceptually workable size (neither too large nor too small), but this often produces more pitches than can be processed within the limits of short-term memory. Remember that the number of elements that can be handled by STM at any given time is seven, plus or minus two. While our own European tuning system has twelve pitches per octave, for example, the diatonic scale used in much traditional European music has only seven. Generally, we find that scales actually in use have five to nine pitches per octave in them.[10]

Scales, Categories, and Schemas

Like the tuning system within which they are contained, the pitches and intervals of a scale are established *categorically* (see Krumhansl, 1990: 16–20; Dowling and

Harwood, 1986: 90–95; Burns and Ward, 1978; Burns and Ward, 1982: 243–246). One indication of this is that each pitch and interval category within a scale has a *different name*. These pitch and interval categories are a type of encoding that can greatly enhance memory for melodic information.

Pitch and interval categories are learned better by some individuals than others. Certainly, professional musicians have a stronger perception of interval categories than nonmusicians, although exposure to music creates some sense of this in almost everyone (Dowling, 1993: 12). For example, if asked to sing a familiar melody, a person might start on any pitch in an absolute sense, but will usually reproduce the intervals (scale positions) of that melody with reasonable accuracy. Most people judge the accuracy ("in-tuneness") of a particular pitch by how it fits into an interval; for most listeners, a single isolated pitch cannot be in or out of tune.[11]

I have previously noted that categories are the elements or slots from which schemas are constructed. Generally, although the instances that fill these slots are variable, the *relations* between the slots or categories are fixed—the relations between the events or objects in the schema do not change much between different instances of the schema. Indeed, these relations *are* the schema. Because the metaphors used to describe the structure of scales are spatial, a scale can be seen metaphorically as a *spatial* schema, with interval categories as its slots.[12]

Scales, Categories, and Nuance

That the intervals in a scale are perceived as a set of categories means that, in relation to a scale, the absolute frequency of a pitch is not perceived as such, and small errors in the frequency value of a particular pitch are possible without changing the perception of that pitch's position in the scale. This means that each frequency actually heard is taken as an example of one of the interval categories of the scale. This type of conceptual categorical structure is very pervasive in human experience.

The small deviations that occur in different examples of the same pitch are *pitch nuances*. If pitches were not perceived categorically, every deviation from the correct frequency value of a pitch (every instance of being "out of tune") would make it impossible to identify that pitch within the context of an interval or scale. This is clearly not the case: frequency deviations on the order of 0.5 percent are quite common in musical performance and do not interfere with our perception of interval relationships in the music. These small deviations occur constantly in musical performance. Examples of common types of pitch nuances are vibrato, pitches

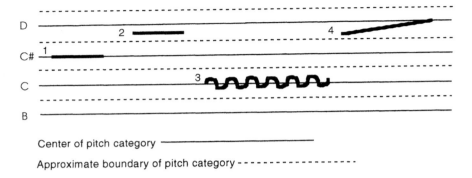

Center of pitch category ————————————

Approximate boundary of pitch category - - - - - - - - - - - - - - - - - - -

Figure 11.2
Pitch nuances. 1. "In tune" C-sharp. 2. "Flat" D. 3. C with vibrato. 4. Slide up to D. These pitch nuances would usually be heard in relation to an interval category.

played slightly out of tune, and pitches bent slightly toward the following pitch (figure 11.2). As noted in chapter 7, these small deviations are very important, and along with small deviations in timing, can carry much of the emotional content of the music. It is rather like the way in which the pitch inflection of voice adds emotional nuance to the semantic categories of speech.

Also note that these nuances are *continuous* variations of the pitch of musical events, unlike pitch and interval categories themselves, which are *discrete*. Reducing continuous nuance information to a small number of discrete categories makes it possible for memory to deal with musical interval as a syntactical parameter.

Musical pitch nuances vary from musician to musician, from piece to piece, from performance to performance, and even from note to note in the same piece (Rakowski, 1990). They constitute part of what is referred to as a musician's "interpretation" of a particular notated piece, although not usually an *explicit* part in Western music. That is, although Western musicians (especially players of stringed instruments and singers) certainly use pitch nuances, these are not usually explicitly notated.[13] This means that the notated music only provides certain aspects of what is required for an effective (and affective) performance—what we have previously referred to as its "structure" or syntax.

It is also significant that nuances, being within-category distinctions, are difficult to remember. As we noted in chapter 10, the reason that nuances can be immediately heard, but not remembered is related to our ability to make many fine distinctions of frequency in a discrimination task (a function of echoic memory), but our inability to remember and identify all but a few of these distinctions in an identification task (a function of short-term and long-term memory).

Nuance is an important factor in making fixed renditions of music such as recordings interesting to listen to many times. Even though we may know the patterns of pitch categories (syntax) of the music quite well, the nuances will continue to surprise us time after time because they elude the grasp of long-term memory.

Blurring Pitch Categories: Ornamentation

The function of categorization was described earlier in this book as the reduction or removal of small-scale detail, which can be viewed as a kind of perceptual "noise" (The term noise is here used to mean small-scale irrelevant variations, rather than a type of acoustical waveform). In some musical systems, however, especially those having scales with few pitches, certain controlled types of small-scale variation are allowed precisely to blur categorical pitch boundaries. Called "ornamentation," these variations may consist of a wide variety of trills, continuous slides, oscillating patterns, or even occasional stable pitches that are not part of the tuning system. All of these can introduce uncertainty into the perception of pitch categories. They are most typically introduced at the beginning or end of a stable pitch event, creating uncertainty either about what the stable pitch will actually be or about where it will lead. That is to say, they usually "attach" themselves to a stable pitch event. Many ornaments consist of continuous pitch movement and may cross pitch category boundaries. In some musical styles, extensive use of pitch nuance and ornamentation can introduce uncertainty about the size of interval categories.[14]

Melodic Grouping and Streaming

Grouping operates vertically in pitch space as well as horizontally in time. Similarity at the melodic level is vertical rather than horizontal.[15] Of the two aspects of interval similarity introduced in chapter 10, chroma and pitch height, we shall consider pitch height here.

Pitches similar in pitch height tend to be grouped together vertically, just as pitches close to each other in time tend to be grouped together horizontally (rhythmically). Our nervous system seems to assume that most sounds from single coherent sources occur within a limited pitch range and do not move out of this range quickly; that

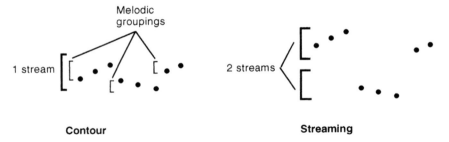

Figure 11.3
Melodic contour and streaming.

sounds in different pitch ranges are often produced by different sound sources. Thus, as we hear them, sounds close together in pitch seem related, whereas sounds appearing quickly out of this range seem to have originated from a different source. This is called the "streaming effect" (figure 11.3). A *stream* is a constructed acoustical image of a coherent sound source, and may consist of sounds that happen either simultaneously or sequentially. Streaming is an example of what has previously been referred to as "perceptual categorization."

When a sequence of sounds takes place with pitch events far enough apart in pitch, groupings may actually break apart from each other and form streams, separate groupings in the *vertical* dimension of music. Because musical streams are independent "lines" of melody heard as being separate from each other, sounds far enough apart in pitch are heard as coming from different sources, even if they are actually being produced by the *same* source.

Streaming is also responsible for our ability to hear several different kinds of sounds simultaneously and to identify them as coming from separate sources. This is what makes the musical phenomenon of counterpoint possible. On the other hand, although we can perceive the *presence* of multiple streams simultaneously (up to at least four), we cannot closely *attend* to more than one at a time (Bregman, 1990), thus we cannot attend to the details of acoustical events in more than one pitch range at a time. For example, in a situation where a number of verbal conversations are taking place at the same time, we may be aware of how many there are, but can only listen to the content of one at a time. The unattended conversations will form a relatively undifferentiated background, although our attention may be drawn to them by the appearance of something either novel or familiar (our own name, for example). This seems to indicate that the unattended conversations are still being at least minimally monitored in some way outside of conscious awareness (Neisser, 1976: 79–105). In musical streams, the time order and rhythm of events can only be perceived with accuracy in one stream at a time, although our attention may shift between different streams very quickly.[16] We can of course also hear an overall texture consisting of multiple streams holistically.

The speed at which melodic events happen is also a factor in streaming—the faster these events occur, the narrower the range of pitches must be to form a single stream (Bregman, 1990: 61). Conversely, the slower they occur, the wider the range of pitches (larger the leaps in pitch) can be that still form a single stream. This means that the pitch range of a single stream cannot be defined absolutely: it varies with both the speed and melodic intervals of events. All of which seems to suggest that streaming is the result of some kind of limit on the amount of melodic information we can process at one time.

Although frequency separation and speed are the most important factors in stream segregation, there are other factors that can also affect it, and that may define what would usually be a single sound source. These include

1. Glides. Sounds that are connected by sliding transitions (as in speech) tend to form a single stream.

2. Continuous or directed progressions (continuity). Sequences of elements that change in a particular direction in regular intervals tend to form coherent streams much more easily than sequences of irregular values: progressions are more predictable, and hence easier to track. For example, isolated large pitch leaps (which violate continuity) tend to pop out of a melody and form a separate stream.

3. Regular timing. Sounds that recur at equal time intervals tend to form streams more readily than sounds that do not. Again, predictable sequences of elements tend to bind together into streams more readily.

Streams that occur at the same time but that have differing degrees of repetition can also have a relationship referred to as "foreground-background." This was previously explained in relation to the phenomenon of habituation in chapter 2. In this case, one stream (the less repetitive one) can be perceived as *out in front of* another. If the two streams are in different pitch ranges, the more repetitive stream may be regarded as an *accompaniment* to the other stream. Patterns of musical accompaniment are often structured in a repetitive way.

Melodic Motion

We noted in chapter 3 that perceptual grouping is generally a bottom-up process, guided by proximity, similarity, and continuity. We shall now take a closer look at how proximity, similarity, and continuity operate at the melodic level.[17]

If we consider successive pitch intervals as the basic units of melodic motion, we see that all intervals have two basic aspects, metaphorically described as "size" and "direction." (Note that we never experience these aspects separately.) The *size* of the distance between two pitch events may be smaller (a step) or larger (a leap). Here again, we find an abstract musical process being defined by a physical metaphor. Note also that in this case the metaphor refers to the idea of melodic motion by referring to pitches as though they were *alive*. Stepping and leaping are activities pursued by living organisms that can move. As general, bottom-up categories, *steps* and *leaps* are relative terms defined at least in part contextually. A *leap* may be defined as the smallest size of pitch interval that will form a grouping boundary in a given context. (Context here includes both the scale the interval is part of, and the immediately surrounding pitch intervals.) The *direction* of motion of an interval is absolute, not contextually defined: it may move up, down, or stay the same (see figure 11.4). Change of direction can form a weak grouping boundary without change in interval size.

Although the two pitch events that constitute an interval can create expectation by moving in a particular direction, to get a clear sense of how that expectation is realized, we must consider at least three pitch events (two intervals; Narmour, 1990). This is a kind of minimum size for a typical melodic grouping. Melodic groupings are in turn the basic units of a melodic phrase. Thus a sequence of three pitch events

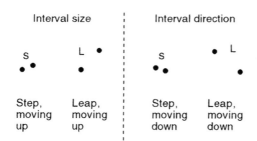

Figure 11.4
Melodic motion.

consists of an interval that creates an expectation, and another interval that either confirms, partly confirms, or disconfirms that expectation. The way an interval functions is therefore usually determined by the interval that precedes it, which makes a three-note grouping a basic unit for the analysis of melodic grouping, especially if the second interval is different from the first one. If the second interval is identical in size and direction to the first, it is the *third* interval that is important.

Looking at melodic groupings in this way, we can see how each pitch interval implies the next and how grouping boundaries are formed. That melodic grouping boundaries are usually rather weak helps to support the integrity of phrases. Because a phrase is seen as a continuous gesture, its components must not segment too radically.

Interval sequences may imply continuity or reversal. Motion in similar intervals in the same direction implies continuation, whereas larger changes in interval size or change in direction of motion (reversals) imply segmentation. The expectation of continuation or reversal may be in relation to either pitch interval, direction of melodic motion, or both.

Thus an interval may be continued with a similar type of interval or reversed with a dissimilar one. (Note that the interval reversal is a reversal of *implication*, not of direction of motion.) For example, a step followed by a leap in the same direction would be a reversal of the implied interval (another step), but not a reversal of direction of motion (figure 11.5 [3]).

Pitch motion may also be continued by moving in the same direction or reversed by moving in the opposite direction. This kind of reversal *is* a change in direction of motion. The strongest kind of reversal involves both a reversal of interval type and a reversal of direction of motion.

These aspects of pitch motion are thought to be processed in a bottom-up fashion (Narmour, 1992a: 69–74), which suggests there may be specific neural feature extractors whose function is to detect whether a small step or a large melodic leap has occurred, and whether a change in the direction of melodic motion has occurred.[18] We have seen that the majority of intervals used in most music are the smaller, steplike intervals. When several of these intervals move consistently in the same direction, they strongly imply continuation in the same direction with similar small intervals. When a leap occurs, it creates a "gap" in this continuity. The implication created by this situation is that the gap will then be "filled in" with the expected steplike intervals (Meyer, 1973: 145–157). To fill in this gap, the subsequent steplike intervals must move in the *opposite* direction from the leap. Thus,

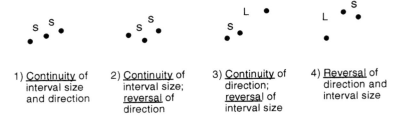

1) <u>Continuity</u> of
interval size
and direction

2) <u>Continuity</u> of
interval size;
<u>reversal</u> of
direction

3) <u>Continuity</u> of
direction;
<u>reversal</u> of
interval size

4) <u>Reversal</u> of
direction and
interval size

Figure 11.5
Melodic implication.

although a step implies continuation with another small interval moving in the same direction, a leap implies reversal in *both interval direction and size* (not continuation in the same direction in another large interval).[19] To fill in the gap that a leap creates, motion should proceed in the direction *opposite* that of the leap, in step-size intervals. This also tends to stabilize pitch range and keeps melodies moving back toward a center.

Basically, continuity is nonclosural and progressive, whereas reversal of implication is closural and segmentive. "Closural" here does not mean absolutely final, but having any kind of segmentation, however weak. The degree of melodic closure achieved depends on context. If supported by closure in other parameters, such as duration and metrical position, melodic reversals can be strongly closural. If unsupported by closure in other parameters, they will have what has been described as "soft closure," which may not actually "end" anything, but which helps articulate the contour of a phrase. This is how the lowest level of melodic grouping boundary is established. In other words, although a reversal unsupported by closure in other parameters will not usually create a phrase ending, it may articulate a grouping within a phrase, giving that phrase shape and definition and creating expectations about its further progress. Groupings constitute the identifying features of a phrase, and can be important for some types of musical development, where a phrase is dismantled into its constituent groupings, which are then treated as separate musical elements. How these grouping boundaries relate to metrical stress points is also an important factor in creating subtle metrical tensions between the interior of a phrase and the metrical structure.

The question arises, where do the boundaries of melodic groupings actually occur? Are they *between* pitches or do they occur *on* pitches, which then become the boundary points of two different groupings? In the case of reversal of interval

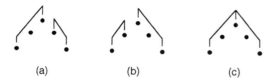

(a)   (b)   (c)

Figure 11.6
Possible groupings of a reversal melodic direction.

type it is clear that the new grouping generally starts with the pitch that constitutes the reversal, but what about a reversal of melodic direction? In this case, there are several possibilities (figure 11.6), and which potential grouping results can depend on how the music is actually performed (see Deliege, 1987: 346, 353–354).

Another factor important in melodic grouping, and one that interacts with the factors presented above, the presence of a *central pitch* in a tonality can have strong closural significance. This of course involves long-term memory to some extent.

Contour

The horizontal accumulation of upward and downward movements by melodic intervals creates what is metaphorically referred to as "contour".[20] In this spatial metaphor, a melodic phrase, which actually occurs one tone at a time, is referred to as if it were a single physical object with a horizontal outline, as though we could scan the melody in time the way we scan the outline of an object in space. We can think of melody in this way because of our ability to retain more than one pitch event at a time as a short-term memory. (Of course, we use STM in the scanning of a physical object, too.) Along with the qualities of particular intervals, contour is the main factor that gives melodies their recognizable individual melodic characteristics.

Contour is the most memorable characteristic of nontonal melodies (Dowling and Harwood, 1986: 133–134). For melodies constructed around the central pitch of a scale, the hierarchical schematic structure of the scale pitches contributes redundancy that is useful for memory. Whereas for those constructed with no central pitch, there are no hierarchical pitch cues to act as memory aids. Memory of nontonal melodies thus depends on other types of organization, and contour is the primary other type of organization available: listeners remember the "bumps" and "depressions" and their relative size, which is more general than remembering specific interval categories. Indeed, nontonal melodies can often be repeated with some pitches changed by one or two steps, and as long as contour is retained, many listeners may not notice (Imberty, 1993). Generally, this same type of pitch change is quite obvious in tonal melodies.

Continuous Contour

Melodic materials are not always organized in terms of discrete intervals or steps. Pitch space may be used in a continuous way. This is usually accomplished with musical instruments that do not have fixed pitches built into them, such as the unfretted string instruments, the trombone, electronic instruments such as oscillators, and the voice. In this case, rather than "stepping" between pitches, a melody will slide between them continuously. This makes perceptual estimation of the size of intervals more difficult and less precise, although certainly the difference between large and small intervals can still be clear. The perception of contour, however, remains undisturbed. Note that the intonation of speech in nontonal languages (such as English) is a pitch contour phenomenon of this type. The precise pitch at which a sentence is intoned is not important, although its relative pitch often carries emotional information. Certain kinds of pitch contours are even associated with certain types of content. (Tonal languages, such as some Asian and African languages, actually use pitch interval to carry semantic meaning, and are closer to being "sung" than other languages.)

Progressive linearity is still possible in pure contour melodies, where speed of motion is also an important variable. As in speech (with which pure contour melodies are often compared), the speed of a slide provides emotional inflection. Fast-sliding motion tends to produce tension, while slower-sliding motion is more relaxed, and leads to resolution.

There are also many types of music which use both stepped intervals and slides. African-American jazz, for example, is a combination of European stepped interval music and some speechlike aspects of traditional West African music. This makes possible the precision and specificity of European interval structure, while at the same time allowing emotional inflection and nuance within the interval structure by "bending" individual notes, and sometimes sliding between them. The music of India also uses a combination of stable pitches and sliding ornaments of various kinds. Indeed, it is rare for a music to use *only* sliding pitches, which are most often used as a way of moving between or inflecting stable pitches. In these cases, because we get our sense of where we are in pitch space from the stable portions of pitch events, the proportion of time between the stable pitch and the sliding pitch is important. The slides are perceived as nuances; not amenable to categorical perception, they cannot function syntactically. Thus a music that consisted only of sliding pitches would probably not be able to support many syntactical pitch relations.

A System of Melodic Organization: Tonality

The third type of constraint on melodic materials, after tuning systems and scales, tonality is a set of constraints on the use of the particular pitches of a scale. Unlike a tuning system or a scale, a tonality is a limitation not on *whether* a particular pitch will occur within a scale, but rather on *how often* it occurs, and on the *relative importance* of the places where it occurs. In a tonality, a particular pitch of a scale is made to seem *more central* or *more important* than others.[21] This central pitch (and the intervals that other pitches form with it) thus becomes a special kind of pitch category. Although tonality is not necessary for the establishment of interval categories in general, it seems to be a major way of establishing a *hierarchical* arrangement of interval categories.

As we have seen, when a scale is notated, its "tonic" or central tone is notated as the first pitch, at the "bottom" of the scale (symbolizing the closural function of this pitch). The rest of the pitches of the scale are then notated as "rising up," moving further "away" from the central pitch. Note that these are all spatial metaphors.

The centrality of a particular pitch within a scale is not completely fixed by the structure of the scale; it has to be continually established and reestablished contextually in the music. Because tonality only exists *in time*, it needs a real musical context to be established. The order in which particular pitches are presented can strongly affect our perception of tonality (Butler and Brown, 1994: 198–208), thus making it considerably less abstract than the previously established structures of tuning system and scale.

The primary way a particular pitch becomes central is through repetition: because it has occurred frequently in the past, we expect it to return in the future. Our perception of other pitches becomes colored by expectations of return to the central one, and in this sense the other pitches become subordinate to the central one. Because repetition can be a form of closure, returning to this central pitch can define important grouping boundaries on larger levels, and withholding return can create tension.

The centrality of a particular pitch is generally established by more than brute repetition. This reinforcement is accomplished in parameters other than pitch. For instance, the central pitch may occur in a rhythmic position in the meter that is itself central, or it may have longer durations, establishing centrality in several parameters at once. There are a number of different possibilities for this type of multi-parametric reinforcement that allow for many degrees of emphasis on the return to the central pitch. This is an important aspect of establishing different hierarchical levels of closure. Generally, the higher the structural level a return to the central pitch is, the larger the number of parameters on which the return will be reinforced.[22] In nontonal melodic patterns, tension and closure are established through means other than pitch centrality, such as duration, rhythmic position, and direction of motion.

Tonality and Implicit Memory

Most people, whether they have musical training or not, can identify the central pitch of a passage of tonal music. This is often true even if the music is not from their own culture. The ability to hear the central pitch of music is learned, but appears to be learned *implicitly* (see Cuddy, 1993: 24; Krumhansl, 1990: 18–25). Remember that one of the kinds of things that implicit memory seems to operate on is syntax, or the rulelike distributions of events. Because it is a distribution in time of particular pitches, tonality is a syntax in this sense. It has been said that implicit memories are established slowly, over time and through repeated practice. We probably learn to identify central pitches simply by being exposed to so much tonal music in our environment, and we learn this without ever knowing that we are learning it (see Dowling, 1993: 12, 1999: 613–616, 620–21). Although untrained listeners are not good at categorizing isolated pitch intervals, in real musical contexts they can detect wrong and out-of-tune pitches remarkably well if the music is tonal. Most untrained listeners can also sing the intervals of familiar tonal melodies. All of this seems to indicate that most people have some kind of implicit schema of the intervals within a scale (see Dowling, 1978).

Melodic Schemas

We have seen that much of experience is comprehended using schemas. Because melodies are structures in experience, we might suspect that there are schemas for particular types of melodies (figure 11.7).

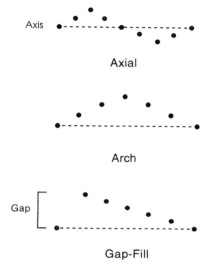

Figure 11.7
Melodic schemas.

Note that tuning systems and scales are category structures that exist outside actual music: they are highly abstract sets of materials out of which music is made; they are part of a musical culture. But such categories have no time order—they tell us little about the actual ordering of events in real time. They give us expectations about what categories of events are likely to occur, but not when or in what order. A temporal schema, on the other hand, is a general model of the ordering of events in time. It not only tells us where we can expect things to be, it tells us when we can expect them to be there. As a general kind of temporal schema, tonality leads us to expect that the central tone will probably appear in some central metrical locations, with longer durations, and so on. Although still an abstraction, it is nonetheless closer to actual music. Melodic schemas are even more specific in that they give a set of expectations about the order of pitches necessary to create a specific contour.

Although the analysis of melody in schematic terms is a relatively new field, there are several types of patterns that appear to be sufficiently generalized that they may be thought of as melodic schemas. Some are learned within particular styles and cultures. These are part of the syntax of a style. North Indian ragas, for example, are partly defined by particular melodic contour schemas within a particular scale.[23]

Because, however, we do not deal with top-down, learned syntax organization (unique to particular styles) in this book, we shall not deal with this type of schema here. Other types of melodic schemas seem much more universal, and it is to these that we now turn.

Image Schemas and Melody

We have already suggested that image schemas may be operative in music as well as in language. The idea of centrality, which we have defined in relation to tonality, is image schematic in nature. It is a basic feature of the way in which we orient ourselves in space, whether that space is physical or metaphorical.

We might expect that melodic schemas could be metaphorically derived from abstractions of basic physical experiences, and I shall now suggest that they are. The kind of melodic schemas we shall be dealing with here are schematic *contours*. These melodic contours are clearly metaphorically related to actions and objects in physical space. The most general kinds of melodic schemas are certain types of generalized contours, which generate large families of melodies on many different time scales. These types of schemas also can be found in the music of many different cultures.

Axial Melodies

One of the oldest ways of organizing a melody in some types of ancient music, especially chants, an *axial melody* is motion *around* a central pitch (Meyer, 1973: 183–191). Axial melodies are the clearest demonstration of the idea of centrality as it is expressed at the melodic level. In them, melodic motion alternately rises above and sinks below a central pitch, always eventually returning to that pitch. This makes the axial schema balanced; axial melodies thus tend to have a static quality. Although the rising and sinking motion can perfectly balance each other, in most axial melodies, rising motion tends to predominate slightly.

Melodic Arch

Unlike the axial melody, the *melodic arch* is a form of melodic schema that generally does not use pitches below its central pitch; rather, it rises to a climactic high pitch and falls back down (see Guck, 1997). Also unlike an axial melody, a melodic arch usually develops a fairly linear pattern of tension. An expectation is created that the melody can only move upward for so long, and will then reach a point of reversal, eventually falling back to the pitch on which it started.

The melodic arch can vary in regard to where its central climax is located, often not in the exact temporal center of the pattern, but somewhat closer to the end. This is especially true of larger-scale arch forms, such as those occupying an entire section of a piece (see Guck, 1997). Much more rarely, it can be closer to the beginning.

Melody and the Filling of Gaps

Another type of melodic schema found in many kinds of music, the *gap-fill* schema is derived from the metaphorical idea that when a melodic leap is made, it leaves a "hole" or gap, which then needs to be filled (Meyer, 1973; see also "Melodic Motion" above). The leap in a gap-fill schema is usually made upward so that the "fill" consists of downward motion that not only closes the gap, but provides the type of release of tension which has been mentioned previously.

The interest in a gap-fill melody is generated by the ways in which the basic downward pattern is elaborated. Because the leap creates the expectation of the fill, interest is created by delaying the fill, utilizing reversals, and incomplete closures of various kinds. Often, gap-fill structures occupying longer time spans reach the bottom note in some inconclusive way, then "bounce" back up several times, creating a sequence of increasingly smaller gap-fills. Note that the gap-fill schema is highly directed, that is, the return to the initial tone is a goal, and the entire filling of the gap is directed toward that goal. We shall now look at how the basic ideas introduced earlier in this book apply to the rhythmic dimension of grouping.

Notes

1. I am aware that this definition says nothing about the function of melodies in musical contexts. It is meant to be a general characterization of melodic *information*.

2. In traditional musical analysis, these basic groupings can be referred to as "motifs," "cells," or "figures." See Nattiez, 1990, 156–157.

3. I shall refer to pitch sequences that are not structured around a central pitch as *nontonal*. I use this term rather than for instance "atonal," a word that can have specific stylistic connotations in Western European music.

4. *Tuning system* is another musical term that does not have a single meaning. My usage follows authors such as Mandelbaum (1962), Barbour (1972), and Krumhansel (1990). I

prefer this more general definition, because to me the term tuning *system* implies the most inclusive level of intervals and their relations to each other. Dowling and Harwood (1986: 113–114) use the term "tuning system" to mean what I mean by "scale," and use the term "tonal material" to mean what I mean by "tuning system." I shall use the term *pitch category* when speaking of single (isolated) pitches, and *interval* or *interval category* to describe distance between pitches. Most listeners judge the "correctness" of a particular pitch contextually, by its relation to the pitches around it. See Burns, 1999, p. 218.

5. Some musical cultures use two tuning systems, such as the Slendro and Pelog of Indonesia and the Bac and Nam of Vietnam.

6. Note that this means that neither the distinction between nuance and category nor that between expression and structure is absolute. What constitutes structure in one musical culture may be heard as nuance in another. This is what we would expect given the learned (conceptual) nature of interval categories.

7. In a musical culture where tuning system and scale are the same, this may not be the case.

8. The term *microtonal* refers to any tuning system that uses intervals other (usually smaller) than those found in twelve-tone equal temperament. A general survey of microtonal tunings can be found in Mandelbaum, 1961.

9. A concept that could be introduced at this point is that of *mode*. One definition of mode is that a number of versions of a particular scale can be produced, with a different pitch of the scale being central in each. These would be the modes of that scale. However, I have chosen not to include the concept of mode in this book because, as *The New Harvard Dictionary of Music* (Randel, 1986: 499) says: "No single concept usefully embraces all that has been meant by the term throughout the history of Western music as well as all that is meant by the terms associated with non-Western music that have at one time or another been translated as mode."

10. For an interesting cognitive critique of a type of music that attempts to use more than nine pitches, see Thomson, 1991.

11. Individuals having what is called "perfect pitch" are able to name isolated pitches accurately; they may encode pitch in such a way as to use their short-term memory capacity more efficiently than individuals who lack this ability.

12. I call scales "spatial schemas," rather than "temporal schemas," because scales describe the relations between categories in metaphorical pitch space, but *do not specify their time order*. On the other hand, I call melodic schemas "temporal schemas" because they specify an archetype for the temporal order in which pitches occur. Just as the same categories of objects or events can appear in different relationships in different temporal schemas, so the same scale pitches can appear in different patterns in different melodic schemas.

13. Pitch nuances are especially obvious in African-American hybrid music such as jazz.

14. Two examples are the Maqam system in Arabic folk music (Cohen and Katz, 1997) and the modal scales associated with the Vietnamese Dan Tranh (Keefe, Burns, and Nguyen, 1991).

15. Note that pitch is an example of a musical parameter where the both the terms *proximity* and *similarity* are used. In fact, the "purest" use of the term "proximity" is usually

reserved for temporal proximity, probably because metaphors involving the spatialization of time are very common. However, most authors also use the term "proximity" to describe the relative distance between pitches, although grouping effects involving change of register or widening of interval are often referred to as *similarity effects* (for instance, see Lerdahl and Jakendoff, 1983, pp. 45–46, and Deliège, 1987, p. 332). These usages may be distinguished as follows: successive *pitches* may be more or less close together (proximate), and successive *intervals* may be similar or not. Therefore the interval categories of step and leap are similarity categories. All steplike intervals are similar, as are leaps. Also, the pitches in steplike intervals are proximate, and tend to group together, while leaplike intervals are heard as gaps in proximity.

16. Note also that in traditional European contrapuntal music (fugues, for example), important thematic material is often introduced in one melodic stream at a time. In this kind of music, thematic material usually appears in different streams of melody at different times so as to structure the motion of the listener's attention between different streams. That way, listeners do not have to closely attend to the details of more than one stream at a time.

17. Many of the ideas about melodic motion in this subsection are derived from those of Eugene Narmour, called the "implication–realization model" (Meyer, 1956; Narmour, 1990). Narmour's ideas about melodic motion, however, are very strongly related to metrical factors. Because I wish to consider melodic movement without also considering metrical factors at this time, my description of melodic motion will be far less detailed than Narmour's. Also, my aim is not to present a complete analytical model so much as to give an indication of what the basic variables of melodic organization are, because organization affects memory. Readers interested in a much more thorough presentation of Narmour's ideas about melodic analysis should consult Narmour, 1990, 1992b.

18. Note that, thus far, no perceptual mechanism has been discovered that specifically extracts reversal of melodic direction. Nevertheless, it is certainly clear that reversal of direction is one feature of a melodic contour; however, it appears to be a relatively weak factor in segmentation. See Deliège, 1987, pp. 353–354. Note that the categorization of intervals as simple steps or leaps is a bottom-up process, whereas the *identification* of the particular intervals that constitute a scale is a top-down process. Also note that although the perception of intervals as steps or leaps is contextually related to the tuning system that the intervals occur in, Narmour classifies the distinction for Western 12-tone equal temperament as breaking around the center of the octave. He classifies the intervals of minor second, major second, minor third, and major third as clearly steplike, the perfect fourth, tritone, and perfect fifth as ambiguous and subject to local contextual interpretation, and the minor sixth, major sixth, minor seventh, and major seventh as clearly leaps. See Narmour, 1990; pp. 76–81. Interestingly, in tests where musicians are asked to produce isolated intervals, they produce intervals that are too small for steplike intervals, and too large for leaps, reproducing the intervals the best at the center of the octave. See Rakowski, 1990.

19. Note that not all possible types of melodic motion are considered here. Narmour also defines what he calls "retrospective" melodic motion patterns, such as a pattern of two successive leaps, where the quality of motion is realized in retrospect. See Narmour, 1989, p. 52.

20. Indeed, the word for melodic pattern in Persian classical music, "*gusheh*," literally means corner or angle.

21. Most functioning tonal systems have more than one important pitch: one primary and one or more secondary and even tertiary pitches.

22. While tonality can serve as a powerful organizational factor for listeners on time scales up to a minute without relatively continuous reinforcement, it may not do so on larger time scales. See Cook, 1990, pp. 54–58. Although much more research needs to be done in this area, Cook's experiments with tonality seem to challenge long-held assumptions about the significance of tonality as a large-scale formative element in music, especially from the listener's (as opposed to the musician's or the analyst's) point or view. One system in which tonality can clearly be maintained over long time periods is the drone-based raga system of Indian music, where a continuous drone sound acts like a constantly refreshed long-term memory of the tonal center.

23. For a definition of what constitutes a raga, see Bagchee, 1998, pp. 282–284. Bagchee compares a raga to a kind of grammar. See also Danielou, 1995, p. 89.

12
Rhythm

I have used the term *event* to describe a perceptible change in an acoustical environment. When two or more events take place within the length of short-term memory, we have what will be referred to as a "rhythm."

Basic Rhythmic Concepts

A number of terms are useful in talking about rhythm. A *beat* is a single point in time.[1] It is an imaginary temporal reference point, which is often but not always represented by an actual musical event. Beats have no duration, only temporal position. Beats are the components of a pulse. An *attack point* is the perceived location in time of the beginning of an event, and the primary cue from which locations of beats are inferred.

Pulse refers to a series of identical and regularly recurring (isochronous) beats equally spaced in time, underlying music and providing a framework against which durations and patterns are heard. No beat in a pulse is emphasized more than any other. Pulse is inferred from the occurrence of temporally equidistant events in music. Because the beats of a pulse are mental reference points, each beat of a pulse does not have to be represented by an actual musical event. *Tempo* refers to the repetition rate of a pulse, the number of beats per time unit. This is often measured in beats per minute (bpm). A pulse always has a tempo. The term *basic pulse* is used here to refer to the tempo that is felt by a listener to be the central organizing pulse in a piece of music.[2]

An *accent* gives a particular beat the quality of having more "weight," "emphasis," or "stress," and hence more importance or centrality than immediately surrounding beats. Accent is based on the quality of the event that occurs on a particular beat. It is a way of *marking* a particular beat, of making it stand out.

An accent may be established by any of the grouping factors previously mentioned, such as a change in loudness, duration, or timbre, or a leap in pitch.

Time interval refers to the length of time between the onsets of musical events, regardless of duration. Rhythmic patterns are patterns of time intervals and accents.

Duration refers to the time between the beginning (or onset) of an event, and the end of that event. Two rhythmic sequences of sounds can have the same attack points, but the actual durations of the sounds can vary. Duration here refers to the actual length of time that is filled with sound. *Articulation* refers to relatively small differences in the actual length of time that is given to notated durations.

Rhythmic groupings are the actual patterns of time intervals and accents that form music. An accent or larger time interval in the ongoing flow of events will usually form a rhythmic grouping boundary. Paralleling the terms *melodic grouping* and *melodic phrase* in chapter 11, the terms *rhythmic grouping* and *rhythmic phrase* indicate, respectively, the lowest and the next higher level of grouping in the rhythmic dimension. Rhythmic phrases, then, consist of one or more rhythmic groupings; they are distinguished from these by stronger, more closural boundaries, often delineated by longer event durations or by pauses. Rhythmic (temporal) and melodic grouping factors interact with melodic grouping forces to a large degree, and a particular grouping is usually the result of the interaction of both of these forces. Rhythmic grouping boundaries are the primary factor in establishing the repeating accent patterns of meter.

Meter is the organization of the beats of a pulse into a cyclically repeating accent pattern. This pattern is inferred from accented events in the music and, once established, tends to persist. Meter has a reciprocal relationship with grouping—that is, meter is inferred from accents, primarily at grouping and phrase boundaries, and groupings and phrases are heard as either conforming to the accent pattern of meter or not. When grouping boundaries do not reinforce the established accent pattern of meter, *metrical tension* is the result.

Metrical structure is a primary way of establishing important points of temporal reference in music. This is accomplished by accenting particular beats more than others, which makes them central temporal reference points. This forms a framework for rhythmic expectation, where the central beat is "listened forward to." In this sense, meter is a type of schema. The most strongly accented beat in a metrical cycle is usually found at the beginning of the cycle and is called the *downbeat*. One cycle of meter is referred to in Western music as a *measure*. Just as a pulse forms a basic structure of beats repeating at a regular interval at the lowest rhythmic level, so meter can form a repetitive structure of accented beats at the next higher level. In this sense, meter is like a higher-level pulse.

Metrical tension is tension between the rhythmic groupings of actual musical events and the accent pattern implied by meter. It is established by producing an accent pattern within a rhythmic phrase that does *not* conform to the accent pattern implied by the meter—placing strongly accented events, such as beginning or ending events in a rhythmic phrase or grouping, on *weak* (unaccented) beats in the meter.

Rhythmic contour is the profile of changing timing patterns in a rhythmic grouping, metaphorically thought of as having a "rising and falling outline" formed by changes in time intervals between events. Faster rhythms with shorter time intervals form the high points of a rhythmic contour. The "height" of a rhythmic contour indicates the amount of purely rhythmic (nonmetrical) tension present at any given moment.

Rhythmic tension is tension established within a rhythmic grouping by rhythmic contour. The larger the number of events occurring in a given amount of time, the higher the rhythmic tension. Rhythmic tension is completely internal to a rhythm, and is *not* dependent on comparison with meter. Hence it is different from metrical tension. Rhythmic tension can be established without a meter or pulse, in a situation of *free rhythm*, where events are organized into patterns without meter, pulse, or both, that is, without the possibility of inferring any regularly repeating accent or pulse structure.

Rhythm and Short-Term Memory

My definition of rhythm is very general, and includes many types of patterns of events that would be excluded from the ordinary definition of the word. Rhythm is often associated with regularity or repetition, but by my definition, irregular sequences of events are also rhythmic. From this point of view, almost all types of temporal distributions of events have rhythmic qualities.

By my definition, *rhythm* describes only events on time scales within the limits of short-term memory; I consider use of the word for events on larger time scales to be essentially metaphorical and to belong to the realm of musical *form* (Clarke, 1999: 476–478).

The length of short-term memory is important in the definition of rhythm because to form a pattern, the component events of a rhythm must seem directly *connected* (see Parncutt, 1994: 450–451). Remember that for this to be the case, events must be inside of the 3- to 5-second length of short-term memory—the length of the longest phrases. It is also important for estimating the time intervals between the component events of a rhythm. When two events are farther apart in time than the length of short-term memory, perceiving their temporal relationship involves the use of long-term memory, and the events do not seem connected. Under these circumstances, it is very difficult to make accurate judgments about the proportions of time intervals between events, and hence it is impossible to directly perceive their rhythm. (Remember the previously introduced example of a sentence spoken with each word separated by a pause of 30 sec, and the difficulty of constructing relations between those words—the same would be true for a rhythm.) This means that the components of a rhythm must in some sense all be *immediately available* to consciousness, so that we can make comparisons about the relative time intervals between events.

Conversely, when successive events are closer together than about 1/16 sec (62 msec), they become so connected that it is impossible to hear them as separate events. (Interestingly, this is also just slightly more than the upper limit on how fast human beings can produce successive physical actions.) As previously stated, relations between events in this case are processed by the peripheral auditory system, and are so fast that their patterns are perceived holistically, and they begin to fuse together into a unitary pitch perception. This rate of event succession falls within the level of event fusion and represents an example of *pitch* and *timbre* rather than rhythm.

Beats

It has been said that a beat is an imaginary time point, often inferred from an actual event in the music. The main requirement for a musical event to represent a beat is that it have an attack point—a precise position in time at which we hear the sound begin. (The time period over which a sound declines in amplitude is called its "decay"; see figure 12.1.) Note that a sound can have many different durations and still have the same attack point. This means that the locations of attack points are more important in defining a rhythmic pattern than its durations.

Not all sounds have clear attack points: some kinds of sounds are better than others for clearly delineating rhythm. To have a precise position in time, a sound must begin and reach its maximum loudness very quickly. This is what makes its

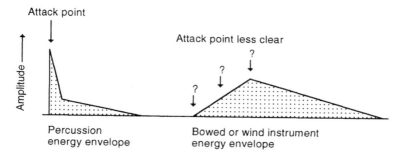

Figure 12.1
Energy distribution and position in time.

attack point clear. Music that is primarily rhythmic often uses percussion instruments, which produce sound by being *struck*. Sounds so produced achieve their maximum loudness virtually instantaneously, and hence have a very precise attack point in time. This is in contrast to instruments that produce acoustical vibrations by other means, such as bowing or blowing, where the sound has a more gradual buildup of energy, and hence does not begin as clearly at a particular time. Although these kinds of instruments can delineate rhythmic patterns fairly clearly, they may also be used to project a kind of temporal vagueness.

The rapid onset of a sound can be thought of as being like "an edge in time." Just as it is easier to visually perceive the position of objects with clearly defined edges, it is easier to perceive the time proportions and details of rhythms executed with sounds having "sharp" attacks. This can be made clear by playing a tape of percussion music backward. The rhythms are not merely reversed, they become *less clear* or *precise*: the more slowly changing decay portions of the sounds, when reversed, become slower attacks, and this causes a kind of blurring of the temporal edges.

Pulse

Given a sequence of musical events, most listeners try to infer an underlying regular series of beats from it, perhaps making use of an internal "clock" (Povel and Essens, 1985). A *pulse* is here defined as a regularly recurring (isochronous) series of *identical* imaginary time points, or *beats*, at a distinct, stable rate of repetition, or *tempo*. Pulse is a nearly universal characteristic of music and forms the basis for rhythmic organization in much of the music of virtually all cultures (Parncutt, 1987).

There are limits on the tempos at which a listener can construct a pulse. We know that there are definite limits on how fast or slow a regular chain of events can be and still be perceived as such. We have already seen that if similar events happen closer together than a certain speed (16 per second), we can no longer perceive them as separate events: they seem continuous and begin to form a pitch. We also know that because of the limits of short-term memory, if events are too far apart in time they will no longer seem connected.

A pulse can be thought of as a kind of limiting case of rhythm. Indeed, a completely regular pulse, represented by a stream of identical musical events, like a completely regular stimulus of any kind, will usually cause habituation and move into the background of awareness. Because it does not change, a pulse does not *articulate* anything. A pure pulse, although it consists of individual events on the lowest time level, has no change on any higher level, and hence is totally predictable. Because the time interval from one beat to the next is well within the limits of echoic and short-term memory, we do not need to use long-term memory to construct the regularity of pulse—we can perceive it directly. Hence the anticipation created from one beat to the next is an example of the primitive grouping principle of continuity, not the long-term memory phenomenon of schema.

Pulse is primarily useful as a basic frame of reference, a background or time base on which other levels of pattern can be superimposed. Its purpose is to make musical time flow in a uniform way. Most important, it creates the possibility of *anticipation* of the next beat, and gives temporal *predictability* to the basic flow underlying the music. It also allows us to "count" time intervals and durations. Once we have heard several events in a row separated by equal amounts of time, we come to expect that subsequent beats will follow in the same way. Note that the existence of a pulse is *inferred* from the time intervals between actual events at the surface of the music, and ultimately depends on those events for its continued existence (see Povel, 1984).

Pulse is important both in the synchronization of performance, and in individual listeners' attention to the music. It has been established that listeners can reproduce (remember) rhythmic patterns much more easily if they are introduced in relation to a regular pulse than if they are not. The same is true for listeners' estimation of durations of events and time intervals, which are also far more accurate in relation to a regular pulse (see Povel, 1981b, and Dowling and Harwood, 1986: 185–186). Indeed, this happens even if the pulse is introduced and then stopped, thus proving that once established, the expectation of a pulse can be used as a framework for comparison, even when it is temporarily no longer there.[3]

Because we tend to expect a pattern to continue in the way it has been established, pulse may be felt as continuing for some time after it is no longer present on every beat, and events will continue to be referenced to it, often in the face of considerable rhythmic contradiction. This is our mind's way of maintaining a "simple" or organized situation. (More will be said about this in "Meter" below.)

Pulse as Temporal Category

We first encountered the phenomenon of categorical perception in chapter 2, noting that its function was to reduce a huge amount of perceptual data to a manageable number of categories with relatively sharp boundaries. In chapter 11, this phenomenon was discussed in relation to pitch categories. An interesting question arises. Is there a similar mechanism for temporal categorization? Do we categorize the position of events in time the way we categorize events in pitch space? It appears that the answer to this question is yes, although a great deal of research on this phenomenon remains to be done (see Clarke, 1987a: 221–224; Fraisse, 1982: 166–168; Parncutt, 1994).

There are several reasons why an understanding of categorical perception in relation to rhythm is important. One is that the phenomenon of categorical perception could explain how we can perceive rhythm and tempo in actual musical performances, where there is considerable deviation from perfect timing (see, for instance, Clynes, 1986; Clarke, 1999: 489–496).

According to current research, rhythmic categorization appears to take place on three different levels: *beat*, *measure*, and *pattern*. The temporal position of an event may be rushed or dragged in relation to the position of a single beat, and sequences of beats may deviate from strict tempo, beats are categorized in relation to their functional position in a measure, and sequences of time intervals are categorized into rhythmic patterns (see figure 12.2).

The lowest hierarchical level on which rhythmic categorization can function is the *beat* level, where the basic category is the position of events in relation to a pulse, and where the category width is a length of time extending from somewhere before each beat position to somewhere after it (see Parncutt, 1994: 416; Parncutt, 1987: 135–136). Events that happen at smaller time intervals from the beat position tend to be interpreted as examples of the same beat, with a certain "feel" of rushing (ahead) or dragging (behind) that particular beat.[4] Thus small deviations from a pulse would be examples of within-category distinctions (rhythmic nuances).

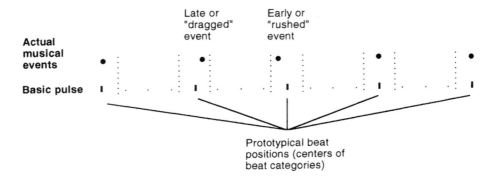

Figure 12.2
Beat categories. The vertical dotted lines represent the approximate boundaries of beat categories.

The size of a beat category undoubtedly varies somewhat (especially in different metrical contexts; see Clarke, 1987a). It has been defined as extending outward from the prototypical beat position a distance of between 1/8 and 1/4 of the time interval of the basic pulse (see Sternberg and Knoll, 1994; Parncutt, 1994: 432). That is, a musical event can deviate on either side of the prototypical beat position by this much, and still function as being on the same beat. This means that our ability to hear rhythmic subdivisions accurately extends to a little more than four times the tempo of the basic pulse. When a musical event is in between beats at this tempo it is simply heard as a version of one of those beats.

Rhythmical nuances are a powerful tool for giving a "human" feel to rhythms. It is important to realize that in actual musical performances, this kind of temporal nuance is occurring constantly (Clarke, 1999). For example, important musical events are often slightly delayed in relation to their prototypical beat positions (Parncutt, 1994).

When several events in succession systematically deviate from their beat positions there is a variation in tempo. Tempo itself is variable in many styles of music. Close study of pulse speed of performing musicians shows that subtle systematic variation of beat positions is going on all of the time (see Clynes, 1986: 169–224).[5] Extraordinarily nuanced ensemble tempos can often be heard in Indonesian Gamelan music, where an entire ensemble of as many as twenty musicians can speed up and slow down together over a fairly large range of tempos.

Conflicts between different players' placement of the beats, especially if large enough that events happen on *both* sides of the center of the beat category, can create a type of nuanced rhythmic tension. Usually, if this type of difference in the interpretation of the beat position is fairly large, the feel of the music passes out of the realm of interesting tension and into the realm of "sloppy" playing (see, for instance, Berliner, 1994: 396), although the distinction between expressive nuance and sloppy playing is certainly contextual to some degree.[6]

Because beat position nuances are examples of within-category distinctions, it also follows that they are hard to remember. And because unremembered nuances can remain fresh, even a fixed musical performance like a recording can continue to surprise us after many listenings.

It is not clear whether the size of a beat category is learned or not. I suspect that it is. If this is the case, cultures whose music is very rhythmically oriented, such as the music of West Africa, might have smaller, tighter beat categories than music without such an orientation. This would mean that small rhythmic changes we might perceive as expressive nuances could function structurally for listeners brought up in that musical culture.

Tempo

Here defined as the number of regularly recurring beats in a given amount of time, *tempo* is the speed of a pulse. The standard way of measuring tempo in Western European music, usually by a *metronome*, is in *beats per minute* (bpm).

Figure 12.3 reproduces the melodic and rhythmic time level of table 1.1. In this version, a new column, labeled "Beats per Minute," has been added in boldface. This column shows the equivalent beats per minute measurement for the "Events per Second" and "Seconds per Event" measurements already in the diagram. In addition, the number of milliseconds between beats for each bpm measurement is shown in parentheses. This new diagram further subdivides the melodic and rhythmic level into three ranges of tempo that are important in human rhythmic perception and cognition.

1. *The moderate tempo.*   This is a tempo of 100 bpm. This is the average tempo that is judged by most people to be neither fast nor slow (see Parncutt, 1994: 418–420, 436–437). It is also a tempo at which judgments of tempo are the most accurate. Note that the moderate tempo is located roughly in the center of the range

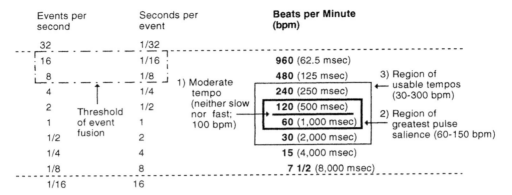

Figure 12.3
Time and tempo.

of values on the rhythmic level. A given piece of music usually implies a number of possible pulses, with different but closely related (e.g., 2:1, 3:1, 4:1) tempos. From these, listeners unconsciously choose one tempo that acts as a central framework in relation to which all the other tempos and rhythms are organized (see Parncutt, 1994: 413; and Povel and Essens, 1985: 414). This is what I have termed the *basic pulse*. The particular tempo that is heard as the basic pulse is usually as close to the moderate tempo as possible, and almost always falls within the region of greatest pulse salience. The selection of the rate of basic pulse in any given piece of music is not always completely consistent across listeners. Generally, the faster the tempo of a piece of music, and the more complex its rhythmic patterns, the more ambiguous its basic pulse (see Parncutt, 1994: 418). The moderate tempo is roughly in the center of a range of tempo values that are referred to as

2. *The region of greatest pulse salience.* This tempo range (60–150 bpm), which surrounds the moderate tempo, is the range from which listeners are most likely to infer the basic pulse of a piece of music if there are no events present that establish the moderate tempo. It is also a range of tempo that we can easily respond to physically in various ways, such as by tapping our feet. Note that tempos outside this range can and do exist in music, but are usually not heard as the basic pulse, which all other rhythms and tempos are related to. Note also that the tempo we feel as the basic pulse of the music may not always correspond to the notated tempo of the music (if there is one). Indeed, our sense of the relative fastness or slowness of

the music is often based, not on the tempo of the basic pulse, which usually falls within a relatively small range, but on the fastest subdivisions of that pulse that are present. This means that it is quite possible for a person to tap their foot at the same speed during two different pieces of music that produce very different impressions in terms of their overall speed. Outside the region of greatest pulse salience is

3. *The region of usable tempos.* This tempo range (30–300 bpm; or between 5 events per second and 1 event every 2 seconds) is the range within which streams of musical events can be heard to have a tempo at all. Rhythms and tempos in this range that are outside the region of greatest pulse salience will generally not be heard as constituting the basic pulse, but as multiples or subdivisions of it. Note that this region is still not quite equivalent to the totality of the rhythmic dimension itself because there are still tempos above and below it at which we can still resolve individual events, but these occur too slowly or quickly for us to perceive clear rhythmic patterns. This would apply to speeds above 5 events per second, and below 1 event every 2 seconds. Above 16 events per second, chains of regular events begin to fuse into pitches, and below 1 event every 8 seconds, events become elements of form. The top limit of the range of usable tempos is 300 bpm— a tempo of 5 events per second. Because this is about the rate at which the order of individual musical events begins to be unclear, it is almost impossible to clearly identify rhythmic patterns at faster tempos. Indeed, sequences of events that occur faster than this (up to a rate of 16 per second) are processed "holistically," like a waveform. Although we can still perceive the separateness of events inside of sequences at this speed, we cannot discern any detailed rhythmic patterns.

While the concept of pulse has been defined as a completely regular succession of beats, tempo in actual musical performances is almost never completely stable: it is speeding up and slowing down by small amounts almost all the time. These tempo changes are usually executed in relation to structural aspects of the music, such as phrase endings and sectional downbeats, and can exist on several structural levels of music at the same time. Nevertheless, because of categorical perception, such deviations from regularity do *not* undermine our sense of pulse. For a rhythm to sustain our interest for any length of time, however, we need more change than provided by a simple pulse.

Accent

Generally in music, some events are emphasized more than others. This emphasis can be established by making a particular event stand out through increased loudness, or through any of the boundary-forming grouping factors previously mentioned. These include relatively large changes in duration, timbre, and changes in pitch contour or time interval. Events that are so emphasized are referred to as being "accented."

Accented events are very important in the formation of rhythmic groupings and phrases. Because accents make one event stand out from others and hence define a change, they are generally closural to some degree. Writers on the subject of rhythm often define three kinds of accent, based on where the accented event is likely to occur.[7]

The first type of accent, referred to as a "phenomenal accent," is created whenever any event is perceived as standing out from the musical surface by being sufficiently different from the events immediately surrounding it (see figure 12.4). This may be the result of any of the above mentioned grouping factors. This type of accent can occur independently of the accent patterns of phrasing or meter. For instance, a phenomenal accent can occur when an event inside a phrase stands out in relation to surrounding events. This type of accent often creates low-level grouping boundaries inside a phrase. It is not dependent on being at the beginning or ending of a rhythmic phrase (as is a structural accent) or on being in the position of a strong beat in a measure (as is a metrical accent).

The second type of accent, referred to as a "structural accent," is perceived at important points in a rhythmic phrase. These points naturally occur at the first and last events of a phrase. Isolated events and the second event in an isolated pair are also perceived as structurally accented (Garner, 1974; Povel and Essens, 1985: 415). Note that structural accent is a perceptual phenomenon and occurs even in sequences of identical events (Povel and Okkerman, 1981). Structural accents may or may not coincide with strong beats in a measure, depending on the amount of metrical tension being established at a given time.

The third type of accent is referred to as a "metrical accent." When phenomenal and structural accents occur at regularly spaced intervals in the rhythmic flow of events, listeners often infer a regular pattern of emphasis or strength of beats called *meter*. Metric accentuation is found on beats that initiate metrical groupings (measures). (In a four-beat meter, the third beat of a measure is also metrically accented, but to a lesser degree than the first.) Note that metric accents are initially inferred from recurring phenomenal and structural accents; the construction of meter by the

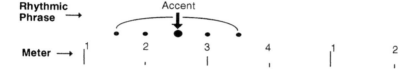

Phenomenal accent: louder event in middle of phrase is accented.

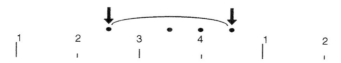

Structural accent: first and last events of phrase are accented.

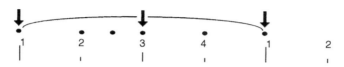

Metrical accent: first and third beats of measure are accented.

Figure 12.4
Three kinds of accent.

listener is not automatic, but must be at least partially maintained by accents naturally occurring in the music. This is especially true at the beginning of a piece of metrical music, where a metrical framework is being established. After such a framework is established, it is possible for a musical event to be heard as accented just by virtue of occurring on a metrically strong beat.

Note that accent is one of the primary ways that melodic and rhythmic grouping interact. Melodic contour features such as melodic leaps and changes of direction can create accents, which may be of any of the above kinds. Melodic features may therefore be organized so as to be congruent with meter or not.

Meter

Researchers have found that when people are presented with a series of events occurring at identical time intervals (a pulse), they subjectively divide these events into recurring groups of two or three (Fraisse, 1982: 155–157). This suggests that we tend to superimpose order on any regularly occurring acoustical stimuli, creating groupings of a constant size. Of course, this tendency is even stronger if there is any change in the quality of events that might support the regular repetition of one particular size of grouping.

When the individual events that constitute a pulse are *no longer perceptually identical*, we have the beginning of the possibility of *meter*. Meter is created when some beats of a pulse are *accented* in a *regularly repeating* pattern.[8] Thus again we see that change forms boundaries in our perception. When an event is sufficiently different from previous events, it is interpreted as the beginning of something new. Initially the most intense beat in a metrical pattern will tend to be interpreted as the *first* beat in the cycle, although the beat perceived as first is affected both by the very first event we actually hear in a piece, and by where we hear the largest change in the cycle. All other things being equal, we usually interpret the first event we hear in a piece as the first beat of a metrical cycle. Exceptions to this occur when the first event or events we hear are made intentionally weak, and are soon followed by a much more strongly accented event. This kind of pattern of emphasis makes it possible to begin a piece of music in the middle of a metrical cycle. It cannot be emphasized enough that the very first events we hear in a piece of music powerfully affect our expectations about the metrical framework to follow (see, for instance, Lee, 1991: 89–90).

Thus we might define meter as a regularly recurring pattern of difference in emphasis of beats within a pulse, which at a given time may be more or less clear, giving a sense of regular progression in time. Indeed, meter is like a pulse on a higher hierarchical level. Its *cyclical* pattern of strong and weak beats creates a small-scale imbalance, with some beats being more central, more important, or having more weight than others. Like the beats of a pulse, this pattern of accents must be *inferred* from events actually present in the music. This means that there are many possibilities for ambiguity in the perception of meter.

In Western music, the first and most centrally important beat of a metrical grouping is referred to as the "downbeat," which acquires stability from being given more accentual weight than the other beats, and from the constant repetition of the cycle in which it is imbedded. Both of these factors work to establish the cycle, and make the downbeat the first beat of the cycle (see Fraisse, 1982: 162).[9] In European music, a single cycle of meter is referred to as a "measure" (see figure 12.5). The centrality of the downbeat is established by the fact that the repetition of its accent is such that we return to this beat again and again. It is almost as though we are returning

Pulse

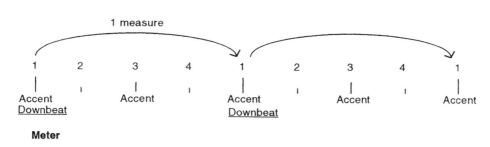

Meter

Figure 12.5
Pulse and meter.

to the same "place" each time the metrical cycle starts over (the expectation of return to the downbeat is represented by the arrows in figure 12.5). Note however that meter is not a given; it is constructed by listeners, although once inferred, it will tend to persist for some time. The stability of the downbeat is established by the degree to which it is accented. The particular way the accent of the downbeat is established can and often does vary from measure to measure. That is, the particular grouping factors that establish the accented quality of the downbeat can differ from measure to measure (figure 12.6).

The regularity and predictability of meter are critical to establishing meter as a framework in relation to which all other rhythmic activity is organized. Moreover, for reasons just explained, the downbeat's central position in the metrical cycle makes it a point of maximal temporal closure. This means that a condition of maximum stability (minimum metrical tension) exists when a rhythmic grouping or phrase of events begins, and especially when it ends, on this beat.

A typical measure of an even-numbered meter would be a four-beat pattern, with a strongly accented first beat (downbeat), a weak second beat, a somewhat accented third beat, and a weak fourth beat (see figure 12.6).

Again we encounter the notion of establishing a framework for perception and cognition through *centrality*. Just as we are able to perceive and remember many

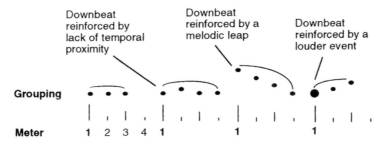

Figure 12.6
Grouping and the maintenance of meter.

more pitch patterns when those patterns are embedded and stabilized in the centralized pitch organization of a scale, so we are also able to perceive and remember rhythmic patterns much more efficiently when they are presented within the stable framework of a metrical system (Summers, Hawkins, and Mayers, 1986). Pulse and metrical frameworks are to temporal perception what tuning systems and scales are to pitch perception (Dowling and Harwood, 1986: 186). They are frameworks that help us to orient ourselves and to have a sense of "where" we are.

Meter establishes a basic temporal tension pattern, where the weaker beats create expectation of the stronger beats. This expectation allows listeners to "hear ahead" to the stronger beats. In relation to meter, this means that the points in time immediately before, and to a lesser extent immediately after, a downbeat have great tension value. Expectation builds as we get closer to the downbeat, and if it does not occur, we continue to expect it for a short while after it should have occurred. This creates a zone of tension surrounding strong beats, much like the zone around a central pitch. There are many possibilities for utilizing these areas of the meter to create metrical tension. Standard rhythmic techniques such as "drum fills," are an example of this. Drum fills are an increase in the level of rhythmic activity right before a downbeat, where the weaker fourth beat of a measure is "filled" with activity. The tension created by placing this more intense activity on a weak beat strengthens the impact of the downbeat when it finally does occur.

An interesting aspect of meter is that at some points its accent pattern may only be implied. That is, the accent pattern of actual musical events does not always have to conform to that of the meter. Once established, the accent pattern of meter can shape rhythmic expectation *even though it may not always be present.* This is possible because once we hear a particular pattern of strong and weak beats presented several times, we tend to assume that the accent pattern will continue in the same way. Indeed, it takes a rather lengthy discrepancy in meter to completely dislodge our assumption that it will continue as it has been before. Thus once a regular meter has been set up, all of the component beats of its pattern do not actually have to be present for us to hear currently present events in relation to them, provided they do not deviate from the meter for too long a time. This means that a kind of metrical tension can be created by deviating from and returning to rhythmic accent and grouping patterns that conform to the meter.

Although it has not been established experimentally, our ability to correctly categorize a musical event as a downbeat may well be an implicit memory phenomenon, like our ability to identify the central pitch of a tonality. In our musical culture, we are constantly exposed to metrical music (usually in four-beat meter); we could easily get the practice we need to identify downbeats implicitly.

Metrical Hierarchy

Generally, there is more than one tempo that is implied by the time intervals between events in the rhythmic groupings and phrases of metrical music. These other tempos usually appear as even multiples and divisions of the basic pulse tempo,[10] and indeed are like other subsidiary levels of pulse. Often, the basic pulse is subdivided into tempos that are twice and four times as fast as it is. Subdivisions smaller than this are not perceived as rhythms at most tempos because they would be inside a particular beat category, and thus would be perceived as nuances rather than as another level of tempo. Also present may be tempos that are one-half and one-fourth as fast as the basic pulse. All of these other tempos can also be metrical because they have the same alternating strong and weak beat structure as the basic pulse (figure 12.7). Note that some of these subdivided beats have the same "strength" as the beats one level above, and some do not. This is the way in which the different pulse levels reinforce each other. In figure 12.7, this reinforcement defines a hierarchy of five levels of strength:

1. At the highest level (SSSSS), the strongest beat of all is the first beat of the measure at the basic pulse tempo (the downbeat), which is strong on all levels.

2. At the second highest level (SSSw), the next strongest beat is the third beat of the measure at the basic pulse tempo. It is weaker than the first, but stronger than all other beats.

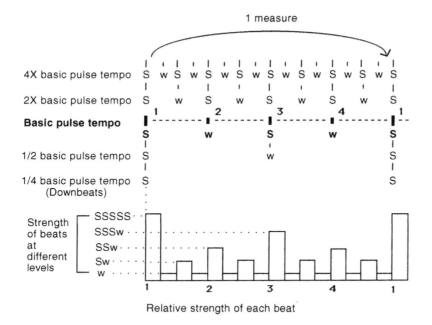

Figure 12.7
A metrical hierarchy. S = strong beat; w = weak beat.

3. At the third highest level (SSw), beats 2 and 4 are the weak beats of the measure at the basic pulse tempo.

4. At the fourth highest level (Sw), weak beats of the first subdivision of the basic pulse tempo are at twice the tempo of the basic pulse and are sometimes called the "off-beats."

5. At the lowest level (w), weakest of all, the eight weak beats of the highest subdivision of the basic pulse tempo are at four times the tempo of the basic pulse and fall between all of the other levels of beats.

Notice that the distribution of strength of beats within a measure is somewhat like a wave that peaks on the downbeat.

These levels of strength are closely related to the creation of metrical tension. The *weaker* a beat, the *greater* the metrical tension created by placing an accented event on it. Placing accented events on weak beats strongly undercuts the stable, closural qualities of those events. Placing the final event of a grouping on a weak beat, for example, creates the contradiction of closing the grouping at a nonclosural position in the meter. Like all nonclosural situations, this creates a strong drive forward. The weaker the beat on which the strong grouping event is placed, the greater the metrical tension created.[11] The greater the number of accented events falling on weak beats, the greater the overall metrical tension. At this point, we can make some distinctions that will establish different degrees of metrical tension; these are illustrated in figure 12.8. In the most stable situation, the rhythmic and melodic groupings in the actual music (phenomenal and structural accents) coincide exactly with the grouping implied by the meter (panel 1). This rhythm holds little interest: the accent pattern of the phrase and that of the meter match exactly, hence the rhythm is very predictable or "square."

In the second, slightly less stable situation, one grouping boundary on the phrase level, in this case the ending boundary, coincides with a strong beat in the meter, but the beginning boundary does not (panel 2). This creates a grouping that "pushes" toward the downbeat, creating a small-scale tension within the measure, which is immediately resolved.

In the third most stable situation, no boundaries of the phrase coincide with metrical grouping, but lower-level grouping boundaries inside the phrase still do (panel 3). I have described this type of phrase as "floating" because it is not anchored to a downbeat at either end. A string of such phrases would probably eventually be "closed" by a phrase that ended on a downbeat.

In the fourth most stable situation, both important phrase boundaries occur on a weak subdivision of the basic pulse (panel 4), whereas in the least stable situation—*syncopation*—the grouping established by phrase structure is in conflict with the metrical structure (panel 5). Here major metrical boundaries, such as downbeats, have continuous rhythmic motion moving right across them.

Meter as Temporal Schema

On the next higher level of rhythmic categorization, the level of the *measure*, events are categorized not only by the position of beats in a pulse, but by their metrical position as well (Clarke, 1987a). That is, in a four-beat meter, they are categorized as being first, second, third, or fourth beats (or first, second, and third in a triple meter). Remember that knowing exactly *which* beat of the measure a rhythmic pattern starts on is crucial to apprehending its metrical tension value: the same rhythmic pattern moved ahead or behind in relation to the meter by a beat or a fraction of a beat can have a very different metrical tension value. Thus metrical categorization is essential

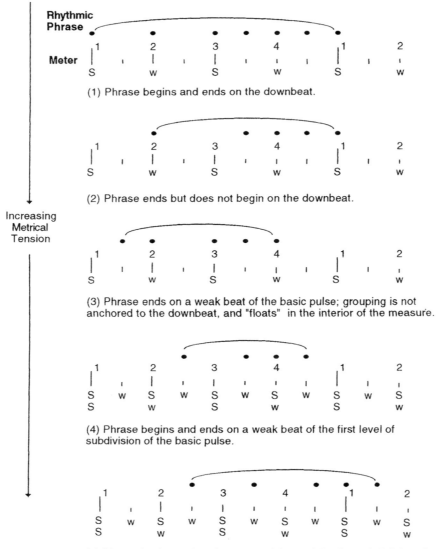

Figure 12.8
Metrical tension. (It is assumed that these patterns take place in a context where the meter has already been established.) This diagram is meant to show, not that metrical tension is precisely quantifiable, but only that it can exist to varying degrees.

for determining the relative degree of closure achieved by a pattern in metrical music.[12] We cannot know for certain how much closure a particular phrase achieves metrically *without knowing where the downbeat is.*

Categorizing a musical event as a downbeat can be a fairly complicated judgment. Although the downbeat is a temporal category (the first beat of the measure), as we have seen, it is often established through *other* than temporal means. Because metrical organization is related to grouping, any of the factors that help to establish grouping boundaries can help to establish a particular event as the downbeat.

In chapter 8, I defined schemas as sets of expectations about sequences of events, and the components of schemas as categories. We know that categorical slots in a schema are variable and can be filled in with different exemplars of a category. The type of musical event found on a particular downbeat can vary—and even be no event at all; different types of grouping factors will establish the identity of the downbeat to varying degrees. The structure of the category of possible downbeat events is therefore graduated, with some types of grouping factors producing more prototypical (stronger) examples of a downbeat than others. The downbeat need not and often is not marked in the same way on each repetition. In the absence of clear marking by intensity, other grouping factors usually determine which beat gets categorized as the downbeat. If a particular beat in a pulse regularly appears at the beginning or ending of groupings, it is often judged to be the downbeat. In music where there are several streams of events going on at one time, there may be competition for the status of the downbeat. Here it is often a combination of factors that is decisive, although music may be designed to be metrically ambiguous. Because our perception of rhythms is based to a large extent on predictability, that is, we establish a norm and perceive subsequent events as conforming to or deviating from it to various degrees, meter falls within the realm of schemas as previously defined. The positions of the individual beats that constitute meter are categories, with boundaries that act as limits within which an actually occurring event is interpreted as falling on one beat or another, and the downbeat is the most important of those categories.

It seems that there are limitations on the size that basic metrical groupings can have. Metrical groupings of more than four beats are generally referred to as "compound meters." This means that a meter consisting of patterns of five beats, for instance, would tend to be heard as a pattern of three beats, followed by a pattern of two beats (or vice versa). As the number of beats in a metrical pattern increases, the overall feeling of a unified meter gets weaker, and "pulls apart" into smaller meters. Note that the longer a metrical cycle gets, the more the listeners have to depend on long-term memory to comprehend its pattern, and hence the more schematic (as opposed to simply categorical) it will be.

In addition, the longer the repetition of a pattern takes (especially if it exceeds the capacity of short-term memory), the harder it will be to perceive its repetition. Therefore, musics that use "long" meters, such as North Indian raga music, which theoretically can use up to 108 beats in a single metrical cycle (Massey and Massey, 1996: 110), tend to use relatively strict repetition of a basic metrical pattern to make that pattern clear. Indeed, if the metrical pattern is to be made clear in the listeners' memory, there is often a kind of inverse relation between the length of meter and rhythmic freedom. Each accented beat in this kind of meter is rendered in a particular way, with a particular kind of drum sound, and this is usually kept relatively consistent over each repetition of the metrical cycle. Certain sounds at important points in the meter act as landmarks that recur with each cycle, giving listeners a sense of where they are in the progression of the meter.

An interesting aspect of meter is that the lengths of some kinds of metrical cycles fall within the time frame of short-term memory, and some do not. Because of this, meter can have some aspects of schematic structure, and some aspects of category structure. Generally speaking, the longer the time length a meter covers, the more schematic it will be.

Patterns of Time Interval as Rhythmic Categories

Remembering the exact proportions of the time intervals between sounds is difficult. Experiments where subjects try to reproduce the duration proportions of different sounds *outside a pulse framework* show relatively large margins of error. It seems that to make accurate judgments about time intervals between events, we need some sort of regular "clock" to compare them to (Michon, 1985: 28–32). (Keep in mind that the term time interval refers to the time distance between two successive events, *whether that time is completely filled with an event or not*.)

As previously noted, time intervals seem to be easiest to remember when they can be represented by ratios of small whole numbers, such as 2:1 and 3:1. One proportion of time interval that seems to have a special status is the ratio of 2:1. Many experiments on our ability to remember rhythmic relationships indicate that in memory, especially in the absence of a pulse, we tend to reduce more complex time proportions of long and short to a 2:1 ratio (Summers, Hawkins, and Mayers, 1986, Fraisse, 1982): we have a very general capacity for time interval categorization that operates outside the more precise interval judgments that can be made in the presence of metrical "clocks." It is also worth noting here that the basic system of durational notation used in Western European music is built on successive levels of 2:1 duration proportions. That is, each basic notated rhythmic value is either double or half of the duration of the next element in the series.

Clearly, interval proportions are another kind of categorical distinction. That is, it is as though there are two kinds of interval categories, long and short, and long durations are about two or three times as long as short ones (see Fraisse, 1982: 167). Indeed, duration seems to be categorized into long and short in much the way pitch intervals are categorized into steps and leaps. Both types of categorization probably represent, not learned, but primitive perceptual categories. In the presence of a metrical framework, judgments of durational proportion seem to be related to meter. That is, the particular metrical context in which a long and a short duration occur can determine whether it is interpreted as being a 2:1 ratio, or a 3:1 ratio (Clarke, 1987a).

If duration perception were not categorical, small variations in performance would completely alter our sense of rhythmic proportion, and this is definitely not the case. In addition to beats having a particular location in time, groups of beats have particular qualities *as* patterns; they divide up or color time in various ways. These patterns are formed by different time intervals between events. Rhythms are also categorized at this timing level. This means that rather than all possible rhythmic patterns having unique identities as particular timing sequences, there are probably a *somewhat limited number* of recognizable types of rhythmic patterns (Clarke, 1987a). This limitation is of course in relation to syntactical considerations. Even though there may only be a limited number of identifiable patterns that can function in a rhythmic syntax, each of these patterns may have many degrees of nuance. This means that we can immediately *discriminate* many more patterns than we can repeatedly *identify*.

In figure 12.9, eight different rhythms are generated by moving the third beat of a four-beat measure later in time in regular intervals of 1/8 of a beat. The dotted lines show that these rhythms are heard as three different rhythms rather than eight.[13] It is especially interesting that the uneven rhythms seem to lump together, as Clarke (1987a) suggests. Each of the rhythms *feels* different, but the actual

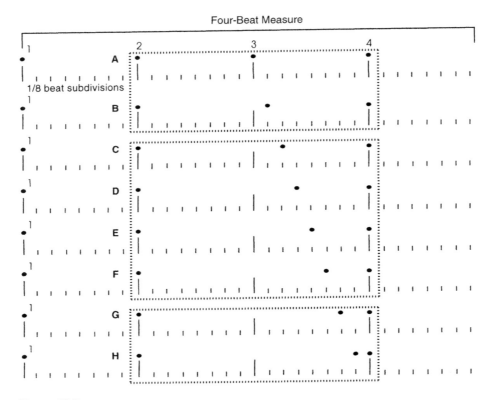

Figure 12.9

Rhythmic pattern categories. This diagram illustrates categorization of eight rhythms created by repeating a four-beat pattern eight times, and making the third beat of the measure later by 1/8 beat on each successive repetition. Each repetition is represented by one horizontal row. The dotted lines indicate rhythmic patterns heard as being roughly the same. The categorical effect consists of three rhythms being heard, rather than eight. A and B are heard as two versions of the same rhythm with a different "feel"; C, D, E, and F are heard as four versions of the same rhythm, and G and H are also heard as two versions of the same rhythm. Note that the discrimination of different rhythms is best close to the prototypical or central positions of beats 3 and 4, and is worst at the points between those beats.

number of identifiably different patterns for the average listener is only three. Note that this is a categorical effect: although each of these patterns differs from the one before it by the same amount, they are not heard as a continuum, but as a few discrete categories of pattern. All eight different patterns cannot therefore be reliably reidentified. Current theory is that durational proportions between successive rhythmic events are categorized as being simply "even" or "uneven." They may consist of equal or unequal timing relationships (Clarke, 1987a). An unequal rhythm would consist of a long and a short event. In figure 12.9, rhythms A and B represent *equal* timing interval categories, whereas rhythms C, D, E, F, as well as G and H, would be categorized together as *unequal*. Because the lagging third beat is so close to the fourth beat, it no longer floats between the third and fourth beats, and its distance from the fourth beat can be heard more clearly. Hence G and H are heard as another rhythm. In the case of the pattern illustrated here, a long timing interval is followed by a short one. The actual proportions of long and short are only perceived as nuances of the basic unequal rhythm category.

In the sense that it functions as a recognizable pattern (syntactically), a rhythm thus consists of particular categories of time interval superimposed on beat and measure categories. A given rhythm may be played many different ways, (with many different small variations of its time intervals) and still retain its identity as that particular rhythm, provided all its component events stay within the temporal limits of their respective beat, metrical, and interval categories. The rhythm may also be shifted in relation to its position in the measure, in which case it will retain its identity as a pattern, but will create a different degree of metrical tension.

Rhythmic nuances constitute what we have referred to as the "feel" of a rhythm. The same rhythm may be played with many different feels, just as the same melody may be played with many different pitch inflections. Indeed, we can think of rhythmic feel as a kind of rhythmic inflection that gives a rhythm its subtle dynamic and emotional qualities. Nuances produced by live musicians are generally systematic— for example, when a drummer rushes (places beats "in the front of" the beat category) as the rhythm moves toward an important downbeat—and are closely related to the grouping structure of the music. One of the problems with drum machines that purport to introduce a "human feel" into rhythms by randomly displacing beats by small amounts of time is that these displacements are not systematic, have no relation to the larger structural levels of the music, and hence do not feel natural.

Rhythmic Contour and Rhythmic Tension

We have seen that time intervals can operate much like pitch scales, that is, we can organize intervals into fixed categories of proportions, and doing so allows us to perceive and remember patterns much more clearly. Time intervals, can be seen as somewhat analogous to pitch intervals. Both of these concepts of interval involve metaphorical concepts of distance. Because we use contour as well as intervals to remember and identify pitch patterns, the question naturally arises, is there such a thing as rhythmic contour?

In a melody consisting of pitches, the pitch intervals form the ups and downs of a contour. An interval moving upward (to a higher frequency) serves to increase intensity, and an interval moving downward (to a lower frequency) serves to decrease intensity. If we look at rhythm from the standpoint of frequency relationships, we see that a rhythm can contain different frequencies (intervals) of attack points, and move through time intervals that are longer (slower) and shorter (faster).

Changes in the time intervals between the components of a rhythm can also be thought of as having a contour: the faster parts of the rhythm are the "higher" parts of the contour, which generate tension, and the slower parts are the "lower" parts of the contour, which release that tension. (Note that this purely *rhythmic* tension does not need meter to work.) Large changes of time interval may be thought of as "sharp corners" in the contour; small changes, as "dull corners." The interesting thing about this metaphor is that rhythms actually do seem to work like melodies. Parts of a rhythm with shorter time intervals and durations are perceived as generating tension, which is resolved by longer time intervals and durations (figure 12.10).

Because tension is always a factor in closure, rhythmic contour is also a closural factor. A closural rhythmic phrase typically ends on a low part of its contour. Contour thus combines with position in the metrical hierarchy to create the total tension profile of a rhythmic phrase. In the lowest tension profiles, a rhythmic phrase ends on a downbeat with a long duration (low contour), whereas in the highest tension profiles a rhythmic phrase ends on a very weak subdivision of the beat with a short duration (higher contour). In between lie various possibilities, such as ending a phrase with an upturn in contour on a stable downbeat.

Each rhythm has its own contour, and this contour is often the *most recognizable* form of organization a musical pattern can have in *any* parameter—usually

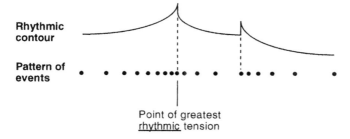

Figure 12.10
Rhythmic contour and rhythmic tension.

more recognizable than pitch contour (Dowling and Harwood, 1986: 179). Famil-iar musical patterns can often be recognized from their rhythm alone, with no pitch information supplied. The reverse is clearly not true. In addition, like pitch con-tours, rhythmic contours may be transposed. That is, a rhythmic pattern may be speeded up or slowed down, and if its interval proportions remain the same, it can be recognized as a version of the same pattern (see Dowling and Harwood, 1986: 187–188).

A common method of musical transformation is to alter pitch contour, timbre, and so on, while keeping rhythmic contour the same. This results in a family of pat-terns that are clearly similar, yet obviously different at the same time. Rhythm is a strong force in establishing the similarity of different musical patterns.

More Complex Types of Metrical Tension

Our earlier discussion of meter centered on the relation between simple meter and rhythmic grouping. More complex types of metrical tension can be created by con-structing rhythmic groupings that, though they repeat, also conflict with meter. Because repetition is the primary factor that sustains meter, creating another repet-itive rhythm that conflicts with the basic meter can throw that meter into question, especially if the new rhythm is anchored on a weak beat. It becomes unclear which repetitive pattern is the basic one. Let us now consider two kinds of metrically con-flicting rhythms in order of increasing complexity and metric tension.

The first, *syncopation*, is a systematic shifting of rhythmic grouping so that the strong beats of rhythmic groupings *consistently* fall on *weak* beats of the meter for some length of time. A set of rhythmic patterns that line up with the meter is shifted

ahead or behind by some fraction (often 1/2) of a beat (figure 12.11). It is important to remember that a syncopated rhythm (unlike a true polyrhythm) is still *synchronized to the same basic tempo as the meter*—it is merely shifted ahead or behind
in time by some simple fraction of a beat, creating two close but conflicting interpretations of where the downbeat actually is. Note that by putting the metrical
framework into question, extended syncopation can create a considerable amount
of metrical tension. New World musics derived from African music, such as ragtime,
and jazz, commonly use syncopation, but they do so intermittently, moving into it
to create metrical tension and out of it to release that tension at fairly small time
intervals.

The second kind of conflicting rhythm used to establish short-term metrical tension
is *tuplets*, divisions of a half measure or measure into groupings based on numbers
of equally spaced beats other than that of the metrical cycle. Tuplets are only synchronized with the basic pulse for *one* beat at some regular interval of *one measure
or less*. In notated music, they are expressed as ratios, with the number of notes in
the tuplet coming first, followed by the number of beats in the pulse it occupies. For
example, 3:4 is three beats evenly spaced over four beats of the pulse (see figure
12.11). Tuplets subdividing the beat into units of three (called "triplets") are fairly
common in notated Western music, and occur in many unnotated traditional world
musics as well, whereas those subdividing the beat into five, seven, nine, and higher
numbers of beats are less common, and are much harder to actually play.

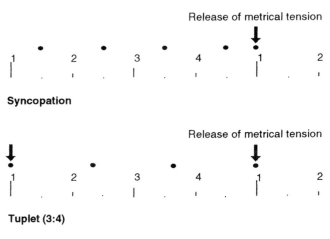

Figure 12.11
Syncopation and tuplets.

Extended Meters and Large-Scale Metrical Tension

The metrical structures discussed thus far, while certainly the most analyzed and written about, represent only a fraction of the possibilities for metrical organization. Those structures all involve regularly repeating units of four beats or less, a type of meter characteristic of much Western European music written between the fourteenth and twentieth centuries, and various popular and ethnic musics.

There are, however, musics that use longer repeating metrical structures, musics with a different "time feel" from that of Western European music. Some Eastern European folk music, for example, uses rhythms that pulsate in irregularly alternating groupings of two, three, and four beats, which, like the long meter of Indian raga music, generally repeat on some higher level.

A more complex type of metrical organization, one that occurs in multipart music is *polymeter*. Polymetrical music has a *common pulse*, in which different (simultaneous) parts are in *different meters*. The metrical accent patterns of different parts are thus different, with downbeats occurring on different pulses, and coming together in some larger pattern when the downbeats of the two meters coincide. This creates a mild rhythmic tension between the meters of the separate parts, which come in and out of alignment in a higher-level structural rhythm. Much of the orchestral percussion music of West Africa is polymetrical (and often polyrhythmic as well).

The most complex type of metrical organization that can still maintain meter of some type is *polyrhythm*, defined here as multipart music whose different parts are synchronized to *different basic pulses*, which come together at certain points.

Tuplets occur when two parts of the music are synchronized to different pulses, but the two different pulses come into synchronization at *each repetition* of the metrical unit (measure) or less. Polyrhythm, as defined here, occurs when two parts of the music are synchronized to different pulses, but the two pulses come into synchronization at *some level higher than a single cycle* (measure) of either meter. Whereas tuplets *reinforce* the downbeats at the level of the measure (the tuplets and the measure they occur in have the *same* downbeat), polyrhythm *undercuts* the authority of the downbeat of *both* its parts. Polyrhythm represents a whole new level of rhythmic complexity, with two independent tempo streams and with metrical tension sustained for fairly long periods of time at high structural levels. Indeed, for long periods of time there is *no regular, single location for the downbeat*. Rather

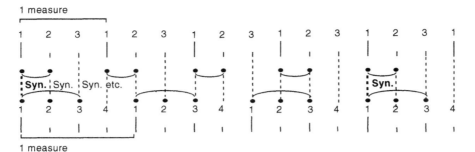

Poly*meter*: 3/4 and 4/4. One basic pulse tempo. Note that *syn*chronicity occurs at the beat level *and* between downbeats at the multimeasure level.

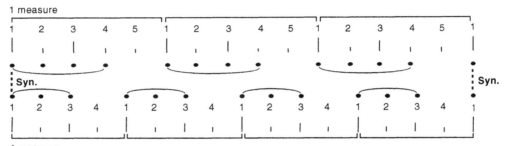

Poly*rhythm*: 15:16 (3x5 and 4x4). Two basic pulse tempos (and two meters). No synchronicity of pulse. Note that *syn*chronicity between downbeats occurs at the multimeasure level only.

Figure 12.12
Polymeter and polyrhythm. Synchronization at the measure downbeat level is indicated in boldface.

than tension being generated by conflict between rhythmic grouping and meter, it is created by conflict between meters running at different basic tempos. It is not clear *which* component of a polyrhythm is the basic level: the listeners' sense of which stream is the basic level may fluctuate because only one tempo stream can occupy the listener's attention any given moment (figure 12.12).

The ratio between the tempos of the layers of a polyrhythm determines the length and tension value of the rhythm. Rhythms of this type can be thought of as consonant or dissonant, just like pitch intervals. When the ratio between the two tempos consists of two large numbers with no common factor, say 15:16, the rhythm will cover a larger time span and will have more tension value. When the ratio consists of two small numbers, the beats of the two tempos will come into phase in a relatively short time.[14] Like pitch interval, this demonstrates a basic fact of perception: things close enough in value so as to not seem entirely separate, but far enough apart to not be identical are unstable, and have high tension value because the mind wants to resolve them either into two separate things or one single thing.

There are types of recent Western European polyrhythmic music where the component groupings of the polyrhythms do not remain stable in size or internal pattern.[15] Here the internal structure of each part is not consistently repetitive. Each rhythmic tempo forms an independent stream and it is virtually impossible to attend to more than one of these streams at a time, different streams compete for attention, which vacillates between them. Such polyrhythmic music may represent a limiting case of complexity: it stretches both the Western notation system and the listeners' ability to hear rhythm to the utmost.

Free Rhythm

Although, as I have defined it, *rhythm* includes completely irregular phenomena (such as computer-generated random rhythms), it is worth noting that even when we are highly trained, we cannot accurately identify many different time intervals or durations accurately without a pulse as a framework of reference, although we can easily recognize regular changes of time interval, such as speeding up, and slowing down.[16] Irregular rhythms operating outside any pulse framework therefore have a quality different from that of rhythms within a pulse and metrical framework. Indeed, irregular rhythms as a whole may well be processed as rhythmic nuances: we might be able to immediately differentiate between different irregular rhythms, but not be able to remember and identify them if they were repeated at a later time.

Although many people equate rhythm with meter, it is quite possible to have *ametrical* rhythms. Because most traditional forms of music notation are metrical (although newer forms of graphic and proportional notation are not), ametrical rhythms are more often found in improvised music of various types. We shall refer to such rhythms—those not organized within a pulse or metrical framework—as "free rhythm."

An interesting issue is the question of how tension is established in free rhythmic music, since the opposition of metrical and rhythmic groupings is obviously not possible. The answer is that tension is created in free rhythm by changes in intensity, described previously as rhythmic contour. This means that timing intervals, durations, and accents become functionally very important for defining tension. This is true *rhythmic* tension, rather than metrical tension. Free rhythm often uses continuous changes of speed—accelerations and decelerations—to allow for easy perception of time intervals: each can be compared to the one directly before it. Indeed, this type of rhythm might almost be considered a "midway point" between metrical and free. Denied metrical accents, free rhythm instead uses phenomenal and structural accents.

In relation to large-scale tension, free rhythmic passages are generally less stable than metrical passages. The two may even be used in contrasting sections. In North Indian classical music, for example, there is often an introductory section in free rhythm, which is "resolved" by the metrical main body of the piece. It is possible that, in the absence of the conceptual categorizations that accompany meter, free rhythms may actually be encoded in a different way than metrical rhythmic patterns (see Povel and Essens, 1985: 436).

Next, we shall consider organization in music that takes place on a level clearly outside the limits of short-term memory and always requiring long-term memory for its comprehension—the third level of musical experience, that of *form*.

Notes

1. The usage of terms relating to rhythm and meter is inconsistent. The term *beat*, for example, can be used to designate either a single event (as in "the third beat") or a succession of events (as in "keeping the beat"). I use the term in the former sense, because this makes it much easier to explain the term down*beat*, which has a single position in a measure. The term *pulse* can also be used to designate either a single event or a series of events. Here I prefer to use the term in the latter sense because this is closer to everyday (and medical) usage. I make no claims as to the universality of my usages, although they are shared by other writers.

2. I use the term *basic pulse* in an attempt to relate this idea to recent categorization theory. Another term long used to describe the same thing is *tactus*.

3. For an explanation of how events that do not happen can have as much impact as events that do, see Metcalfe, 1995, p. 329.

4. A discussion of rhythmic feel for the position of events within beat categories in African-American jazz can be found in Berliner, 1994, pp. 349–352.

5. For a study of how this subtle variation occurs in an ensemble situation (a jazz rhythm section), see Progler, 1995.

6. For two excellent examples of the contextual nature of what constitutes an appropriate level of nuance, see Waterman, 1995, p. 93; Keil and Feld, 1984, 133–134.

7. My usage of *phenomenal, structural,* and *metrical accent* follows Lerdahl and Jackendoff, 1983, pp. 17–18.

8. Note that there are usually several metrical interpretations possible for a given musical passage; which interpretation a listener settles on often does not seem to be determined by any simple set of rules. Lee (1991) gives an overview of some of the complexities involved in listeners' metrical judgments. Also note that under some circumstances, top-down factors such as knowledge of musical style can facilitate a listener's construction of meter in the absence of accents.

9. One interesting exception is that in some forms of Asian music, notably some Chinese and Indonesian music, the factors of initiation of metrical grouping and weight of a beat are placed in opposition. In these musics, more weight is given to what is clearly the last beat of the metrical cycle, although rhythmic and melodic phrases start on the first beat of the cycle. This creates an inherent syncopated tension between metrical and rhythmic grouping. My experience with this music is that often Western listeners hear the accented fourth beat as a downbeat, rather than the real first beat.

10. However, this is not always the case. See Zbikowski, 1991, p. 209.

11. For a good explanation of metrical hierarchy, see Locke, 1987, pp. 33–34. Note that what Locke refers to as "pulses" are what I would call the "fastest subdivisions of the basic pulse." What he calls "beats" I call the "basic pulse".

12. It has been found that the timing of strong beats in a measure is usually more "accurate," or closer to the prototypical beat position, than the timing of weak beats. See Parncutt, 1994, p. 449.

13. The time interval proportion categories I have given here are based on informal experiments on me and my students. The rhythms in figure 12.9 (and the same process at higher levels of detail, such as moving the third beat behind in increments of 1/16 and 1/32 of a beat) were presented as a sequence at 100 bpm. Listeners were given a form with a square representing each repetition of the rhythm (8, 16, or 32 squares). After being played the sequences several times, they were asked to mark a square when they thought they heard a new rhythmic pattern. Almost all the listeners categorized the rhythms into fewer categories than the actual number of different patterns, especially in the middle of the temporal area between the third and fourth beat. (A few professional drummers who have turned up in my classes are able to categorize these rhythms in a finer degree of detail then that shown in the figure.) Note that these results are roughly consistent with both the idea of a rather broad beat category of 1/4 of a beat on either side of the first subdivision of the third beat, and with the idea that patterns of uneven time intervals are lumped together into a category. For a study on categorical perception of rhythms, see Clarke, 1987a; for a study of beat fractions, see Sternberg and Knoll, 1994.

The size of a beat category is probably at least in part a learned conceptual category, and is also contextual to some extent. In cultures where complex rhythmic music is the norm, such as certain West African cultures, the beat category is probably finer grained, at least for the musicians themselves, than in our own. Just as we may hear music in a foreign tuning system as an out-of-tune rendition of our own tuning system, we may hear rhythmic nuances in another music as "bad timing" or even fail to hear them at all because of the larger grain of our own beat categories—thus reducing a complex experience to something *apparently* simpler.

14. One way to differentiate between tuplets and polyrhythm is; small ratios like 2:3, 3:4 etc. are tuplets, while ratios like 25:24, etc. are polyrhythms. By this definition, a tuplet could *not* have a 2nd number which is larger than the number of beats (or subdivisions of beats) in a measure. Polyrhythms defined in this way would extend over more than one measural unit.

15. This is the case in some of Elliot Carter's music. See Schiff, 1983.

16. Interestingly, a tempo that is slowing down is perceived more quickly than a tempo that is speeding up. Tempo change is also harder to hear at rates below 60 bpm. See Royal, 1994.

13
Form

Traditional considerations of musical form are typically concerned with historical musical *forms*, particular cultural schemas that most often have names, such as sonata, fugue, symphony, variations, blues, or raga. This book will attempt a more general discussion of our ability to perceive and remember higher-level musical shapes, where "higher-level" means outside the temporal limits of short-term memory, and "musical shapes" refers to having separate bounded parts that seem genuinely different. This chapter will focus on the establishment of higher-level boundaries and the memory issues associated with the larger time scale of the formal level, that is, on how the mechanisms of memory establish musical form.

The third of the time levels of musical experience described in chapter 1, the formal level differs from the melodic and rhythmic level in that it always requires the use of long-term memory. Indeed, because all the higher-level details of a piece of music cannot be present in consciousness at one time, there is no way to talk about any aspect of music larger than a phrase without talking about long-term memories.

The structure and limitations of long-term memory, which differ from those of short-term memory, place certain kinds of limits on the articulation of large musical forms. These limits and other kinds of order that can be established only on the formal level are the subject of this chapter. Because of the way short-term memory shades into long-term memory, and because the time limit of STM can vary with the amount of information remembered, the exact time scale form occupies is not absolutely clear. In figure 1.2, I have placed the boundary between short-term and long-term memory at 8 to 16 seconds, about the length of a very long phrase.

The basic unit at the formal level that corresponds roughly to phrases at the melodic and rhythmic level is what I shall call a "section," loosely defined as a relatively self-contained grouping of musical events that is usually larger than a phrase and that requires long-term memory for its comprehension. Sectional units have relatively clear boundaries and may be of many different sizes.

Music is often structured in such a way that some of its aspects (parameters) maintain similar configurations of values for some time. At certain points some of these parameters may change more radically, eventually arriving at a new, comparatively stable configuration of patterns or values. These changes may be large or small, depending on what has been established as "normal" in a particular context. These points of multiparametric change are what I shall call "sectional boundaries." Like any other kind of boundaries, they may be sharp or not. Sections are separated from each other by multiparametric *change*, and the internal coherence of sections is established by relative parametric *constancy*. Because hierarchical order may be built up from groupings on different levels, sections occupy no clear range of temporal "sizes." In addition, higher-level "sections *of* sections" may be established. On rare occasions, if sufficiently differentiated from its surroundings, a section may consist of only a single phrase, or even a single event. It is possible to imagine a piece of music consisting of single sounds, each of which is very different from the others and separated from them by a considerable amount of time. In such a piece, each individual sound might function like a section. By the same token, an entire piece that has no clearly articulated internal sectional boundaries may be viewed as a single large section.

Various types of sections may also be identified with particular functions. Typical sectional functions include beginnings, endings, and (in music that is in some sense linear) transitions. These types of sections often assume general forms that are not random or arbitrary, but that are structured metaphorically. Just as the various "scenes" of our lives are defined by different physical locations (physical boundaries) and by different goals (psychological boundaries) (Schank, 1982: 95–97), so musical sections may be defined by musical boundaries and goals.

Finally, because sections have duration and are heard sequentially, we shall briefly consider the psychological nature of time itself and review ideas about time as it bears on music. To begin with, we shall examine exactly what it is that may change on the formal level in music.

Stephen McAdams (1989: p. 182; see also pp. 181–198) has said that "musical form is built upon relations among perceptual qualities." These perceptual qualities are often referred to as "parameters," defined here as particular aspects of a sound or sounds that can change and have discernibly different values at different times. As we shall see, many different kinds of things may be viewed as functioning parametrically in different musical contexts. Parameters may be divided into "primary" and "secondary" (Meyer, 1989: 14–16; Hopkins, 1990: 4–31).

Primary Parameters

Musical variables that can be organized so that similarities and differences between different values are relatively constant and identifiable at different times, *primary parameters* can have relatively fixed proportional relationships between them, like the fixed proportions of a tuning system and the fixed proportions of a system of time intervals and durations.[1] This makes it possible to identify patterns and their variations within a piece of music. It also facilitates the construction of culturally learned and identifiable syntactical patterns that signify musical functions such as closure. With primary parameters, we can construct a number of different fixed conceptual categories, such as the pitch interval categories of a tuning system or a system of time interval categories, and both perceive and remember relations between these categories. Because these are *conceptual* categories, they are learned and can vary across cultures.

The distinction between primary and secondary parameters is not absolute: parameters such as timbre may be primary in certain limited respects, but may not be primary in terms of pattern recognition.[2] Note that primary parameters are not more important than secondary parameters; rather, they operate in a different way. The existence of primary parameters is not a culturally determined phenomenon; it is based on perceptual abilities selected by our biological evolution, by means of which our nervous system has become finely tuned to certain aspects of sounds in our environment. Pitch and duration are primary parameters for all cultures, all music uses some form of pitch and rhythm patterns. However, within basic psychological limits, which of these primary parameters predominates and the particular ways they are organized into systems of categories differs from culture to culture. In traditional European music, for example, multiple pitch structures of harmony and counterpoint predominate; in Indian raga music, melodic pitch and long-metered rhythmic patterns; and in much West African music, complex rhythmic textures.

The *number* of primary parameters is probably limited by our nervous system and the way it has evolved to extract information from the environment. Pitch and rhythm are two clearly primary parameters, with harmony being a third, higher-level primary parameter based on combinations of pitches. (That is, individual pitch intervals can have discrete identities, and so can chords that are composed of multiple intervals.) In all three primary parameters, fairly complex patterns can be articulated and recognized at a later time. This ability may have evolved because the pitches and rhythms of voices and animal sounds would have been important things for our ancestors to hear and identify later.

The clearest example of a primary parameter is *pitch*: we can proportionally categorize pitches into tuning systems and scales, and construct many different melodic patterns from these scales that can be recognized when repeated. As mentioned in chapter 11, the parameter of pitch can be further divided into pitch interval and direction of pitch motion, the variable aspects of pitch patterns. Identifiable pitch intervals can vary widely in size, whereas direction of pitch motion can only be up or down, or remain the same. As we have seen, both pitch interval and direction of pitch motion are important in the shaping of melodic groupings and phrases.

Related to pitch is *harmony*, the second primary parameter, which involves combinations of simultaneously sounded pitches called "chords." Harmonies or chords can also be categorized, and these categories organized into patterns that can be identified when they recur. This is based on the ability of the ear to break down or analyze simultaneous groupings of pitches into their individual pitch components.

The third primary parameter is *rhythm*, the perception of accents and proportional intervals of time between sounds. Like pitch, rhythm can be organized into scales of values with discrete, recognizable intervals. (As we noted in chapter 12, the accurate perception of proportional time intervals is dependent on the inference of a regular background pulse.) Rhythms constructed from proportional time intervals and accents can be organized into patterns that can be remembered and identified. Indeed, rhythms are often the most identifiable characteristics of musical patterns.

Secondary Parameters

Secondary parameters are aspects of musical sound that cannot easily be divided up into very many clearly recognizable categories. Loudness and tempo would be examples of secondary parameters, because there is no way of establishing standardized scales of proportional values for them that are *repeatedly identifiable across different experiences*. For instance, although it is possible to recognize (identify) a later recurrence of a particular pitch interval after an intervening passage of music, we find it very difficult to do the same for either a loudness interval or a tempo. (Note that these are examples of *identification* rather than discrimination tasks.) We also cannot identify two loudness values or tempos as being *different by the same amount* if separated in time. Because we can neither establish different re-cognizable intervals between values, nor identify patterns of those values, we cannot construct the equivalent of a recognizable pitch melody or a rhythmic pattern using loudness or tempo. Note that this does not mean that loudness, tempo, or other secondary parameters cannot be used to structure music, only that such structure does not function syntactically by itself.

Thus we tend to hear secondary parameters simply in terms of their *relative amounts*: we cannot recognize change in these parameters in terms of any but the most general categories, such as "much of" or "not much of," and "more of" or "less of."[3] Secondary parameters are therefore generally used in music in simple increasing or decreasing progressions or in large contrasts. Secondary parameters can, however, be important in reinforcing patterns in primary parameters. Note that it is also possible to use primary parameters as secondary parameters, although the reverse is usually not true. This would involve using a primary parameter not to define complex patterns but in fairly simple increases and decreases in *value*. Examples of this would be a series of time intervals that simply get longer and longer, a series of pitches that simply get higher and higher, or a series of chords that become more and more dissonant. In all of these cases, the patterns do not require precise proportional relationships to be effective, only increase or decrease.

Secondary parameters seem to be neither limited in number nor fixed in the way that primary parameters are. It is my contention that new secondary parameters can be created. All that is necessary is to establish some quality of music that can support a recognizable relation of "less of" / "more of". The creation of new secondary parameters would be an example of the kind of metaphorical extension discussed in chapter 9.

The lack of identifiability is central to the definition of a secondary parameter. As we have noted, a particular pitch can be recognized as being related to another pitch by a specific interval, and this interval may recur in different parts of a piece. This interval has a recognizable identity, even when transposed to different sounding pitches. None of this would be true for a particular loudness interval, however; hence loudness is a secondary parameter. Note that in Western European music notation, loudness is indicated only by a small number of very general symbols meaning loud, medium loud, and so on, which indicate, not fixed proportions, but only relative levels—attesting to the secondary character of loudness as a parameter. In traditional Western music notation, virtually all of the graphically detailed, *spatial* parts of the notation system are devoted to the representation of primary parameters. When they are specifically indicated at all, secondary parameters are usually indicated with language: loudness indications, names of instruments, tempo indications, and so on.[4]

The lack of recognizability bears on our ability to have expectations. Whereas primary parameters can be formed into patterns about which we can have very detailed expectations and in which we can perceive fairly minute alterations, secondary parameters cannot.

Related to the primary parameter of rhythm, *tempo* is a secondary parameter because it cannot be organized into discrete, perceptually identifiable intervals: most people find it very difficult to identify the same tempo occurring at different times. Related to tempo, but not identical to it, is the secondary parameter of *density*, the average number of events in a given amount of time—which may be higher, lower, or changing while the tempo remains the same.

Duration could also be considered a secondary parameter. Remember that duration is the length of time between the onset of a sound and when the sound stops, not the *time interval* between onsets. Identifiable rhythmic patterns consist primarily of time intervals between onsets, coupled with accents. Durations represent the degree to which these time intervals are "filled in" with sound. Our ability to make accurate judgements about the exact durations of sounds is much less acute than our ability to judge time intervals. (Time intervals themselves are of course much easier to judge in relation to pulse and meter.) Duration shades into *articulation*, another secondary parameter that is related to the way that particular notated durations are actually performed. Articulation is a way of making small differences in performed durations of events, and affects how closely events seem to be connected. Articulation may be notated in verbal form, as in the Italian terms *legato* and *staccato*, or it may be indicated by unquantified symbols like dots and lines.

Related to the primary parameter of pitch is the secondary parameter of *timbre*, or sound color, largely determined by the complex time-variant behavior of frequency components that make up a musical event. One group of timbres is the sounds of traditional Western European acoustical instruments, which are grouped into families. These families are not based on any systematic organizing principle other then the constructed forms that musical instruments have taken. The identity of the timbres of particular instruments are learned categories (in Western music notation, these timbre categories are indicated with the names of instruments, written on the left side of the score). These categories do not seem to form a single identifiable scalar order (Sethares, 1998: 28–30). Timbre is a complex parameter which is not entirely understood at this time, that seems to consist of several independent dimensions (Hajda et al., 1997). Timbre is also related to our sense of pitch: certain kinds of timbre changes can actually change the pitch content of a sound (see Sethares, 1998: 32–37). Hence pitch and timbre are not entirely separate parameters, although sequences of different timbres do not have the kind of identifiability across time that patterns of pitches do (Dowling and Harwood, 1986: 158–159). Much remains to be learned about the mechanisms of timbre perception and how they relate to our ability to organize groups of related frequencies into pitches.

Just as harmony is the primary parameter that results from the combination of pitches, so *sonority* (orchestration) is the secondary parameter that results from the combination of timbres. Different combinations of instruments produce different global sound qualities, and these qualities form a higher-level secondary parameter.

Another secondary parameter related to pitch, but not organizable proportionally, is *pitch range*, which has two different aspects: *register*, the *actual* overall or average range of pitches in a section—this may be higher, lower, or changing; and *compass*, the *extent* of the range—this may be small if the pitches are compressed together in a narrow band, or large if they are spread out over a wide range.

The *number of instruments or sound sources*—the number of *different* entities we perceive as producing the sounds we are hearing—is yet another secondary parameter. (Note that even if we can categorize a number of sound sources as being different, if we cannot construct a *continuous scale of values* from these categories, they still constitute a secondary parameter.)

Because secondary parameters operate in a "more of" or "less of" way, I believe that *any* aspect of music that can be organized in this way may be used as a secondary parameter. Thus aspects of music such as phrase length, amount of repetition, amount of continuity, section length, or amount of noise content may be used as secondary parameters. Essentially, this means that secondary parameter is an open concept, and no complete listing of such parameters is possible: they may involve any aspect of music that changes but does not involve the identification of specific patterns.

To repeat: the use of the term secondary in no way implies that secondary para-meters are less important than so-called primary parameters. Secondary parameters present *different* kinds of possibilities for organization: gradients and simple con-trasts rather than more complex patterns.

It is worth noting at this point that different musical cultures choose to exert different amounts of control over various musical parameters. Obviously, no musical culture can exert the same amount of control over the many possible para-meters in a musical situation. Thus part of what constitutes a particular musical culture is the knowledge of which parameters are consciously controlled. For instance, in Western European music, the intonation of pitches on a detailed level (essentially, pitch nuances) is not really specified, but is left up to the performer, and is an implicit aspect of a performer's style. The intonation of particular pitches played on instruments of variable pitch (such as stringed instruments) can vary con-siderably in relation to the emotional and structural demands of the moment. In the raga music of North India, by contrast, the precise intonation of pitch is much more consciously controlled through a system of nuanced ornaments, and there is some-what less room for individual freedom in this particular parameter. There are many other examples of this sort of thing, and every musical culture emphasizes various parameters to different degrees.

An interesting fact about basic secondary parameters such as loudness, timbre, and number of instruments is that large changes in these parameters seem to stand out in the initial memory formation of musical sequences, especially for less expe-rienced listeners (see Pollard-Gott, 1993; Berz and Kelly, 1998).

Syntax, Parameters, and Closure

The meaning of the term *syntax* as it is used in this book is somewhat more general than the way the term is often used. I will define syntax here as sets of relations between identifiable patterns. This is a broad definition in that it includes both tra-ditions of rules for the use of particular kinds of functional patterns in particular musical styles, and relations between patterns that are developed in (and unique to) particular pieces. Primary parameters, as previously defined, are central to the cre-ation of syntax because they are the *aspects of music by which patterns are identi-fied and related to each other*.[5] The ability to identify a pattern as similar although occurring at different times is the essence of syntax. This is true for many forms of communication. Thus syntax is made possible by categorization and memory.

Musical syntax consists of learned rules that generate certain types of patterns or gestures that in turn can signify specific types of musical functions. Note that this can operate on both the immediate level, as with pattern variation within a section, or on larger levels, as with the recapitulation or variation of a pattern in different parts of a piece. It can also work across different pieces of music: syntax is an important component of musical style. Because this depends on the perception of patterns occurring at different times as very similar or identical, syntax depends on the perception of *identity*. The rules of syntax may be part of a tradition, or they may be established within the context of a single piece of music. It is important to note that the actual patterns signifying closure, for example, may be relatively arbitrary, but they come to mean closure through consensus or repeated use. An example of this would be the standardized patterns of harmony that signify closure in Western European music of the classical period. These patterns are called "cadences" (from Latin *cadere*, to fall). Almost anyone in Western European culture, when hearing one of these patterns, even out of context, would immediately recognize it as an ending pattern. Another example would be the melodic *mukhra* (Hindi for face, feature) patterns that signify the closure of a metrical cycle in the North Indian Khayal style of raga music. The meaning of learned syntactical patterns must constantly be maintained by repetition or it will be lost, both on the immediate and historical time scales.

Note that syntactical closure works in a way that is distinctly different from the "natural" closure of downward motion, long duration, and so on. Indeed, it is musical syntax that makes possible a gesture that can achieve closure by moving *up* in one or more parameters (Meyer, 1989: 16). In a sense, syntactical closure is the most complete form of closure because its meaning and the expectations it generates can be quite specific.

Closure that is realized through other means, as through downward motion of parametric values, on the other hand, is not as precise. When we hear a falling series of values for a single parameter, we are probably not sure what the *last* value in the series will be—there is no specific implied final point. This kind of closure cannot therefore be developed in many different degrees. We only realize that the final point in this type of series was final *after* we hear it, whereas when syntactical closure is reached, we know this *while* it is happening.

This other type of closure does not seem to be learned[6] and its understanding does not require a tradition of syntax. Thus, music that is not part of an established tradition often relies heavily on this type of closure. This is also often the case with music in "transitional" periods between stable styles.

This type at closure seems to operate in a similar way in the music of many times and cultures. We have previously mentioned that devices such as a "drop" in loudness, brightness of timbre, and a slowing of tempo all seem to signify closure in music of different times and places.

Constancy

Not all parameters need to be varied all of the time in music—this would only produce a situation of unprocessable complexity. Generally, some parameters remain within relatively stable limits, while others change. Indeed, keeping some parameters relatively *constant* for a length of time is one way order is created on the sectional (formal) level.

One of the principles defining formal units whose length exceeds the limits of short-term memory is *constancy*, a psychological concept that explains how our mind "reconstructs" a stable world even though the appearance of that world is constantly changing (see Miller and Johnson-Laird, 1976: 54–57).[7] Constancy is the establishment of invariances in our perception of the environment. For example, we tend to see the color of objects as constant despite changing lighting conditions. If we carry a piece of white paper from bright sunlight into a room lit with a greenish light, we normally do not see the color of the paper itself as changing, even though the actual wavelength of the light that is being reflected off of the paper changes considerably—we still see it as *the same* white sheet of paper.[8] Most often we do not notice these types of changes at all.

We also see objects as having constant size and shape, even though the size and shape of the retinal image of an object changes a great deal as we move in relation to it, and even though we are constantly moving our eyes. Indeed, the "shape" of the object *as sensation* is not a single thing at all, but an entire family of different shapes which are constantly transforming geometrically over time, from which we construct the percept of one invariant object. (This is an example of what has previously called perceptual categorization.) It is really the relations between these transformations which constitute the "shape" of the object. This shape is actually reconstructed in memory, and is never perceived in its entirety at any single time. As we move in relation to an object, we travel through different parts of this family of transforming retinal images, but we *perceive* the object as *staying constant*.

As an example of acoustical constancy, even though a number of musical instruments produce sounds in different pitch registers that are quite different in their acoustical details, we nonetheless hear all of these sounds as coming from a single, constant, and unified instrument. Indeed, in the acoustical realm, many sounds coming from the same source can be quite different in their physical waveform, and yet are readily identified as coming from the same source.

Constancy and Sectional Coherence

Just as our mind, operating unconsciously through the principle of constancy can establish "things" in our perception, so we can consciously construct musical "things" at the sectional level by keeping some musical parameters relatively invariant or constant.[9] There may be many degrees of constancy. Because music has many parameters, each of which may have values and patterns that stay relatively constant for different lengths of time, sectional boundaries, like lower-level forms of closure, may be partial.

We have seen that boundaries are established by discontinuities of some sort. The principles of similarity and proximity were defined as basic grouping mechanisms in chapter 3, and dissimilarities and lack of proximity were therefore established as factors that created boundaries. On the formal or sectional level, this still holds true, although in somewhat different ways.

Certainly, similarity is still the glue that holds formal units together, and constancy is a constructed high-level similarity over time. Through the associative mechanisms of long-term memory, similar patterns can still be recognized over fairly long time distances *with many events intervening*. On the other hand, temporal proximity is not as strong a factor. Remember that the use of the term proximity in the first part of this book only referred to adjacent events, and did not include the concept of intervening events over periods of time longer than the length of STM. That is, events were closer together or farther apart, with only silence between them. If all parameters are kept constant, a fairly long pause will establish a lower-level phrase boundary, but will not generally establish a sectional boundary unless reinforced by multiparametric change (see Deliege and El Ahmadi, 1990: 39–42). Such a silence will simply be heard as a pause in the ongoing activity. Thus temporal proximity is not as strong a closural factor at higher structural levels as it is locally.

Proximity does, however, work over longer time spans in the following way. If two events separated by a time interval longer than the limits of short-term memory are similar enough, they tend to be more easily related to each other if they are closer together in time than if they are farther apart. Indeed, the *farther* apart in time two patterns of events are, the *stronger* their similarity will have to be in order for that similarity to be *recognized*. The repetition of thematic material from the beginning at the end of movements that can occur in sonatas of the classical period is an example of this idea.

A sectional boundary is formed when multiparametric change creates sufficient dissimilarity. Changes may be introduced in any of many parameters. The question then arises, can a change in a *single* parameter constitute a sectional boundary? I believe that the answer to this question is, generally not. Although there has been little research on this subject, a useful rule of thumb is this: change in only one parameter away from constancy generally constitutes, not a sectional boundary, but rather articulation or variation *within* a section. Examples of changing only one parameter include repeating a pitch contour at a higher or lower pitch (transposing it), speeding up or slowing down a pattern while keeping the rhythm the same, and making everything louder. Even change in two parameters at the same time (such as in pitch level and timbre or loudness and tempo), depending on which parameters are involved and how much they change, may not constitute a sectional boundary. On the other hand, change in *three or more* parameters at the same time almost certainly constitutes a sectional boundary (see Miller and Johnson-Laird, 1976: 88–89). Thus, as with the types of lower-level closure discussed previously, there can be many different strengths of sectional closure, from weak articulations within a section to major structural boundaries within a piece. All of this depends of course on context, at least to some degree. If the overall level of change in a piece is very low, a change in a single parameter will have more significance than it would in a piece where sectional boundaries are established by large-scale parametric change. Generally, the greater the number of parameters that change at a given point, the higher the hierarchical level of the boundary created at that point.

Also, parametric change must be established for a certain *length* of time in order to establish a strong sectional boundary. Generally, this means that parametric changes must last for a length of time longer than the limits of short-term memory, so that the new section is firmly established. Multiparametric change that occurs over a *shorter* length of time, with parameters then returning to a previous set of values, is usually perceived, not as establishing a new section, but as an anomaly or interruption in a continuous, ongoing section. This is of course not an absolute principle: interesting formal ambiguities can be created by making many different sections of very short length, with interruptions just different enough so that they are not clearly new material or old material. Indeed, the manipulation of similarity is a major factor in establishing sectional boundaries.

A sectional boundary in a primary parameter tends to be a change in the *type of pattern* present, such as a change in pitch intervals, melodic contour, or rhythmic patterns, whereas a sectional boundary in a secondary parameter tends to be a change in the *value* or *range* of a parameter, such as a change in overall loudness, pitch range, or orchestration. The notion of similarity and difference in the pattern of a primary parameter is not a simple issue because what constitutes a completely new pattern is not at all cut-and-dried (see for instance, Selfridge-Field, 1998: 13).

In many cases, a change in a primary parameter has a stronger effect than a change in a single secondary parameter. For example, keeping melodic and rhythmic patterns constant and changing only loudness or tempo usually constitutes, not a sectional boundary, but an articulation within a section.

Where multiparametric change occurs gradually, I shall generally refer to the area of gradual change as a "transitional section." Thus sections may be relatively stable or relatively transitional—I say "relatively" because most sections are both, at least to some degree. The primary difference is whether the changes in a section are relatively stable around a particular set of values or changing cumulatively in a particular direction. We shall now look at how the organization of sections relates to memory.

Information and Redundancy

The following discussion is primarily about music as a form of communication, although I am aware that this is not the only possible view (see Nattiez, 1990: 16–24) and shall discuss other views where appropriate. My special, somewhat technical use of the terms *message* and *information* in this chapter is drawn from the mathematical discipline *information theory* (see Baars, 1988: 188–201).[10] Although the overall theory, especially the theory's rigorously quantitative approach, has proved problematic with respect to art, some of its basic concepts are generally accepted as useful (Noth, 1990: 143). My interpretation of some of those concepts is meant to emphasize the active role of memory in listeners' understanding of music. As John Blacking (1995: 231) said, "Listening to music is a kind of performance." In this and the following subsections, music will be viewed as a kind of *message*.

"Message" is actually used in two different senses in everyday speech. First, it is used to mean someone's intentions or thoughts, as in "Do you get the message?" Second, it is used to mean some sort of physical trace or pattern of energy *representing* of someone's state of mind, as in "She left him a message."[11] These two meanings of the term message are often confused, as though someone's thoughts were *in* the physical representation (Reddy, 1993). Reflection reveals, however, that a message in the first sense never leaves a person's head. Our states of mind are not transferred directly from one mind to another (that would be telepathy) but only through some representation in a physical medium. This representation is usually in some sense publically available. Music is an example of a representation using sound as a physical medium.

Further reflection reveals a third type of message—the listeners' states of mind as influenced by the second type of message (the sound, in this case).[12] This "third version" of the original message must be reconstructed out of elements of the listeners' memory (figure 13.1). Note that the rightmost arrow points to the left—this represents the idea that listeners must actively reconstruct most of the organization in the music.

These elements of memory are cued by the musical sounds. Note that in order for this type of *communication* to work, there must be some kind of correlation between the repertoires of elements in the memories of the musician and the listeners. These repertoires would consist of a largely unconscious context of categories and schemas.

Thus we may describe the situation of musical communication as having three levels of messages: (1) the original message in the mind of a musician; (2) the physical sound of the music; and (3) the reconstructed message in the minds of the listeners.[13]

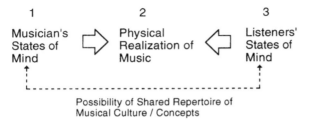

Figure 13.1
Three aspects of a musical message.

Reflecting the second sense described above, the term *message* will be used to mean an organized pattern of musical sound. A function of musical sound is to cause states of mind to arise in listeners that are in some way related to the states of mind that originally arose in the musician.[14] As previous chapters have tried to show, how this representation is organized can have a major effect on the cuing process.

Thus a function of musical sound is to *influence* the state of mind of listeners, to get us to think and feel some things rather than others. It does this by limiting our states of mind to a manageable number of alternatives through specific memory cues. What music ultimately does, then, is to provide a sensory experience that activates combinations of elements in memory. This is why limitations on musical messages are related to memory limitations. From this point of view, the musical sound is a *sequence of memory cues*. (And, as we have seen, some of the memories that are cued may be implicit.) In addition, there are parts of the musical sound that can be directly experienced, bypassing the formation of long-term memory, what we have referred to as "nuances."

The meaningful reception of a musical message therefore depends on an appropriate context in memory, a *repertoire* of schemas and categories that can be activated by these cues (Noth, 1990: 176–180). This repertoire is both personally and culturally acquired, and in fact these shade into each other (Sperber, 1996: 49). Creating a message with the desire to communicate is an attempt to influence others to make a selection from their repertoire of memory schemas that is similar to one that we have made from ours—to think and feel things that are similar to what we are thinking and feeling. This implies that, for communication to occur, there must be some sort of correlation between different people's repertoires. (In the case of music, part of this correlation could be called a "musical culture.") This correlation of schematic repertoires is clearly important in the case of messages taking the form of language. Note, however, that musical meaning is *much less constrained* than linguistic meaning. Music does not have literal meaning. Therefore the repertoires that listeners may use to derive meaning from music can include many types of metaphorical interpretations of experience. These may be related to the repertoire of the musician in a rather distant way (see Geertz, quoted in Blacking, 1995: 227). This would allow for many different kinds of personal as well as cultural repertoires to be used in the understanding of music (Higgens, 1997). I believe that music can be interpreted in many ways, across cultures as well as within them, that listeners can construct meaning for a piece of music that the musician who created it never imagined, although this meaning would still be cued by perceptible features in that music. Such a meaning would be metaphorical (transformational), some of it unique to a given individual.[15] Indeed, because music is a unique type of experience, I would say almost all verbal descriptions of music are metaphorical.

As we have seen, musicians employ a number of bottom-up principles, such as similarity, proximity, and continuity to mark out various kinds of pattern units (see Meyer, 1994: 288–289). These principles operate largely in the context of early processing, and hence rely to a considerable extent on innate perceptual and cognitive mechanisms. Hence listeners will tend to agree about organization at this level (Deliege, 1987). In most cases, listeners will agree about where a phrase ends or where a shift in melodic contour occurs, especially if different grouping principles are not in conflict. As "higher-level" relations between basic pattern units involving long-term memory enter the picture, however, listeners' personal and cultural schemas have a larger influence. That is to say, the conceptual repertoires (schemas) of the musician and listeners are more likely to differ at higher structural levels, especially across cultures. Having defined a message as an organized pattern of energy (a *signal*), in the next two subsections we shall explore the meaning of "organized" in that definition.

Limits on Patterns

As we noted in chapter 2, a feature of many nerve cells is that if they are continuously stimulated, their output of neural impulses does not stay the same, but drops off fairly quickly.[16] This habituation response is an important way an organism deals with change in its environment: when no change is taking place, almost no new information is being activated in memory. (Note that the state of the environment is here being viewed as a kind of message.) Unchanging events are quickly perceived as a background against which more informative, changing events may be foregrounded. In music, for example, accompanimental patterns are usually more repetitive than the patterns they accompany, and hence tend to be backgrounded. As we have seen, this is one of the ways our attention is used efficiently, so that we are not constantly overloaded by paying equal attention to everything, or by constantly reprocessing sensory data that remain the same.

It is also worth remembering that information and redundancy are related to context. That is, everything is new or repetitive *within a framework*. A change in context can bring a change in information content. For example, once, for nearly six months, I listened to almost nothing but North Indian Khyal singing, music whose intricate intonation structure includes many small pitch slides and ornaments. I remember very clearly the first time I listened again to Western music, a recording of a Beethoven string quartet by the Budapest quartet. Although I had listened to this particular recording many times in the past, it was newly alive with details of intonation I had never really heard before. Because my unconscious context and expectations had been altered by repeated exposure to a different kind of music, I found the quartet transformed into a new piece, with new information.

The habituation response is counterbalanced by the fact that the capacity of our short-term memory, hence the amount of new information (change) we can process at a given time, is small. Taken together, these two factors lead to the conclusion that we need a certain amount of change to stay involved and learn about our environment, but that we cannot process too much change in a given amount of time. Or to put it another way, we need information, but within certain limits: not too much and not too little (see Baars, 1988: 188). The limits imposed by habituation and by short-term memory are the two major constraints on the structure of comprehensible messages, and are related to the concepts of information and redundancy, respectively.

Information

In the technical sense introduced above, the term information refers to novelty, and the removal of uncertainty. Thus a message cues memory only to the extent that it cues something in a way we are not completely familiar with, and this is related to change or difference. Note that "difference" in this case need not imply a totally novel event we have never experienced before, but rather can be a pattern of thought we have not had before; the removal of uncertainty means we discover which of the elements in our repertoire the message is meant to cue.

If a message is exactly as we expect, we usually become habituated to it, and thus are not informed by it. As a basic feature of the functioning of many neurons, habituation occurs at many levels of consciousness, cognitive as well as perceptual, and on many different time scales, from seconds to years. It happens both with things immediately experienced and with things stored in long-term memory. Thus we may not notice or remember experiences that keep repeating or are continuous within the present or that we perceive as being the same as at some other time (repeating on a larger time scale). Instead, they may become part of our "background." It is worth recalling that the higher the level of a musical pattern is, the more its information content depends on the knowledge of the listeners. "Higher level" here means dependent on long-term memory. Thus at the level of stylistic norms, say, even what constitutes novelty or repetition can depend on individual knowledge. The perception of higher-level musical structure requires a more knowledgeable listener, whereas low-level similarities and repetition are usually perceived in the same way by everyone.

Redundancy

Proceeding from the definition of information as the amount of novelty something holds for us, we might assume that messages should be as informative as possible. On reflection, however, it becomes clear that a maximally informative message would quickly overload short-term memory: we would never know what to expect next. (Note that the limitation of the capacity of STM to a small set of elements is a limitation on how much novelty it can handle, and hence is an *information* limitation.) Indeed, an unstructured message of this type would be referred to as "nonsense." It would use memory in a maximally *inefficient* way, having no meaningful chunk boundaries, no natural units by which it could be stored; nor would it be easily relatable to any organized context already present in memory. In short, its maximal informativeness would simply create confusion.

To be coherent and memorable, a message must have a certain amount of *noninformative repetition*, or *redundancy*. Redundancy in messages usually takes the form of constraints or rule systems (remember that by definition, a message is a set of *limitations*), constituting what we have referred to as "syntax." These constraints determine how many elements a message can have and how those elements can be arranged, which produces a certain amount of invariance or regularity. This redundancy in messages acts as a kind of implicit memory rehearsal.

Whether as syntax, as repetition of elements and patterns of elements, or as constancy, redundancy thus allows us to have certain expectations about the messages we perceive: it makes them predictable to some extent. This is equivalent to saying that communication is regulated by schemas. (Grammatical structure, for instance, is highly schematic.) Indeed, we can see that there is a kind of reciprocal relationship between redundancy and schemas. Schemas are like condensations of redundant repetitions in our experience over time; constructing messages so that they have redundancy facilitates our development of schemas for them. Schemas help us to derive ways of *understanding* messages and conversely, having rules for *creating* messages allows us to develop schemas for them. Schemas and redundancy effectively reduce the enormous amount of information we have to process to a manageable amount.

Redundancy is useful in many ways, including the reconstruction of signals with elements missing. F-r ins9nce, th*s s#ntence ha& maˆy let!ers mis)ing. Note that the preceding sentence is readable, even though letters are indeed missing. This is because constraints such as English grammar, and rules for the formation of English words give us a fairly good idea of what to expect.

In relation to music, we can define information and redundancy at the three levels of experience defined earlier. At the event fusion level, the idea of redundancy involves repetition of similar waveforms, which, when they occur in very rapid succession, create pitch. At the melodic and rhythmic level, the constraints of tuning systems and scales limit the number of elements used, which automatically creates redundancy in melodic patterns. This is also true of the regularity and repetition of tempo and meter, and systems of limited numbers of time intervals and durations. At the formal level, redundancy includes larger symmetries and repetition of patterns—tonality, constancies within sections, and entire sections that resemble each other. Note that all of these are constraint systems that make music more comprehensible on many levels.

It should be clear, then, that redundancy and similarity are related. The idea of repetition after all presupposes the idea of similarity. Redundancy is based on the repetition of elements perceived as similar; in this sense, it is a kind of management of novelty.

The concepts of information and redundancy are closely related, and all organized messages are *both informative and redundant*. Again, we need change to be informed of something, but our memories are not so efficient that we can be informed of too much at one time.

Our nervous system searches out regularity on many levels. Many traditional European musical forms are based on repetition of musical materials at key structural points, such as sectional and larger-scale endings. This repetition, in addition to being a memory retrieval cue, is a *metaphor* for the process of *remembering itself*. When a pattern that has appeared earlier in a piece of music reappears, it is like a recollection—an image of the past reappearing in the present, and its familiarity gives it stability. Such associative repetition is thus often a factor in establishing closure. As returning to a central pitch in tonality can establish closure, so returning to a previously introduced pattern at a later time can establish higher-level (formal) closure. Conversely, points that introduce new and unfamiliar material (higher information), such as transitions, generally have a higher tension value and are less stable. Information can therefore be related to tension factors in music. Beginnings, by the nature of their basic orientational function, tend to have high information, although there are several kinds of beginnings that are designed to ease us into this by presenting highly redundant material first.

In music, redundancy often occurs as various kinds of internal and stylistic *norms*, redundant schemas such as meter, tonality, and orchestration, that remain relatively constant over time, and that provide a framework within which deviations (information) can be appreciated. Some of these redundancies, such as the limited number of tones in the scale, are established immediately in the music, while others, such as stylistic relationships with other similar pieces, require more processing through long-term memory, and hence are more knowledge dependent.

In summary, we can say that organized messages are things that simultaneously sustain our interest (and therefore represent novelty, or information), and are also recognizable (and therefore represent repetition, or redundancy). We shall now turn to how the concept of information is related to ideas about time.

Information, Memory, and Time

Time is often thought of as existing independently of human experience. Certainly, the notion of time travel as presented in science fiction is based on the idea of time having some sort of objective physical existence. The position taken in this book, however, is that time is an abstract construction of the human mind based on certain aspects of memory and the concept of an enduring self.[17] We do not experience time in the way that we experience physical objects. Rather, our subjective notion of time is *constructed from* our perceptions of objects and events, and its qualities at a given moment depend on the relationships between these perceptions. Indeed, what we perceive in a given amount of time to some extent determines our sense of the length of that time.

From a biological point of view, the function of our sense of time is to tune our behavior to the environment (Michon, 1985: 28–32). Events in the environment can act as "clocks" to which we synchronize our behavior. Almost anything can be used as a clock in this way; the whole world can be viewed as an ensemble of clocks that we use at various times for various purposes. This model may explain temporal experience more accurately than a single "internal clock" model (see Block, 1990: 14–19).[18] Knowing when certain kinds of events will happen and being able to predict this on the basis of regular cycles of events in the environment are extremely biologically valuable survival skills for any organism.

The study of time in experimental psychology is usually broken down into three subfields that are often studied more or less independently of each other (Block, 1990):

1. *Duration*, the study of the experience and memory of time lengths;

2. *Succession*, the study of the experience and memory of the ordering of events in time; and

3. *Temporal perspective*, the study of the construction of the linear ordering of the future, present, and past, and the way a particular event occurring at a particular time moves through these three phases of consciousness.

Each of these areas of study has implications for the study of musical form.

Duration

One way the concepts of information and redundancy are related to musical form is that they have a profound effect on our perception and memory of *lengths of time*. The perception of the relative lengths of sections in a piece of music, often referred to as its "formal proportions," is an important aspect of musical form.

Our judgment of the length of a time period longer than the limits of short-term memory is not at all absolute, and depends on the nature of the events that "fill" it. Because we have no absolute sense of time (time is not directly perceived) and are dependent for our sense of time on events as they happen to us, we now need to establish how different kinds of relations between events give us a sense of different durations.

We might imagine that how long a length of time seems depends on how many events happen within it, but in reality it seems to depend not only on how many events "fill" a length of time, but also on *how much information* we process from those events. Thus a time period filled with novel and unexpected events will be remembered as longer than an identical (in clock time) period filled with redundant or expected events. An interesting effect related to this is what is known as a positive time-order effect, in which the first of two equal time periods filled with the same type of events is remembered as having a longer duration (Block, 1985: 175). This is presumably because the first occurrence of anything is new, hence is processed as more information. In this way, the time order of even identical events can change their informativeness, hence their remembered duration.

All of the above implies that our expectations (schemas) are a factor in our sense of duration. For example, after a vacation spent in a novel environment (say a foreign country) the time spent is remembered as much longer than the same amount of time spent in a familiar environment. The many violations of our expectations on many levels in such an environment can stimulate the processing of a great deal of new information. On the other hand, accounts of the sense of elapsed time by people deprived of sensory experience or having highly predictable life routines, people in prison, for example, describe remembering long periods of time as seeming to have been quite short.[19]

It is as though unfamiliar situations that stretch our schemas or do not fit comfortably into them take more processing or attention, and somehow take up more "space" in memory, as though the amount of space taken up determines our memory of the duration of the time interval. This metaphorical idea of memory space was introduced by Robert Ornstein (1997: 37–52), and is referred to as the "storage size metaphor." Novel events described as taking up more memory space are then remembered as having taken more time to happen. On the other hand, ordinary events, which fit comfortably within our schemas and require little attention and processing, are described as taking up little memory space and in retrospect seem to have taken less time to happen.

Note, however, that the above are descriptions of duration *as remembered*, and duration remembered is not the same as duration *experienced*. Indeed, duration as experienced tends to be the *opposite* of duration remembered (see Block, 1990: 9–11). This is to say, "boring" time periods with little information are experienced as being long, but *remembered as shorter*. Conversely, because our attention is actively engaged in the events themselves, time periods filled with unusual, informative sequences of events, can seem to flow very rapidly while actually occurring, but are *remembered as longer*. Thus a musical passage filled with repetitive events can seem, in retrospect, shorter than one filled with unpredictable events (see Kramer, 1988: 333–345). Note that many of the factors contributing to predictability that may affect our sense of the duration of a passage of music are not purely temporal. Example of this could include pitch patterning, orchestration, and any other recognizable musical relations that contribute to its information. In addition, a particular listener's knowledge, because it would affect expectations, would also be an important factor (see Kramer, 1988: 342–343).

In relation to music the above idea implies that attempts to establish perceptible sectional proportions by constructing section lengths with proportional amounts of clock time may not be an effective procedure. Proportional relations of clock time do not necessarily establish similar relations of proportional remembered time length. Two sections of music that have the same length in clock time are not necessarily experienced or remembered as being the same length. Two other factors can affect this, however. First, this effect seems to diminish with repeated listening; that is, the more times we hear something, the closer our sense of its durational proportions comes to being accurate in relation to clock time. In addition, regular pulse and metrical frameworks seem to make it easier to get a more accurate sense of larger durational proportions. In fact, by acting as a kind of "perceptual clock" in music, metrical organization can be as important a factor in duration perception as information (see Kramer, 1988: 347–367). Not only do we perceive sequences of events as lasting longer or shorter, we perceive them as occurring in *succession* and in a particular *order*.

Succession

The idea of succession in the study of time is primarily about *time order*, the relation of before and after. In the long term, we do not automatically remember the time order in which events happen: our ability to remember time order varies with different time levels, and with the different kinds of memory that function on those time levels.

Clearly, the few events that can be retained by short-term memory are usually retained in a time order, although it is not yet clear how this is accomplished (see Jackson, 1990: 162–164; Brown, 1997). It is usually the case that *individual chunks* retain the time order of their elements especially if rehearsal is possible. That we remember time order on this level is obvious when we consider our ability to remember short sequences of elements such as telephone numbers and brief sentences, where time order is extremely important. Melodic and rhythmic groupings, as we have defined them earlier, could not function as different types of patterns with characteristic contours if we could not remember their components in order.

Time Order and Long-Term Memory

There does not appear to be any simple time-order mechanism for long-term memory comparable to that of STM, especially in the longest term. Long-term memories are not necessarily organized in a time order: we must usually try to make a special effort to remember the particular time at which something occurred, and we must usually do so with respect to some external frame of reference. The existence of long-term anchoring devices such as calendars and clocks attests to our relative inability to do this sort of thing (note that both of these temporal measurement systems are hierarchical). To determine when something happened in the longest term, we must usually try to date the event either by referring it to the calendar or to some important "landmark" event in our lives[20] (see Jackson, 1990: 174–176). Long-term memory experiments have established that factors such as *where*, *what*, and *how* are much better thematic cues for retrieval of long-term memories than *when*. Of these factors, the most important is *where*. Spatial context is of primary importance in LTM recall. There is no natural mechanism that allows us to access time order easily—it is not necessarily "in" the memories. We must often construct external reference systems to find particular events in the past.

Spatial order is more basic and easier to remember than temporal order, and our spatial memory is much older (in an evolutionary sense) than the sense of time; our memories of these two aspects of the world are probably closely related. The part of the brain that appears to be central to our spatial memory, the hippocampus, also appears to have an important function in the establishment of long-term memories (see Doty, 1990: 148–151). Also note that almost all of the language terms we use (in English) to talk about time are spatial, and that both clocks and calendars use space to represent time. In addition, there are many systems for memorizing large amounts of text (some of them ancient), that use retrieval cues based on spatial models (see Yates, 1966).

That recall of the time order for events persisting as long-term memory is a great deal less accurate than for those persisting as short-term memory is believed to be because recall from LTM occurs in a parallel rather than a serial fashion (see Barsalou, 1992: 100–102). A parallel process allows us to access and select from many different memories simultaneously, rather than moving through them one by one in succession. This is how we are able to access the memories we want quickly from the enormous amount of material stored in LTM. The contents of LTM are of course many, many times larger than those of STM. If long-term memory were searched serially in the order memories were created, each item would have to be considered one at a time, and this would take an enormous amount of time. Rather, it appears that many parts of LTM are searched in parallel simultaneously through patterns of association. This is a much more rapid and efficient search procedure for the large amount of memory involved, but it in *no way guarantees* that the items will emerge from memory in the order they originally happened, or the order the memories were created. Rather, they will emerge in some spreading pattern of associations that will be different for different individuals, and even different for the same individual on different recall occasions.

Another factor that probably contributes to the lack of time order in long-term memory is the way episodic memories evolve into semantic memory categories. Remember that episodic memories are usually organized chronologically, whereas semantic categories are not.[21] Therefore, as specific episodic memories become related to a large body of similar episodic memories of similar episodes, they lose their specific time-ordered character, and eventually lose their status as specific memories altogether.

Memory and Hierarchy

Nevertheless, it is clear that we are able to store time-ordered sequences of long-term memories under some conditions, and that some types of information structures seem to lend themselves to more efficient formation of long-term memories than others.[22] As we have seen, a form of organization that is very important from the standpoint of memory encoding is *hierarchy*, defined here as a form of organization where elements are ordered on different levels, and where some levels (the higher levels) include some of the other levels (the lower levels). The elements of these levels consist of memory chunks, with each element in a chunk at a higher level being a chunk on the next level down, and so on. At least one element in a chunk at a particular level can act as a retrieval cue to a chunk on the same or another level, and thus recall can move through the hierarchy of memory to get to the desired level of detail quickly and efficiently. This movement through hierarchically organized memories can take place in either of two directions—horizontally to other elements at the same level, or vertically to elements at other levels of detail.

Hierarchical organization seems to be the best way of overcoming the limits of short-term memory. Remember that the time and information limits of STM apply not only to incoming perceptions and the formation of long-term memories but to *retrieval from LTM* as well. Because material activated in long-term memory and made conscious must be held as short-term memory, when retrieving information from LTM, we can only deal with it one STM chunk at a time. Hierarchy aids this process insofar as it is a type of structure that allows us to break the recall task up into units of manageable size. We can recall one chunk of a maximum of five to nine elements, use one of those elements as a retrieval cue for another chunk of five to nine elements, and so on, and so forth. In this way, we can *reconstruct* some remarkably complex materials from memory, provided they can be structured *in the form of a hierarchy of chunks*. Note that this means that we do not recall long and complex sequences from LTM all at one time, but *in chunks*, which we must reassemble into long sequences. This is because the chunks are initially stored *independently* of each other. And because we can only hold one chunk at a time in consciousness, we cannot have all of the details of a long sequence in consciousness at once, but rather only one chunk of details, and possibly some semiconscious schematic idea of the rest of the sequence.

Thus a message that is structured hierarchically in some way is more efficiently stored, more stable in memory, and more easily retrieved. Hierarchical order facilitates both the formation and retrieval of long-term memories.

Indeed, many forms of music and language display this type of order, as though the form these communications take is a kind of diagram of memory itself. (In music, individual events, groupings, phrases, groups of phrases, sections, and whole pieces would each form a level of a hierarchy.)

As we have noted, the formation of mental representations is what makes music graspable on the formal (long-term memory) level. Our access to musical chunks, like any others, is hierarchical. If we can chunk musical groupings, phrases, and sections, we can access those memories and assemble their time sequence more easily (Deutsch, 1999: 370–373). This is what enables us to contemplate the larger formal aspects of compositions, and to remember patterns across larger time scales. (Note that this type of contemplation is not always the goal of a particular composition, and that by no means is all music organized hierarchically.) It is not clear, however, how many levels of hierarchical organization are obvious to musical listeners. Although musical analysts have tended to assume that high-level hierarchical information such as large-scale tonal and metrical structure is part of the listeners' experience, recent research has tended to throw this into question, especially in relation to less experienced listeners (see Cook, 1990: 43–70; Karno and Konecni, 1992).

It appears that we access memories that are hierarchically organized at major boundary points of hierarchical units (chunk boundaries). These are important closure or change points, and seem to be the anchor points of memories of time sequences. For example, even our memory of a prototypical continuous sequence such as the alphabet seems to be chunked in a simple two-level hierarchy. If asked what letters are near a particular letter of the alphabet, most of us access this information by dividing the alphabet into the following units: ABCD EFG HIJK LMNOP QRS TUV WXYZ.[23] Note that each of these units falls within the five to nine-element limit of short-term memory. Also note that the number of these chunks itself is within this limit, meaning that the entire alphabet is itself a chunk on a higher level. Most of us learn this particular chunking of the alphabet as children. People apparently do not store the alphabet as a continuous sequence, but access the position of particular letters by entering at the boundaries of chunks and are therefore able to answer questions about the positions of letters more quickly if they are close to and after a boundary (see Anderson, 1980: 107–109; Mandler, 1984: 11–12).

We have noted that the theoretical limit on this hierarchical process is the number of items in a chunk raised to the power of the same number—conservatively 5^5, which amounts to five levels of five chunks of (moving upward) 5, 25, 125, and 625, elements, respectively, or about 3,000 elements. Note that this number represents, not the total capacity of long-term memory, but merely the approximate number of items that can be related in a coherent mass—a sort of metachunk or a large schema.

Hierarchy and Time Order

The price we pay for the ability to encode time sequences through chunking is that we cannot access or enter memory sequences at any arbitrary point, but must do so at the chunk boundaries.[24] In addition, it is often easier to do this at higher-level chunk boundaries (which are fewer) than at lower chunk boundaries (which are more numerous). Higher-level boundaries in this case means boundaries that exist on more than one level at a time. In a piece of music, these would often be sectional boundaries. Sequence 1 at the top of figure 13.2 is a simplified representation of an organized time sequence of musical events. Each dot represents a musical event. This sequence is segmented into chunks of various sizes. In the diagram, events that can potentially be consolidated in a chunk are all under one bracket. Chunk boundaries are indicated by the spaces between the brackets. These chunks retain their

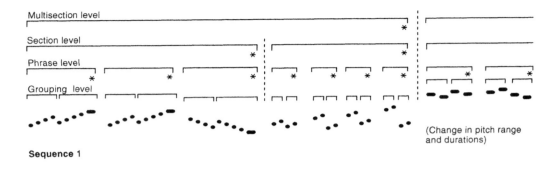

Sequence 1

Sequence 2

Figure 13.2
Hierarchy and time order. These diagrams represent a highly simplified representation of two ways of structuring time-ordered sequences of musical events. Both sequences have the same number of events. Complete chunks at various levels are represented by horizontal brackets; higher-level chunking boundaries, by dashed vertical lines; and cues, by asterisks.

internal time order. If the material has been structured so as to have clear boundaries on a number of levels, these chunks may be then combined into larger chunks, again based on grouping boundaries, with these chunks also retaining *their* time order.

Each chunk can act as a cue for another chunk in the sequence. This is represented by an asterisk at the chunk boundary. These cues are the connections that hold the memory of the sequence together. Because entire large-scale chunks can be cued, the number of cues that need to be stored can be minimized. This chunking process can create the kinds of levels indicated in the diagram. Above the grouping level is the phrase level, the *basic* level, in that it is the highest level at which a chunk can be created immediately, and the level most accessible to immediate recall. It is one "short-term memory full": the size of the units we are likely to recall most easily. It is the level on which we immediately grasp the music. Above this are the higher levels of section and section group. The first three sections are here chunked together in a section group, separate from the fourth section because of a change in pitch range. Higher-level chunks would need to be listened to repeatedly to establish them as complete strings, although some strong higher-level chunk boundaries might stand out immediately. There could of course be more levels than illustrated here.

This process can continue upward, finally terminating in one large chunk, which represents the entire piece, and retains its time order. Thus the time order of the entire piece can eventually be preserved through the hierarchy of levels (although, at this later point, the consolidation of chunks and the reduction of the number of cues would make it hard to recall the sequence starting *inside* one of the chunks). All of these effects strongly depend on careful compositional structuring of the material, so that the structure of the material conforms to the structure of memory itself. This structuring primarily consists of creating clear boundaries of various strengths between units at various levels, distinctive markers at important boundary points, and multiple degrees of closure. These degrees of closure would be a very important factor in making the different levels clear. It is also important to note that the building up of such a hierarchical memory is not a completely infallible process. Small time order errors, usually in the form of shuffling of the positions of elements that are close to each other inside of chunks, may occur at any stage in the process and at any level of the hierarchy (see Jackson, 1990: 165–168).

Our discussion may seem to imply that all chunk boundaries are equivalent, and that they are built up or established in an orderly way in the correct time order. While this might be the case for performers systematically memorizing a piece in its original time order, it would most likely not be the case for listeners.

Indeed, the initial chunking of a piece would most likely *not* proceed in a simple, linear way. In chapter 8, I described the initial formation of a long-term memory of a piece of music as being "peppered" with episodic memories of aspects of the piece that were particularly striking or novel in some way. It is very likely that these points would form chunk boundaries. Even though the locations of the chunk boundaries would be relatively fixed by the musical material itself, *which* chunk boundaries we retained in our initial memory of a piece would be powerfully influenced by their salience for us. Some chunk boundaries would immediately stand out more than others. These boundaries would be places where strong cue events were located. In fact the events that stand out for us would be likely to be high-information events, that is, events that were unexpected. The very first and last phrases in a piece would be an example of this, and would be likely to be remembered. Our initial chunking of a piece would not necessarily proceed in an orderly way through different hierarchical levels, either. It could jump around between levels. Also, at least initially, a particular chunk can cue (remind one of) another particularly salient chunk that is some distance in the future, and not immediately adjacent.[25] Thus the organized cuing of the memory of an entire piece, with each chunk in the correct place in its time sequence, constitutes a theoretical ideal reached by listeners only after many repetitions. Interestingly enough, different listeners often agree to a fairly large extent on which events in a piece of music initially stand out the most (see Deliege et al., 1996; Deliege, 1989).[26]

A question that naturally arises about the idea of large-scale representations of musical form is, how are these representations used *during listening*? It seems clear that even if listeners had managed to construct a fairly complete large-scale memory representation of a piece of music, it could not all be in their consciousness during actual listening (it would usurp the actual experience of the music). It would, however, be something they might contemplate outside the time of the actual listening experience. The answer is that our representation of the larger-scale structure of a piece forms part of the semiactivated context of memory within which the piece is heard, which involves implicit recall, primed by hearing earlier parts of the piece. That is, the hierarchical remindings described above would result in the listeners having a sense of familiarity and increasingly specific expectations around chunk boundaries. In many cases, these would form the listeners' contexts and, although outside their focus of conscious awareness, would be felt in the music *as it unfolded*, not separate from it.[27] This is one way music can have formal meaning without that meaning usurping the experience of the music itself. The situation would of course be different for performers, who would initially be involved in *explicit* recall of the musical material in the correct time order. Listeners are primarily involved in *recognizing* musical materials, whereas performers are primarily involved in *recalling* them. As we noted in chapter 1, recognition is usually implicit, whereas recall is usually explicit.

Another way a time sequence can be organized is *without* intentional higher-level chunking boundaries, with no intentional grouping of events at any level higher than that of primitive grouping. In this kind of music, there would be neither dramatic marker events nor organized closure patterns. More like a list, this type of sequence, represented in figure 13.2 by sequence 2, is not usually generated by means of a syntax. A good example would be a sequence of randomly generated pitches and rhythms with no organized system of boundaries. In a sequence of this type, pitch contour would have no relation to duration; changes in duration would not coincide with the changes in pitch contour; groupings would have no particular typical size; and so on. Repetition would be random. The only immediate memory of time order in this type of a sequence would be inside the phrase, and would emerge more or less automatically as a result of bottom-up grouping. This produces a very "flat" hierarchical structure with only 2 levels—the lowest level groupings, and phases. (A visual analogue of such an unstructured sequence might be a camouflage pattern—a randomly strucured image consisting only of lower-level units, and giving no higher-level sense of order.) With this type of sequence, there are no organized higher-level units that can represent larger chunks of the sequence. Retaining the time order of such a sequence would involve memorizing the entire sequence in order, phrase by phrase, with the last element in each grouping acting as a memory cue for the first element in the next grouping. With no higher-level chunking boundaries, such as those in sequence 1 of figure 13.2, each phrase in this type of sequence would be able to cue the recall of only the phrase immediately following it.

Keeping in mind that the connections between elements are what comprise the uniqueness of a memory, note how many more of these memory connections (represented by asterisks) there are at the highest chunkable level in sequence 2 than in sequence 1, even though it contains the *same number of events*. Because remembering something as a string of low-level groupings is the most laborious way to remember it, building up a representation of such a sequence would take many more hearings than building up a representation of a hierarchical sequence. Such chained memory is also rather fragile. Because the only connections (cues) are between immediately adjacent groupings, any disruption of the sequencing of the recall process would require that recall start over again at the beginning of the sequence.[28] For listeners, it would take much longer for parts of this type of sequence to seem familiar.

Of course, for the majority of listeners, most sequences are somewhere in between the two types just described. Some listeners may not always be able to recognize certain marker events, especially in a style of music unfamiliar to them, and certain events may stand out as markers for them, even in what for others is an undifferentiated musical context. Individual knowledge and preferences are certainly a factor in chunking.

To sum up, our discussion has been primarily about listeners' *recognition* of the structure of a piece of music, not their recall. Although the foregoing remarks could certainly apply to voluntary efforts to freely recall the time sequence of a piece of music, more commonly listeners use this type of memory to know where they are in a piece of music while they are hearing it. Although listeners may contemplate long-term musical structure outside their listening experience, much of their remembering takes the form of implicit recognition during the occurrence of the music itself.

Memory and Association

Hierarchy is of course not the only type of structure in long-term memory retrieval (Lerdahl and Jackendoff, 1983: 17). If the type of hierarchical organization described above were the only type of memory organization, our recollection could only "travel" inside of particular hierarchical groupings of knowledge. In fact, our thoughts can move through quite different kinds of memories in rapid succession. For memory to have this flexibility, our thoughts must be able to quickly jump *between* different memory hierarchies.[29]

Hierarchy is just one form of a more general type of memory organization that I have referred to as "association". In their most basic form, associations are created between things that are near each other or are similar. For example, successive musical events that are next to each other in time may be associated in a chunk. Our memory of a melodic contour or a rhythmic pattern is a set of associations between its individual events. Associations may, however, connect anything to virtually anything else in memory. Remembering proceeds along paths determined by patterns of associations. Day and night dreams and the everyday stream of thought are all examples of the extraordinary flexibility of the associative recall process. Memory hierarchies are highly structured associations of a particular type.

Whereas chunking and knowledge hierarchies are amenable to study, because of their idiosyncratic nature, freer forms of association are much harder to study in standardized scientific experiments. Indeed, very little research has been done on free associative structure in music, although it is clear that our long-term memory representations of most pieces of music must have a considerable amount of it. Just as associative structure allows us to jump between different memory hierarchies, associations between similar pitch and rhythm patterns allow us to jump and make associations across different parts of a piece of music, outside its linear time order.[30]

In this way, we can find ourselves at a "place" similar to somewhere we have pre-viously "been" in a piece. It is even possible for musical material to refer backward across a piece and change the significance of something we have heard earlier. Much of the syntactical connections between different but related patterns in a piece of music are associative.

Note that because they do not require adjacency in time, these associative con-nections would differ from the much more immediate *linear* connections between events, groupings, and the like that the hierarchical structure of music can create. Of course even hierarchically organized music is also remembered associatively. No recollection of music is purely hierarchical or purely free associative—remembering in music is a constant interplay between the two, although music can be designed to emphasize one or the other (or neither, for that matter).

Boundary Effects: Primacy and Recency

Two frequently observed long-term memory effects related to time order, the *primacy effect* and the *recency effect*, reflect our tendency to remember the first and last events in a sequence with the greatest accuracy (see Jackson, 1990: 168).[31] Both effects are in agreement with statements made earlier about information and change, on the one hand, and about chunk boundaries, on the other. Just as the first and last events in a phrase are the most important for defining the relation of that phrase to both melodic and rhythmic frameworks, so, on the formal level, landmark events that mark off important parts of a piece are most commonly found at the begin-ning or end of sections.

The first event in a sequence is certainly a major change from no sequence at all, and gives us a great deal of information in that, by definition, it is novel—generally more novel than the events that follow it. Because the last event is also at a change point, it works the same way, although in retrospect. As previously noted, we tend to recall the time position of intermediate events in a sequence less accurately than that of first and last events; these intermediate events can move around in position as they persist as long-term memory. Thus, we can define a sequence here as beginning with some significant amount of change, and ending with another significant change. The middle of a sequence would be the material between these two novel landmark events. This appears to be true for chunks at all hierarchical levels.[32]

Again, we see that boundary points in time, representing points of change, are the most memorable. If we look at a coherent sequence as a kind of temporal category, we see that, as with other types of categories, it is at the edges of this category that discriminability and memorability are the highest. In a musical context, there are usually markers that help retain time order, such as melodic and rhythmic contour.

Schemas and Time Order

When trying to recall the order of events that happened longer ago than the length of short-term memory (3–5 sec on average), we also come to depend more on structured sets of expectations in long-term memory, and less on any episodic memory of the actual events, especially so when encountering something for the first time (see Michon, 1990: 37–45). As we move outward in time from the length of STM, we have less and less ability to remember the temporal position of particular, specific events. Our memories do not contain specific details at a consistent level out into the past as far as we can remember. If we are listening to a piece of music or a lecture, we do not remember all of it in equal detail. We remember the last few seconds in terms of specific events and a specific time order, but beyond this, unless we have encountered something really novel, our memory gets increasingly sketchy and schematic. The ability to remember sentences verbatim, for example, extends back two sentences at most (see Barsalou, 1992: 232). We have a sense of the present being continuous with the past because all of our short-term memories continuously fade into each other, and because each successive state of the world is similar in many ways to the previous state. Our memory of these "presents," however, contains less and less actual detail as it recedes further into the past. Recycling a particular present (rehearsal) can keep a particular chunk active in short-term memory, preserve its time order and details temporarily, and increase the chance that these will make it into permanent storage in long-term memory.

The concept of a schema was introduced in chapter 8, where it was defined as an abstract, skeletal memory of parts of typical sequences of events that have passed beyond the time limits of our short-term memory. It has been proven, for example, that although we do not remember the exact words of a story, we remember the sense of it quite well (see Jenkins, 1980; J. Mandler, 1984: 17–61). This "sense" is as much a product of our expectations about what we *might* have heard, as it is a product of what we actually heard, with what we *expected* to hear forming the basic framework, and deviations from that forming landmarks that may be remembered.

Indeed, we realize that at certain points where we were not paying attention, we may remember *only* what we expected, whether it actually happened or not. On the other hand, if almost all of what we hear is *unexpected* (is too informative and seems unrelated to most of our schemas), we will tend to remember very little. Remembering must take place within a framework of knowledge already in memory. (Imagine trying to remember a lecture on a subject you know nothing about, or a complex piece of music in a style you are unfamiliar with.) Thus large time structures that greatly diverge from our schematic expectations are much harder to reconstruct later, although we might remember some novel events if they can be related to something that we already know. Here again, we need a certain amount of information, but not too much.

Schematic effects depend on prior knowledge. Because they encode standard time orders for particular types of event sequences, schemas are not only central to our reconstruction of the past, but important for dealing with the future: our ideas of *both* past *and* future events depend on memory. Thus we can use schemas that retain typical time orders for sequences as frameworks on which to hang our episodic memories—as another means to remember time order. Most of our musical memories consist of a combination of built-up hierarchical and previously learned schematic order; indeed, these two forms of memory can reinforce each other.

Often in music, the schemas used to reconstruct long-term time order are standardized in the traditional musical *forms* mentioned at the beginning of this chapter. Just as schemas allow us to categorize and understand different kinds of situations in our lives, we can create musical situations based on schematic kinds of organization so that they will be memorable. One of the functions of stable historical-cultural forms or schemas in music is that, like hierarchical structure, they give us a way of knowing "where we are" in a piece of music, partly the result of the schemas' standardized time order. (Note that this order may also be hierarchical.) Individual episodic memories of event sequences can be stored in association with the general categories of the schema, and in retrieving those memories, we can associate them with particular temporal positions in the schema. These cultural musical schemas are a form of redundancy. Our sense of knowing where we are can also be reinforced by differentiation of the musical materials themselves, with different parts or sections of the schema having different constancies of rhythm, orchestration, pitch patterns, and so on.

In contrast, music without a tradition of stable forms would tend not to give us a strong sense of knowing where we are. We would remember such music in a different way—as a string of local associations. This can have the effect of heightening our sense of immediacy in the music. If the music were constructed so that lower-level chunking boundaries were clear, it would still be possible to form a sequential memory for the piece, but the establishment of higher-level chunks and their ordering would be more difficult. The largest time levels of pieces are where schemas and hierarchical chunking reenforce each other the most.

Temporal Perspective

The idea of temporal perspective concerns not just the length or time order of events, but the construction of a unified time flow with a past, present, and future. This view of time appears to be a uniquely human phenomenon. The physical world has no such distinctions (see Fraser, 1987: 236, 274–280). There is no *consistent* sense in which a representation of the past or future state of the world is contained in its present state; the physical world has no memory or anticipation of itself—it simply *is*. The concepts of the past and future require a mind capable of constructing these states. We seem to have this ability to a far greater degree than any other type of organism. Although many animals clearly have a long-term memory and respond to situations in ways based on previous responses, they do so largely without being *aware* they are doing it. They live entirely in the present, in a kind of episodic consciousness. We on the other hand, are clearly aware of our own memory, a self-concept greatly enhanced and stabilized by language.[33]

There are thus at least two different possible views of time: a human world, where now is always passing from being anticipated through being perceived into being remembered; and a physical world, where it is always now. In the first view, the status of a particular event as future, present, or past, is always changing (see Gell, 1992: 149–155), whereas in the second, the status of events as earlier or later is always fixed. Which of these views we adopt in relation to time can have a profound effect on the kind of music we choose to write. The first of these views of time is related to the idea of linearity.

Linearity

When looking at parametric activity of music on higher (sectional or multisectional) levels, we can see that there are a number of possibilities for organization. Assuming that parametric values are changing, their overall pattern of change can be organized in several ways.

One such way is what has been referred to as "linearity," defined by Jonathon Kramer (1988: 20) as "the determination of some characteristics of a piece of music in accordance with implications that arise from earlier events of the piece."[34] Thus, through linearity, earlier events in a piece create the expectation of later ones, which creates a temporal perspective of anticipation and remembrance. As we shall see, these expectations may have various degrees of specificity.

Structuring music in a linear way makes it possible for listeners to have some idea of "where they are" in the music, as they move forward out of the past into the anticipated future of the music. It facilitates the kind of moment-to-moment comparisons necessary to perceive linear change, usually by marking (drawing attention to) the passage of time through incremental, directional, and often regular changes in one or more parameters. As a type of redundancy, linearity reduces immediate memory load; linearity makes efficient use of short-term memory. It also makes it easier to form a schematic representation of the immediate past. Not all places are equivalent in linear music, and the later places can only be later, because they are made to seem as though they are the *result* of earlier events. There are several ways in which music may be structured to move in a linear way. These may be divided roughly into bottom-up and top-down strategies, or nonsyntactical and syntactical ways of establishing linearity. Bottom-up linearity would give a sense of directed motion at any given time in the music, whereas top-down linearity would operate in music so as to optimize the formation of a long-term memory image of its time order.

Linearity Bottom-Up: Continuity, Graduated Parametric Motion, and Discontinuity

The kind of anticipation created by linear sequences is often referred to metaphorically as musical "motion" (considered in chapter 9). Only certain kinds of relations between musical events create a sense of *motion* in the sense the term is being used here. Interestingly, establishing both continuity and discontinuity can contribute to linear musical motion (see Clarke, 1987b: 213).

In chapter 3, the principle of continuity was described in terms of our basic perceptual processes, the idea being that, once several successive musical events change in a similar way, we expect them to continue along their established trajectory. This trajectory, which consists of graduated parametric change in a certain direction, is the "line" of musical linearity. By causing musical events to "point to" other musical events, it connects those events in a relation of implication. Generally, this kind of implication is created by using events whose parametric values lie close together, and which move relatively continuously in the same direction (up or down). This is described here as "bottom-up" linearity, because it operates primarily from event to event; the local connections it creates take place in the immediate present and do not have to be learned. To operate on higher hierarchical levels, it would have to be learned, at least in some sense, and long-term memory would have to be used. Indeed, at the highest level, this type of linearity would have to be made fairly obvious: the trajectory would have to be quite clear.

Musical linearity is like a metaphor of physical causation, and indeed linearity is an attempt to make musical events seem to cause each other. (Note that much of the linearity in verbal narrative structures is based on causation—events are connected to other events through the earlier events causing the later events.) In physical causation, an event that causes another event usually occurs in close physical proximity to it. Linear musical causation is often also established by proximity, albeit the more metaphorical proximity of musical parametric values.

Although graduated parametric change is a kind of scalar movement, linear progressions generally do not move in a simple scalar way. Simple scalar motion is very linear, but not very interesting. Most linear motion in music deviates from perfect linearity. Rather, musical linearity can in general be said to follow a trajectory, an implied path, along which actual parametric values average out over time. Absent such a trajectory, we have fluctuating, nonprogressive motion, where, at one extreme, every parametric motion in a particular direction is soon canceled out by motion in the opposite direction. The distinction between linearity and fluctuation is not absolute, however: there are many strengths or degrees of linearity.

The occurrence of a particular event in a linear progression to some extent circumscribes the possibility of what the next event will be. Certain events increase the probability of certain other events occurring. The similar motion patterns that characterize linearity are a kind of redundancy; like all redundancy, such patterns act as a memory aid. Linear sequences are easier to schematize and to "keep track of." Note that, because it allows us to have a sense of our position in a progression, a linear structuring of a sequence not only streamlines our expectations of "where we are going"; it facilitates our memory of "where we have been."

Different kinds of events or patterns are found in different parts of a linear piece, and there is a kind of evolution or development from one kind of event or pattern to another. This evolution can be looked at in terms of parametric profiles. Particular parameters, *on average*, increase or decrease in value or intensity as they move toward important structural points in the music; the resultant parametric motion is usually referred to as "tension" or "release," respectively. In any given piece of linear music, parametric progressions may be simple increases or decreases (in secondary parameters), actual developments in patterns (in primary parameters), or (as is most often the case) both.

The musical surface is rarely an unbroken continuum. It is usually segmented and broken into groupings and phrases, by primitive processes already described. This segmentation, which greatly enhances our ability to chunk and remember time sequences, need not work against the establishment of linear motion, however: linearity can be established through discontinuity. In addition to graduated parametric change, linearity operates at the local level through *incomplete closure*. Although the most organized sequences of incomplete closure are syntactical and hence top-down, such closure can also be achieved bottom-up, at the phrase level, by ending phrases on short durations or on weak beats of the measure, or with upward melodic movement, for example. Incomplete closure at this local level is important in developing linear motion, because it allows forward movement to continue *across silences*. This type of incomplete closure is important to establishing a sense of anticipation. This takes the concept of musical motion described above from the event level to the phrase level, and connects separate phrases into linear phrase groups and sections.

Because linear (serial) time order can only be retained on higher time levels through hierarchical chunking, which depends on natural breaks in sequences for its formation, linearity depends, at least in part, on hierarchy for its development in music.

Thus linearity at local levels is established using both the continuity of relatively consistent graduated parametric movement and the "connective" discontinuity of incomplete closure. The continuity of graduated parametric motion helps us relate what we are currently hearing to the immediate past and anticipate what is to come in the immediate future. Discontinuity withholds the immediate gratification of that anticipation and therefore intensifies it. Both factors can help to give us a sense of motion on a larger time scale.

Linearity Top-Down: Syntax

Linearity may be established by means other than graduated parametric progressions, especially on higher hierarchical levels. Our sense of position within the time of a piece may be aided by specific types of syntactical patterns that come to signify beginnings, endings, and the like. Because syntactical patterns also create various kinds of expectations, and because the meaning of these syntactical patterns is learned, they can operate on larger time scales than the more local mechanisms we have considered thus far.

Much Western European Music of the seventeenth, eighteenth, and nineteenth centuries is linear in this way, with certain standardized kinds of syntactical patterns, called "cadences," that signify closure points, which become the goals of graduated parametric progressions within the music. The function of linear progression here is to lead to these goals, and to create tension by temporarily withholding their arrival in various ways. With its standardized syntactical goal patterns, this music displays the clearest kind of linearity: the high probability that a standardized goal pattern will arrive creates a highly specific expectation. Because the music moves in a particular direction toward a defined goal, its linearity is said to be "directed"; the directedness is usually established both by standardized goal patterns in primary parameters and by progressive movement and incomplete closure in secondary parameters leading to those goals.

Tonality (first discussed in chapter 11) affords the strongest possibilities for directed linearity: the goal of a tonal piece of music is usually the arrival back at the central pitch. In such a piece, harmony could progress toward a chord based on the central pitch of the tonality, with loudness and orchestration slowly increasing to reinforce the progression.

Functional tonality affords many possibilities for establishing hierarchical structures through high-level incomplete closure.[35] It fully exploits the detailed patterning possibilities of the primary parameters of pitch and harmony. Pitches and chords can have different degrees of tonal distance from the central pitch, which creates many possibilities both for different degrees of closure and for progression. Unlike the bottom-up mechanisms we discussed earlier, however, syntactical gestures signifying closure can take any number of different forms, and these forms must be learned. Thus comprehension of the hierarchical structure of tonal music depends on knowledge of the traditional schemas governing these syntactical patterns. Without this knowledge, it is possible to miss quite a lot of the hierarchical organization of this type of music.

Certainly it is also possible for nontonal music to be linear and goal directed. In the absence of traditional syntactically defined goal patterns, however, goals are established by mechanisms internal to a piece. Repetition of important patterns plays a large part in this, with particular types of patterns placed at important goal points. Repetition gives those points stability and creates expectation of the arrival of the patterns at those points. Motion toward and arrival at the goal points are usually reinforced by secondary parameters. Whereas it is fairly easy to develop directed linear motion on the phrase and section levels without tonality, it is harder to establish such motion on higher levels without centered pitch organization and syntactical closure (see Clarke, 1987b: 215–221).[36] This is because in nontonal music, much of the burden of creating hierarchy must be carried by secondary parameters, which lack precise pattern characteristics, thus cannot be used to develop as many different degrees of closure as primary parameters. Although much nontonal music can still be described as "linear," it is not structured with clearly defined goals. On the other hand, progressions can be constructed to move toward goals that are *not* precisely defined. This is often the case in music not situated within a tradition of syntax such as tonality, especially when secondary parameters are brought into play. Such music is said to exhibit "nondirected linearity" (Kramer, 1988: 39–40, 61–62). Music of this type can still have progressions, but it does not usually draw on any syntactical information about where these progressions are going. Expectations about arrival at specific types of goals are much weaker, and usually confined to lower and intermediate hierarchical levels.

It is also possible to use the dynamics of linearity in such a way that the goal events and the progressions toward them are separated in time. This kind of music depends on larger scale discontinuities that interrupt the linear flow: although particular progressions have goals, these goals do not occur in places directly following the progressions that lead to them. This can produce effects not unlike the intercutting of different plots in a film. Such music is said to exhibit "multiply directed linearity" (see Kramer, 1988: 46–49).

All these types of linearity may occur on various hierarchical levels. That is, music may be linear on the phrase level, the section level, or even on the level of a whole piece, although linearity on *one* of these levels *need not* imply linearity on the *others*. For example, phrases may be linear and progressive in themselves, yet there may be no progressive organization to their overall sequence. Conversely, an overall sequence of phrases may be directed or progressive in its relation between the phrases, whereas the internal organization of each phrase itself shows no such progressive ordering.

It is possible to construct nonlinear music that makes use of primarily associative memory relationships. Although lacking linear progressions and "deep" hierarchical order, such music uses similar materials in different places to make associations across a piece. Its structure could be described as a "web," rather than a "line." Because it is non-progressive, however, at any given time this type of music gives listeners much less of a sense of location: the places where similar material appears are potentially confusable in memory.

Memory Strategies in Music

In the linear music described thus far, there is an overall balance between continuity and novelty, or between redundancy and information. This helps build the music's hierarchical structure, which enhances the formation and retrieval of long-term memories. It is certainly possible, however, to create music with a different probability or information structure—music on the fringes of, or even beyond, our ability to process information.

Memory is an important consideration when talking about music. Indeed, we can divide music into two broad categories based on the use of memory:

1. Music that attempts to exploit long-term memory by building up hierarchical and associative mental representations of large time structures; and

2. Music that attempts to sabotage recognition and expectation by frustrating recollection and anticipation, thereby intensifying the local order of the present.

In the first type of music, sounds are grouped with different degrees of closure in various, clearly perceivable ways; these groupings are subject to various types of structural (associative) repetition and are hierarchical. Because the music is chunkable and its structure hierarchical, it can be learned—represented and stored efficiently in long-term memory. Consisting of events that clearly exemplify categories of primary parameters such as pitch and rhythm, it supports the possibility of identifiable patterns. All of which means that over multiple listenings, listeners can build up a representation of the music in memory, which can be referred to for "positional" references, for possible linear causal patterns, and for overall form. In other words, in this type of music, we have a sense of where we have been, where we are, and where we are going, and of the overall shape of a piece. Much Western European music of the "classical" period, Indian ragas, jazz, and popular music falls into this category.

The second type of music tries to exist outside of memory by flouting the structural principles mentioned above in what might be referred to as a kind of "memory sabotage." Included in this second type would be some kinds of ethnic and mystical religious music, and some recent European and American experimental music.

Strategies for Memory Sabotage

These may be divided roughly into (1) information strategies; and (2) memory length strategies, although the two are certainly related. Information strategies work primarily by constructing patterns whose distribution of information makes them difficult to process, whereas memory length strategies operate by using events or silences whose time lengths exceed the limits of short-term memory. Information strategies may be further divided into high-information and low-information strategies.

High-Information Strategies

Strategies that involve high information and low redundancy, such as using random pitch and rhythm patterns, produce music that cannot be fitted into a schema (standardized musical form): because each event is unpredictable, all events are equally unexpected. This precludes all but the lowest level of grouping, and even groupings at this level are randomly formed (see figure 13.1) An interesting aspect of high-information music in its purest form is that because style depends on the recognition of various kinds of differentiated and repeating patterns, such music cannot really have a style in that sense (Meyer, 1989: 344). Nor, therefore, can it *develop* stylistically and historically (in a linear way), because it is a kind of limiting case.

One way of producing high-information music is by generating events randomly. That is, the actual values of parameters such as pitch and duration are selected, not through decisions made intentionally by the musician, but by some random process. Because we can never know what to expect in this kind of music, our attention may become more focused on individual events and their particular qualities, each of which is not consistently part of any order higher than the grouping or the phrase level. Removing memory and anticipation from the situation leaves us with nothing but the present to focus on. The ideal of such music would be not to engage long-term memory at all, a state approaching some kinds of meditation.

Another high-information strategy might be called "anticategorical." This kind of music attempts to create events that cannot be easily categorized, that cannot easily be framed in a tuning or durational system. This essentially eliminates the concept of a primary parameter and blurs the distinction between structure and expression (see Clarke, 1987b). Uncategorizable events, such as continuously gliding pitches, noises, and highly irregular rhythms, cannot form easily chunkable patterns: the nature of the events themselves precludes the identification of patterns. Instead, they produce a kind of "nuance overload," where every sound is a unique event and cannot easily be identified as being in the same category as another event. Note that determined listeners, by listening to a particular example of any of these high-information kinds of music many, many times, might eventually be able to predict what was going to happen next, and hence might in a sense create a kind of schema for themselves.

Low-Information Strategies

At the opposite extreme, low-information music keeps change to a minimum, with only the bare minimum of contrast necessary to sustain interest. This is usually accomplished through a great deal of repetition on various levels. The limiting case of a low-information strategy consists of single events sustained for very long times. (Note that some religious traditions use this type of strategy in chanting to focus on the present.)

Usually, low-information strategies at the melodic/rhythmic level involve gestures that are very similar, but not necessarily identical. Because they tend to interfere with each other, such gestures, which I shall refer to as "formatted gestures," are *difficult* to separately identify and remember. If we think of formatted gestures as categories at the melodic and rhythmic level, and small variations in pattern as within-category distinctions, we realize that we are talking about a kind of *syntactical nuances*, defined here as small variations in musical events *at the pattern level*. Which is to say, a particular pattern and other highly similar patterns form a kind of category, with a boundary located at points where perceptibly different patterns occur. Occurrences of these highly similar patterns are within-category distinctions. Because these syntactical nuances are all instances of the same category, they are subject to interference effects, or confusion of similar instances in long-term memory. Being within-category distinctions, they are perceptible but not well remembered. Such nuances often give us the sense that the present is somehow "varying" in relation to the past, but we cannot remember exactly how.

In traditional music using balanced-information (neither high or low) strategies, different rhythm and pitch patterns usually occur at different points, and we can usually put these different patterns into different categories. In the transitional sections of such music some of these categories are transformed into others. These patterns often fall into families, distinguished by characteristic features, such as particular types of contrast in duration or pitch motion.

In formatted gestures, by contrast, these distinguishing characteristics are kept to a minimum. (In fact, one recent Western version of this type of music is referred to as "minimalism.") Patterns are constructed so as to seem equivalent. This greatly lessens the sense of moving through different places in a piece. It is as though we keep being presented with slightly different versions of the same present, and the only distinctions we can make are almost ungraspable nuances. This amounts to musical exploitation of what have been referred to previously as "memory interference effects." Examples of formatted gestures would be the repetition of a particular melodic or rhythmic contour. In the most extreme version of formatted gestures, the rhythmic and melodic contours consist of highly similar durations and intervals: gestures are constructed so as to have very little internal differentiation, such as having all events of the same duration, with a melodic contour consisting of all similar intervals all moving in the same direction. The basic issue with formatted gestures is exactly how much similarity can be used while still maintaining interest. Generally, of course, something has to change to prevent habituation and sustain the listeners' interest. Note that it is quite possible for music to use low-information strategies in some parameters, and high-information strategies in others.

Memory Length Strategies

Although overlapping with low-information strategies, memory length strategies involve, not particular types of patterns and their information content, but duration and silence, using these in ways that make musical information difficult to process. Some memory length strategies attempt to break up the continuity of the present by creating situations in which short-term memory cannot perform its usual function. Because we know that the length of short-term memory is relatively fixed, simply separating events or groupings by more than this amount of time will tend to destroy any higher-level coherence. Separating individual events or gestures by large pauses of 10–12 sec will usually accomplish this. This effectively sabotages coherence on the rhythmic level, and prevents us from having any clear sense of time interval, durational proportion or phrasing.

Other memory length strategies do the opposite, making the present so by creating events so long that it is impossible to put their duration in a framework, which tends to work against closure and thus also to keep us in the present, for example, some contemporary Western drone musics, which consist of a single, slowly changing continuous sound. Indeed, music of this type may be thought of as a single extended event, which begins at the beginning of the piece, and ends at the end.

Notes

1. Note that listeners' perceptions of identifiable rhythmic patterns are largely dependent on the inference of pulse and meter, which are constructed from other, more basic aspects of musical events (time intervals and accents). Because of this, the status of rhythm as a primary parameter could be considered an *emergent* phenomenon. See Hopkins, 1990: 29–30. (In fact any rhythmic activity outside of a metrical framework could probably be considered as the operation of a secondary parameter.) Also note that in this chapter I will refer to rhythmic notation as a system of durations, because that is how they are conceptualized in Western music, even though rhythmic patterns are patterns of time intervals and accents.

2. It should be noted that some musical traditions, most notably, aboriginal Australian didjeridu playing and Mongolian throat singing, do use timbral *contour* somewhat like a primary parameter, but in a limited way. (In both traditions, timbral contour is enhanced by extremely restricted pitch content.) However, neither musical tradition develops the kind of multiple reidentifiable patterns that can be developed with more clearly primary parameters. For a different view, see Lerdahl, 1987.

3. I am well aware that some contemporary composers have attempted to organize the parameters of timbre, tempo, loudness, and the like as though they were primary parameters, but believe that none of these attempts has been successful, at least for the average listener. It is possible, however, that the composers themselves, through a great deal of overlearning, are able to hear these parameters in something like a syntactical way.

4. Some non-Western musical notation systems are not graphic, but language based, such as those used in recent times for North Indian raga music and Indonesian Gamelan music. Generally speaking, these systems devote their most sophisticated notation to primary parameters: indeed, because primary parameters can articulate the most complex patterns, the most complex resources of nearly all musical notation systems are used to represent them.

5. For an excellent summary of the perceptual and cognitive constraints on musical forms in general as well as on syntax, see McAdams, 1989. For an explanation of musical syntax, see Swain, 1997, pp. 25–43.

6. Or if a closural pattern such as falling pitch *is* learned (for example, because it occurs in the intonation patterns of language), it does not seem to be learned in a *culturally specific* way. As previously noted, closure by dropping pitch is a feature of many, many languages, and many musics as well.

7. For a discussion of what constitutes a stable "thing," see Barnett, 1953, pp. 411–448. For a discussion of the possible evolution of the neural basis of perceptual constancy, see Fuster, 1995, pp. 32–33.

8. Actually, there is no way to say what color the piece of paper "really is" without establishing some arbitrary standard of ambient illumination. See Hardin, 1988, pp. 59–91.

9. This usage of the term *constancy* is at least somewhat metaphorical.

10. Note that the problem with the "classical" information theory of Shannon and Weaver (1949) from a psychological point of view is that the physical message is only part of the story. As a mathematical theory, designed to deal with precisely specified and limited groups of symbols in electronic communication systems, information theory did not really take psychological context into account. In relation to people's perceptions, information can change radically with context. It is therefore important that the memory of the listener be included in the concept of information. Rather than being entirely "in" the music, or "in" the listener's head, information is best described as a dynamic, evolving relationship between the two. There is, however, no single term that clearly portrays this type of relationship. In this chapter, I have used the term "informativeness," rather than information *content*, to try to include the idea that information has to be information *for* someone, and is not merely "contained" in a musical message. I should also point out that several sets of terms have been used to describe the situation discussed here, all falling within the area of study referred to as semiotics. The term "message" was used in the original formulation of information theory of Shannon and Weaver. The terms *signal* and *sign* have been used to refer to what I am calling "the musical sound," and the term code has been used to refer to what I call "schemas" and "repertoires of musical culture." For a good summary of the many meanings of these semiotic terms, see Nöth, 1990, pp. 79–91, 206–212.

11. In the musical semiotics of Nattiez (Nattiez, 1990), the level of the physical representation is called the "neutral level." The state of mind of the musician and the state of mind of listeners are referred to as the "poietic" and "esthesic," respectively. Fred Lerdahl refers to the musicians' and listeners' levels as the "compositional grammer" and the "listening grammer." See Lerdahl, 1988. The relevance of the idea of the neutral level is somewhat contested at present. See, for example, Lerdahl, 1997. Note that I am using the expression "states of mind" here in a very broad way, that includes various levels of awareness (from implicit to explicit) of *body states*. Information about states of the body can be an important factor in music.

12. My use of the term "influence" here is purposeful. Some recent writing on music cognition invokes the concept of an "experienced listener" (see, for instance, Lerdahl and Jakendoff, 1983). This is essentially a listener whose repertoire of categories and schemas is very similar to that of a musician. This generally involves musical training. Although I would still use the concept of a *dedicated* listener, who is interested in music and listens to it repeatedly, I think that truly experienced listeners are not as common as is often assumed (see Berz and Kelly, 1998). I would say that the most common relationship between the musician's

states of mind and those of listeners is transformative and often metaphorical or poetic (see Burham, 1999, Sibley, 1993, and Higgins, 1997). Indeed, the further one gets from experienced listeners, the more transformative the relation between the states of mind of the musician and those of the listener can be. I think that, although much more difficult to pin down, the states of mind of less-than-experienced listeners are important.

13. Of course the introduction of notation into the situation entails further complexities, which, for the sake of simplicity (and because much of the world's music is not notated), I shall not consider here. In addition, a further distinction can be made between a musician's and listeners' own descriptions of their states of mind, on the one hand, and inferences made by others about those states of mind, on the other. See Nattiez, 1990.

14. With the understanding that this ideal is rarely if ever perfectly achieved. See Sperber, 1996, pp. 32–61. This is why I have used the term "experientially correlated" in chapter 9, to allow for the listener's own associative and metaphorical construction of musical meaning. My description also assumes that we are talking about musicians whose goal is communication. There are twentieth-century Western musicians, such as John Cage, who do not see the function of their music as the representation of their own states of mind at all. (It is also worth noting that I am using the term *musician* here in a way that includes composers, improvising musicians, and performers who make compositional decisions in their playing. Where listeners are listening to unfamiliar music of a culture other than their own, what is occurring would have to be considered communication in the broadest sense.

15. All of this implies a broad notion of what constitutes communication. See Noth, 1990, pp. 168–172.

16. Under certain special kinds of circumstances, usually involving danger, *sensitization* rather than habituation may result. This actually results in the output of impulses from a nerve cell being *higher* than normal. For more on habituation, see Baars, 1988, pp. 180, 190–195.

17. I am aware that there is a scientifically defined notion of time as "objective" in relation to irreversible phenomena. This does not, however, bear on the *subjective* notion of time I am concerned with here.

18. Note that issues around the existence or nonexistence of internal clocks and their significance are far from solved. Clearly, various types of internal clock models are important in explaining research data from animals. See, for example, Gallistel, 1990, pp. 221–223.

19. For an interesting literary treatment of this phenomenon, see Mann, 1966.

20. For classic articles about the little-studied phenomenon of long-term memory over long time periods. See Wagenaar, 1986; Linton, 1982.

21. Note that episodic memories can have a time order, even though they are long-term memories, probably because (1) they are recalled in chunks, and memories on the chunk level have an internal time order, that is, once elements are associated in a chunk, their time order becomes fixed; and (2) they are often organized by temporal schemas (generalized, abstract, chunked models of typical time orders).

22. Exactly what forms long-term memories (mental representations) take, and even their existence are major issues in the philosophy of mind and cognitive science. For a condensed

discussion of these issues, see Bechtel, 1988, pp. 40–78. For a discussion of the importance of hierarchy to memory, see Barsalou, 1992, pp. 126–127, 140–142; and Bigand, 1993, pp. 254–258.

23. Note that this chunking is reinforced by the fact that the words for the last letters of the first, second, fourth, sixth, and seventh chunks rhyme. The reason why the fourth chunk is larger than the others is probably to get it to rhyme.

24. For a musical example of this, see Benjamin Brinner's description of Javenese Gamelan musicians trying to remember their music out of sequence, in Brinner, 1995, pp. 69–70.

25. In my own experience, it is fairly common that some small musical fragment early in the music will remind me of a larger landmark event some distance in the future. Although somewhat explicit, this "reminding" is usually rather vague, and does not seem to disturb my ongoing experience of the music.

26. Note that the subjects tested by Deliege and by Deliege et al. included both experienced (trained musicians) and inexperienced listeners.

27. For an exposition on the implicit nature of recognition in music, see Levinson, 1997.

28. For a graphic demonstration of extent of recall for two text sequences that are somewhat similar (in relation to chunking considerations) to the two sequences discussed here, see Rubin, 1995, pp. 179–186.

29. This is sometimes referred to as "heterarchical" organization.

30. My definition of linearity is primarily driven by the idea of expectation. The more we have expectations about the eventual goals of a passage of music, the more linear it is by my definition. Associative connections in this sense do not necessarily imply linearity. We can find ourselves in a place similar to somewhere we have previously been *without* the feeling of having *progressively* arrived there.

31. Note that in these experiments rehearsal was prevented, therefore this finding does not conflict with the idea that chunks remembered in the long term can have time order.

32. For an example of how this effect is observed even for the structure of individual words, see Rubin, 1995, p. 73.

33. For an extended discussion of the development of language in relation to memory, see Donald, 1991.

34. My discussion of linearity owes much to Kramer's book.

35. For some observations about whether large-scale tonal structure of this type is actually perceived by listeners, see Cook, 1994, pp. 70–76; Cook, 1992, pp. 43–73; and Karno and Konecni, 1992. Whether these results hold true for truly experienced listeners is an interesting question.

36. Some of Elliot Carter's music attempts to do this by using large-scale polyrhythms. See Schiff, 1983. In addition, much nontonal music relies on "salience hierarchies." See Imberty, 1993.

Postscript

As I noted in the preface, many of the ideas presented here are theoretical, and hence subject to change with the acquisition of new data. Some of the generalizations they make may well turn out to vary across cultures more than we now realize. Many of the phenomena discussed here have been studied in isolation from real musical contexts. Certainly new things will be discovered as research moves toward more realistic situations (Aiello, 1994). One area of developing interest is the variation of listening experience across *individuals* (see Higgins, 1997). The concept of the experienced listener is beginning to be examined on a number of levels, influenced no doubt by the large numbers of people who enjoy and understand music but who are not trained musicians. Related to this is a reexamination of the relationship between "analytical" and "poetic" listening and critcism (see for instance Burnham, 1999, and Sibley, 1993). Since virtually all language used to discuss music is metaphorical, this distinction really represents two ends of a continuum. Another exciting area of research, implicit memory and cognition, may eventually yield many insights into the emotional significance of music.

It is my hope that I have fairly represented some of the larger trends in the field, presenting ideas sufficiently established that they will not be judged completely invalid in the near future. Although my original purpose was to inform young composers of some cognitive constraints on their activity, it is also my hope that general readers with an interest in music and psychology will find my book of interest. If in some small way it honors the sentiment of its opening quotation, it will have accomplished its purpose.

Appendix: Listening Examples

This is a short list selected from the much larger list of recordings that I use in my class. I have tried to include music from a diverse range of cultures to show that the principles demonstrated in this book have some cross-cultural validity. Any music with clearly defined phrase structure is useful for demonstrating grouping. I tend to prefer solo instrumental and vocal music, as this often has very unambiguous phrasing. All selections listed below are on compact disc.

Phrasing by Pause and Duration

· A remarkable example of a melody having only two pitches can be found on *The Igede of Nigeria* (Music of the World CDT-117), track 1. This is also an excellent example of closure by downward pitch movement, and lengthening of duration.

· A Gregorian chant with only three pitches can be found on *Ecole Notre Dame: Messe du Jour de Noël* (Harmonia Mundi HMA 1901148), track 5. This chant is also a good example of pitch closure by downward motion.

· Another good example with clear phrasing and downward pitch and durational closure is "Prochula se Yana," on *Balkana: The Music of Bulgaria* (Hannibal HNCD 1335), track 12.

· An interesting demonstration of the relationship between phrasing and human physiology, on the long end of the phrase length spectrum, is "Sokkan," on *Breath-Sight* (Tall Poppies TP 015), track 1. This shakuhatchi (bamboo flute) music is a meditation on the breath.

· A demonstration of phrasing with musical materials that are somewhat more complex than simple pitches, "Aerobics 2," can be found on *Evan Parker: Saxophone Solos* (Chronoscope CPE2002-2), track 2.

· An example of variable phrase length is "Klavierstück VI," on *Karlheinz Stockhausen: Klavierstücke* (hat ART CD 6142), track 6.

· A good example of rhythmic phrasing using percussion instruments can be found on *Max Roach: Percussion Bittersweet* (Impulse GRD 122), track 1, 4:52–6:52.

Phrasing by Pitch Contour

These are some examples of music that has even note durations, where phrases are established by pitch contour.

· An example of phrasing established entirely by pitch contour is "Music in Fifths," track 3 on *Philip Glass* (Electra Nonesuch 9 79326-2).

· Another example of music that makes clear use of pitch contour to establish phrasing is the first movement of J. S. Bach, *Cello Suite in G major*—on Janos Starker, *Bach Suites for Solo Cello Complete* (Mercury 432 756-2), disc 1, track 1.

Melody: Tuning System

· "Cadence on the Wind," on *Terry Riley: The Harp of New Albion* (Celestial Harmonies 2CD CEL 018/19 14018-2), disc 2, track 1. Played on a grand piano tuned in Riley's system of just intonation.

· "Pavane en Fa Dièse Mineur," on *Les Pièces de Clavessin de M Louis Couperin*, vol. 2 (Astrée E 8732), track 14. A pre–equal temperament piece, played here in its original mean-tone tuning.

· "13-Note Etude," on *Twelve Microtonal Etudes for Electronic Music Media* (Cedille Records CDR 90000 018), track 6. An electronically realized piece by composer Easley Blackwood in thirteen-tone equal temperament, so different from the twelve-tone equal temperament we are used to hearing that its uniqueness is quite clear to the ear.

· "Pishdaramad," on *Behnam Manahedji: Master of the Persian Santoor* (Wergo SM 1508-2), track 1. A performance on the santoor, a stringed instrument tuned in the classical Persian-Arabic tuning system, which approximates a 24-tone equal temperament, although of course all of the pitches are never used in a single piece.

Melody: Pitch Categories and Ornamentation

· "Yogure-No-Kyoku," on *Great Masters of the Shakuhachi Flute: Goro Yamaguchi* (Ethnic B 6139), track 1.

· "Piri Sanjo," on *The Ideal of Korean Traditional Wind Ensemble* (JVC VID-25021), track 2. This example includes the use of a vibrato so wide it actually undermines the perception of definite pitch at times.

· *The Art of the Vietnamese Fiddle* (Arion 60417), track 4. This is a wonderful example of Asian bowed stringed-instrument ornamentation.

· "Raga Mian Malhar," on *The Vibrant Violin of Sangeetha Kalanidhi* (Oriental Records AAMS CD140), track 1. An example of the North Indian Gayaki style of instrumental playing, where an instrumentalist imitates all of the subtleties of a vocal performance. Especially interesting are the sliding pitches.

· *Jacques Champion de Chambonnières: Pièces de Clavecin* (Harmonia Mundi 05472 77210 2), track 1. A consideration of ornamentation would not be complete without an example of the delicate flutterings of early French Baroque harpsichord music.

· *The Art of Ornamentation in Early Music* (Vanguard Classics OVC 2537/38). An excellent collection of examples of Western ornamentation in early music, featuring the same music unornamented and then ornamented.

Melody: Streaming

· An excellent technical demonstration of streaming can be found on *Demonstrations of Auditory Scene Analysis*, esp. tracks 1–5. This compact disk is available from MIT Press.

· A demonstration of streaming in solo instrumental music can be found in the fifth movement of J. S. Bach, "Violin Patita no. 2 in D minor," on *Nathan Milstein, Bach: Sonatas and Partitas* (EMI Classics ZDMB 0777 7 64793 2 3), disc 2, track 5, at 4:22 to 5:33.

· Streaming in materials that are not strictly pitched can be heard on *Evan Parker: Conic Sections* (ah um 015), track 4, starting at about 6:00. This entire compact disc is of interest in relation to streaming.

· "Mode de valeurs et d'intensités," on *Messiaen: Gloria Cheng, Piano* (Koch 3-7267-2 H1), track 9.

• An example of streaming in vocal music through yodeling can be found in "Etudes de jodis," on *Gabon: Musique de Pygmées Bibayak* (Occora HM 83), track 2.

• An interesting example of streaming through timbre can be found in this unusual recording of a bamboo Jew's harp, *Voices of the Rainforest* (Rykodisc RCD 10173), track 5.

Melodic Schemas

• "Teak Domreay," on *The Music of Cambodia*, vol. 2 (Celestial Harmonies 13075-2), track 24. This wonderful little melody is a prototypical axial construction—a central pitch with one auxiliary pitch above, and one below.

• "L'oued tin Mentah," on *Touareg*, vol. 1 (al sur ALCD 122 M7 853), track 1.

• "Kong kiun touan-yu" on *Chine: Nan-Kouan*, vol. 1 (Ocora C 559004), track 2.

• Luciano Berio, "Sequenza VIIb," on *The Solitary Saxophone* (BIS CD-640), track 2. This shows that, far from only being a feature of ancient music or ethnic chant, the axial principle is alive and well enough to generate an 8-minute contemporary piece.

• Franco Donatoni, "Tema," on *Ligeti-Donatoni* (Erato 2292-45366-2), track 1, from 14:56 to the end.

• An example of a piece with melodic arches on several levels is Frederic Chopin's "Prelude op. 28, No. 6," track 6 on *Chopin Preludes Maurixio Pollini* (DGG 413796-2). I use this recording in conjunction with Marion Guck's article on this piece (Guck, 1997).

The following are some examples of the gap-fill schema:

• "Bushfire," on *Traditional Aboriginal Music* (Larrikin Records PTY Ltd. EUCD 1224), track 4.

• "Mama Lucy," on *Roots of the Blues* (New World Records 80252-2), track 9.

• "Pengkolan," on *The Sound of Sunda* (Globe Style CDORB 060), track 6, 1:15–2:15.

• "Douce dame jolie," on *Machaut and his Time* (Channel Classics CCS 7094), track 5. A more complex example, with more twists and turns.

• "Raga Sampurna Malkaus," on *Kishori Amonkar* (Music Today A 91006), track 2, 1:34–3:23. Another more complex example.

Rhythm: Tempo

· An example of tempo taken to the limits of human physiology (near the fusion threshold) can be found on *Tambours de la Terre*, vol. 2 (Ethnic B 6774), track 8. Performed by a father-and-son pair of East Indian master drummers, this duet has passages of breathtaking speed, where individual beats happen in such rapid succession they almost fuse into a timbre.

Rhythm: Meter

Some examples of metrical music with a clearly accented first beat include

· "Houses in Motion," on Talking Heads, *Remain in Light* (Sire 6095-2), track 5.
· "Lagu Iama-Pobin Kong Ji Lokl," on *Music from the Outskirts of Jakarta* (Smithsonian Folkways SF 40057), track 1.
· "Om Schar Asmar," on Ali Hassan Kuban, *From Nubia to Cairo* (Shanachi 64036), track 2.
· "Ryo ou Ranjo," on *Gagaku: Court Music of Japan* (JVC VICG 5354-2), track 5.

Rhythm: Metrical Hierarchy

· A demonstration of the subdivision of a slow basic pulse can be found on *Reinhard Flatischler: The Forgotten Power of Rhythm* (LIFERHYTHM), track 5. Track 6 is a demonstration of accenting various beats of the different subdivisions of this basic pulse. This compact disc is a highly useful teaching tool for presenting certain concepts of rhythm. Available from LIFERHYTHM, P. O. Box 806, Mendocino, CA 95460.

Rhythm: Meter versus Grouping

· A nice example of rhythmic phrasing in 4 against a basic rhythm of 3 can be found on *Reinhard Flatischler: The Forgotten Power of Rhythm* (LIFERHYTHM), track 7. Available from LIFERHYTHM, P. O. Box 806, Mendocino CA 95460.
· "Di, Perra Mora," on *El Cancionero de Medinaceli* (Astree E 8764), track 11. This lovely (and beautifully recorded) example from the Spanish Renaissance pits the grouping of the melody against an uneven 5/4 meter.

Rhythm: Accented Beats without Basic Pulse

· Anthony Braxton, *Creative Orchestra Music* (RCA 6579-2 RB), track 6, 0:52 to 2:39. An example of more or less equally spaced accented events without a consistent tempo for the events in between them, and hence no sense of meter.

· "4-voice canon 5," on Larry Polansky, *The Theory of Impossible Melody* (ARTIFACT RECORDINGS 1004), track 5. This example also has regularly repeating sequences of events, but at different tempos, and the resulting "interferance" patterns between the rhythms produces a very complex rhythmic result.

· John Corbett, "The Silent Treatment" and "Road Rage," tracks 4 and 11 on *I'm Sick About My Hat* (Atavistic ALF116CD). These are interesting experiments with filtering one kind of musical material through the time structure of another, thus preserving the time intervals of the original music, but altering the sounds and accents.

Rhythm: Pulse with Ambiguous Meter

· Paul Lansky, "Idle Chatter," on *New Computer Music* (Wergo WER 2010-50), track 1. This computer-generated vocal piece has a clear pulse, but no strong consistent accent pattern, and hence an ambiguous sense of meter.

· The first movement of Steve Reich, *Tehillim* (ECM 1215), track 1. This piece has a complex overlay of echolike parts, creating a constantly shifting pattern of accents.

· The third of Peter Garland's "Songs of Mad Coyote," on *Border Music* (WHAT NEXT? RECORDINGS WN0008), track 7. Another example of music without regular meter, but with a clear pulse.

Rhythm: Meter without Regular Tempo

· An excellent example of the "rubber time" of Indonesian Gamelan music, which maintains metrical cycles while changing tempo, is "Topeng Panji: Kembang Sungsang-Owet Owetan-Lontang Gede," on *The Gamelan of Cirebon* (King Records KICC 5130), track 4.

Rhythm: Uneven and Compound Meter

· A five-beat meter can be found on *Reinhard Flatischler: The Forgotten Power of Rhythm* (LIFERHYTHM), track 4. Available from LIFERHYTHM, P. O. Box 806, Mendocino CA 95460. Track 8 has a good pattern in a nine-beat meter.

· A seven-beat meter can be found on Marcus Stockhausen, *Aparis* (ECM LC 1404 841 774-2), track 1, starting at 6:18.

· A very nice eleven-beat meter (3 + 5 + 3), established by pitch grouping, can be found on Glen Velez, *Ramana* (Nomad 50301), track 2.

· A seven-beat meter can be found in "Mitro le Mitro" on *Bisserov Sisters, Music from the Pirin Mountains* (Pan Records Pan 133CD), track 12.

· An eleven-beat meter can be found on *Distant Hills* by *Oregon* (Vanguard VMD-79341), track 4.

· An example of a fourteen-beat meter is "Raag Des" on *a flavor of india* (Music Club 50051), track 3.

Rhythm: Long Meter

· An example of an East Indian Tala (the sixteen-beat "Teental") that has a recurring rhythmic cycle about 40 sec long (note that what is referred to as a beat in this meter is equivalent to two beats of what can be felt as the basic pulse). The metrical cycle is clearly reinforced by the recurring melodic mukra pattern. "Raga Bhoop" on *Kishori Amonkar Live* (EMI Gramaphone Company of India Limited CD-PSLP 5130), track 1.

· Another example of Tala with a basic twelve-beat cycle (Ektal). What are referred to as beats in this case are one-fourth the tempo of the basic pulse. This cycle is 68 sec in length, "Raag Yaman" on *Dr. Prabha Atre* (TIPS TCCD-5117), track 2.

Rhythm: Miscellaneous and Complex

· Ronald Shannon Jackson, "Tears for the Earthbound," on *Pulse* (Celluloid CELL 5011) CD, side 2, track 6. An example of music that oscillates between pulsed and non-pulsed, creating an interesting kind of rhythmic tension.

· "Amores, Trio for 9 Tom-Toms and Pod Rattle," on *John Cage: Works for Percussion* (Wergo WER 6203-2 286 203-2), track 3. This piece also has moments of both pulsed and unpulsed rhythm.

• "Damp Ankles," on Frank Zappa, *Jazz from Hell* (Rykodisc 10549), track 6. This example has two layers, one metrical and one nonmetrical, running simultaneously.

One kind of nonmetrical and nonpulsed music is based on speech rhythm.

• A classic example is Eric Dolphy's duet with Charles Mingus, "What Love," on *Charles Mingus Presents Charles Mingus* (Candid CD 9005), track 3, 8:35–12:42.

• Another good example of speech-based rhythm, in the considerably more formalized "rhetorical" style of the early French Baroque lute preludes, is Ennemond Gaultier, *SUITE EN D.LA. RÉ MINEUR*, on *Pièces de Luth du Vieux Gaultier* (Astrée E 8703), track 1.

Form: Ambiguous Sectional Boundaries

• A set of pieces interesting for the ambiguity and brevity of their sectional organization is Gottfried Michael Koenig, *3 Asko Pieces* (Wergo LC 0846).

Form: Linearity

Although harmonic motion, on which much of linearity in Western music depends, is not covered in this book, here are three clear examples:

• A classic, full-blown example of linear harmonic motion is the Liebestod from Richard Wagner, *Tristan und Isolde*, on *Wagner: Greatest Hits* (RCA Victor 60847-2-RG), track 6.

• A very nice traditional example of how discontinuity can contribute to linearity can be found in the third movement of Ludwig von Beethoven, *String quartet*, opus 135, on the Guarneri Quartet, *Beethoven • String Quartets Streichquartette Op. 127 & Op. 135* (Philips 420 926-2), track 7, 2:56–4:48.

• A somewhat more contemporary example of nondirected linearity that progresses harmonically toward increasing dissonance and noise is the beginning of region 3 of Karlheinz Stockhausen, *Hymnen* (Stockhausen 10 A–D), disc D, tracks 1–5. This set of compact discs is available from the Electronic Music Foundation, 116 N. Lake Avenue, Albany, NY 12206.

In chapter 12, I mentioned that the scale is a kind of prototypical pattern of linear transition. Here is an example:

• Paul Hindemith, "Concert Music for Strings and Brass," on *Hindemith: Mathis der Maler-Symphonie* (DGG 429 404-2), track 4, 5:18–5:29.

Linearity can be created by means other than harmonic motion. Here are two examples of linearity created by pitch motion without tonal-harmonic motion.

• A nice example of a multisectional transition can be found on *Kronos Quartet: Witold Lutoslawski String Quartet* (Electra Nonesuch 79255-2), part 2, track 2, 7:34–9:11. Note that the motion of different sections of this transition takes place in different parameters.

• A very interesting linear sequence can be found in Gerard Grisey, "Modulations," on *Boulez* (ERATO 4509-98496-2), disc 4, track 3, 0:00–4:15. This is a progression toward consonance and from opposition to continuity.

Here are two examples of solo music, where linearity is created primarily by graduated pitch motion (in the case of the Berio piece, much of it in the form of continuous contours):

• Luciano Berio, "Sequenza V," for solo trombone, on *Luciano Berio* (Wergo WER 6021-2 286 021-2), track 4, 1:30–5:55.

• Edgard Varèse, "Density 21.5," for solo flute, on *Varèse* (Sony SMK 45844), track 3.

• An interesting improvised example of linearity in secondary parameters such as articulation and timbre is Mats Gustafsson *The Education of Lars Jerry* (XERIC-CD-100), track 1, 0:00 to 5:00.

Form: Nonlinear Pieces

• An early classic of European nonlinear music (on the formal level—the piece is weakly linear at the middle-ground level) is Igor Stravinsky, "Symphonies of Wind Instruments," on *Stravinsky: The Composer*, vol. 8 (Music Masters 01612-67103-2), track 5. This is a multisectional nonlinear piece.

• Another early example is the "Jardin du Sommeil d'Amour," the sixth movement of Olivier Messiaen, *Turanglila Symphonie* (Forlane UCD 16504-5), disc 1, track 6. A single nonlinear section.

• A more recent example of a very weakly sectional nonlinear piece is "Music in 12 Parts," part 1, on *Philip Glass: Music in 12 Parts* (Virgin Records 91311-2), track 1.

· A recent example of a single-section nonlinear piece is John Cage, "Thirteen," on *John Cage: Thirteen* (Radio Bremen CPO 999 227-2).

· A recent multisectional nonlinear piece is Kevin Volans, "Kneeling Dance," on *Piano Circus* (ARGO 440 294-2), track 1.

· There are many cultures that have produced music that is not linear. One example is the dense polyphony of the Central African pygmies. "Chant après la collecte du miel," on *Pygmées du Haut-Zaïre* (Fonti Musicali fmd 190), track 1.

· Another example of non-Western nonlinear nonlinear music is "Solo de Khen Hmong: Evocation de la vie Champetre," *on l'Art du Khen.* (ARION ARN 60367), track 4. This is a solo on the Asian mouth organ known as the Khen.

Form: Memory Sabotage

· An excellent example of the attempt to frustrate a sense of position in a piece of music is some of the later music of Morton Feldman. For instance, *For Samuel Beckett* (hat ART CD6107), track 1.

· Also interesting in relation to issues about the formation of memory images in relation to a sense of "place" in a piece of music is Morton Feldman, *For Philip Guston* (hat ART CD4-61041-4), a huge piece lasting nearly four and a half hours. Note that the two pieces listed above are very different in their overall form. The first is virtually a single section, whereas the second is a huge multisectional piece. Both make highly skilled use of imperfect repetition, and the exquisite sense of temporal confusion that results from it.

· An example of another approach to sabotaging memory—the use of events greatly extended in time—is LaMont Young, *The Second Dream of the High-Tension Line Stepdown Transformer from the Four Dreams of China* (Gramavision R2 79467).

· An example of reducing a sense of linear time through the use of extended silence between sections (which can create an intensified perception of individual sounds) is *John Cage: Sixty-Two Mesostics Re Merce Cunningham* (hat ART CD 2-6095).

· An example of music that avoids clear syntax by using primarily sounds outside what is traditionally considered "musical" is Helmut Lachenmann, "Reigen Seliger Geister," on *Helmut Lachenmann* vol. 1 (Montaigne MO 782019), track 1.

· Another example in this vein, from the realm of improvised music, is the King Ubu Orchestra, *Binaurality* (Free Music Production CD 49).

Glossary

accent. A rhythmic event or beat that has more weight than, and stands out from, surrounding events. Accents may be created by emphasizing a beat in a number of ways, all related to grouping factors. Accents may be of three kinds, phenomenal, structural, or metrical. Phenomenal accents are created whenever any event stands out from the musical surface by being sufficiently different from the events immediately surrounding it. Structural accents occur at the important points in a phrase, most notably the first and last events. Metrical accents occur on the strong beats of a metrical unit. Regularly recurring patterns of accented beats are the basis of meter. *See also* **beat; meter; rhythmic grouping.**

amplitude. The physical aspect of a sound that is correlated with subjective loudness. Amplitude represents the level of change in air pressure caused by a sound.

analog. Pertaining to representation that is essentially a copy of the thing represented. Analog representations have a point-for-point continuous correspondence with the things that they represent, whereas encoded representations make use of discrete symbols. The representation of sounds stored in echoic memory is believed to be analog, whereas many representations of sounds processed through long-term memory are encoded. *See also* **echoic memory; long-term memory.**

association. A process by which memories become connected such that the activation of one memory may cue the other. Associated memories form a context for each other. Association often occurs between memories of events close to each other in space, time, or both. More complex, metaphorical associations may be formed between memories correlated in other ways. Association is a primary organizational feature of human memory. One type of structured, multileveled association is called "hierarchy." *See also* **context; hierarchy.**

attack. The beginning of a sound event, during which its overall acoustical energy is increasing. Some sounds, such as those made by struck percussive instruments, have very rapid attacks (almost instantaneous), while others, such as those of bowed and wind instruments, have slower attacks. The more rapid a sound's attack, the more precise its location in time. Also called "onset." *See also* **decay.**

attack point. The precise point at which a sound is perceived as beginning, regardless of its duration. Rhythmic patterns are distributions of attack points in time. Also called "time point."

basic level.   The level of a conceptual category hierarchy that is the most accessible, and the most frequently used. The basic pulse in a meter and a phrase within a piece of music represent basic levels of tempo and formal hierarchies, respectively. *See also* **basic pulse.**

basic pulse.   A central tempo in a piece of music, around which all other implied tempos are organized. The basic pulse is the tempo to which listeners physically respond most easily, such as by tapping their feet. *See also* **metrical hierarchy.**

beat.   A single basic rhythmic time point, defining a precise position in time. Beats do not have duration. They are inferred from musical events that are equidistant in time, and are the components of a pulse; pulse consists of an undifferentiated succession of identical beats. *See also* **attack point; pulse.**

bottom-up processing.   Information processing at the perceptual level. Unlike top-down processing, bottom-up processing operates primarily on perceptual input and usually does not involve memory. *See also* **top-down processing.**

categorical perception.   A psychological mode of perception wherein things are perceived as belonging to categories with boundaries. Members of the same perceptual category appear to be similar, even though they may be measurably different from each other in some way. By the same token, members of different perceptual categories (especially near a category boundary) may appear to be more different from each other than their measured values would suggest. Perceptual categories may be learned or innate. Categorical perception uses mental processing efficiently, by eliminating discrimination that is not needed. *See also* **category; nuance.**

category.   In cognitive psychology, a grouping together of features of experience or memory. Categories are collections of perceptual representations or concepts that seem somehow related. Categories may be perceptual or conceptual. Some perceptual categories are innate, whereas other perceptual and most conceptual categories are learned. One type of category has a central or prototypical member. A musical scale with a central pitch is an example of this type of category structure. Scale tones and intervals are melodic categories; duration scaling, beat position, and some aspects of meter are rhythmic categories; and sections of musical pieces are formal categories. Categories are the components of schemas. *See also* **categorical perception; conceptual category; schema.**

centrality.   A way of making a particular musical element such as a particular pitch category or a particular beat in a metrical cycle central by repeatedly marking it, and making it stand out in some way. This centrality makes these elements seem more important. Particular pitches and beats are given their centrality primarily through repetition. By being returned to many times, these elements generate expectations of this return. *See also* **meter; tonality.**

chroma.   Any of twelve basic pitch categories of the European equal-tempered pitch scale. Although there are many different frequencies that can be resolved by the human auditory system, there are only twelve different chromas in our tuning system, each identified by a different name, such as C, C-sharp, D, D-sharp, or E. Because each chroma repeats at the octave, after eleven intervening pitches, pitch names often have an octave designation added, such as C1, C2, or C3. Owing to the unusual status of the octave relationship within human perception, notes with the same chroma (for example, two E-flats an octave apart) can be heard as highly similar even though they are different in pitch height, a phenomenon known as "octave equivalence." Chroma therefore forms a second dimension of pitch similarity, after pitch height. *See also* **octave; pitch; pitch height.**

chunking. A way of reducing short-term memory load by coding at a higher level. Chunks are small groups of elements (5–9) that, by being frequently associated with each other, form higher-level units, which themselves become elements in memory. An example of chunking might be memorizing a telephone number by converting it from single to double digits, from two-eight-one, one-four-eight-four, say, to two–eighty-one, fourteen–eighty-four. Chunking is essential to the hierarchical organization of information, which makes its mental representation in memory much easier and more efficient. *See also* **hierarchy; short-term memory.**

closure. The tendency of perceptual groupings to have beginning and ending boundaries. Closure tends to occur at points where changes in degree of similarity or proximity occur. That is, boundaries tend to be created where new kinds of events occur, or where the distance in time or pitch interval between events changes. Closure may be partial, and establishing degrees of closure is essential to establishing hierarchies, or multiple levels of organization in music and language. *See also* **grouping.**

conceptual category. A long-term memory structure that groups related items together, treating them as somehow the same. Conceptual categories are usually learned. Many of the organizational aspects of musical cultures are systems of conceptual categories. *See also* **category.**

constancy. A perceptual-cognitive mechanism that maintains our perception of a single thing or quality, even though sensory input may be quite variable. For example, we are able to maintain the perception of a physical object that has a stable size as we approach it, even though the retinal image of this object gets larger. Constancy is a result of perceptual categorization.

context. In cognitive psychology, a web of associations connected with a particular memory. When a particular memory is recalled, much of its associated context is primed for recall as well. Just as a particular memory can cause the priming of a context, so a rich context can provide many alternative pathways to recall of that particular memory. Not all contexts are conscious, however: unconscious contexts, which include schemas, can guide consciousness without ever entering awareness themselves. *See also* **association; schema.**

contour. In music, a particular and characteristic pattern of upward and downward melodic motion, which, following the spatial metaphor of melody, is described as though it were visual. Contour is one of the pattern aspects of melody, and under some conditions, melodies can be recognized by their contour alone. Contour can also be applied to rhythms, describing their movement through longer and shorter durations or time intervals.

musical culture. An aggregate of evolving musical concepts and practices shared by a group of individuals. Through schemas and conceptual categories (contexts) formed in the minds of those individuals, musical culture structures expectations about many aspects of music. *See also* **context; schema.**

decay. The ending of a sound, during which its overall acoustical energy is decreasing or dying away. Some sounds, such as drumbeats, have very rapid, short decays, while others, such as piano notes played with the damper pedal held down, have long decays. *See also* **attack**.

downbeat. The first beat in a metrical cycle, and the beat usually receiving the greatest emphasis in the whole cycle. Meter is established by the repeated emphasis of the downbeat. *See also* **meter**.

duration. The length of time that a rhythmic musical event actually lasts. Duration is distinguished from the time interval between sounds, which is the distance between event onsets. Not every musical event lasts until the beginning of the next event. *See also* **time interval**.

echoic memory. The first stage of auditory memory, echoic memory is a sensory memory of large capacity that decays rapidly, like an echo. Information persisting as echoic memory is in the form of raw sensory data that are not coded or conceptualized yet. Its function is to allow sensory data to persist long enough so that coding and recognition can take place.

episodic memory. A type of long-term memory for specific events, in a specific time order, and in relation to the self. Episodic memories are autobiographical, whereas general knowledge, another type of long-term memory, is not. Episodic memory records events as they happen to us. Because, however, remembering is itself an event, episodic memories are copied when they are recollected, and the copy replaces the original. This makes our episodic memories vulnerable to various kinds of transformations and distortions, especially through their interaction with our semantic memory (conceptual) categories and schemas. In a piece of music, episodic memories would be of the details of the sound of particular passages of music and their time order. *See also* **semantic memory**.

event. In cognitive psychology, the perception that something has happened, caused by a detectable change in the environment. Acoustical events are the fundamental perceptual units of music, from which all musical groupings, phrases, sections, and the like are built up.

explicit memory. A type of long-term memory whose contents are available to consciousness, in contrast to implicit memory, another type of long-term memory, whose contents are not. Explicit memory can be further divided into episodic memory and semantic memory, also referred to as "autobiographical memory" and "general knowledge." *See also* **episodic memory; implicit memory; long-term memory; semantic memory**.

feature extraction. A basic process of perception. This happens very early in the perception process, during the persistence of echoic memory. Different features of sounds are believed to be extracted by various special-purpose feature detectors. These features are then "bound" into units that represent objects or events (perceptual categorization). This process must happen before higher-level coding and recognition can take place. Long-term memories are often referred to as bundles of features. *See also* **echoic memory**.

feedback loop. In information processing, a loop connecting the output of a process back into its input. Examples of this are the short-term memory rehearsal process, the connections between long-term memory and feature extraction, and the connections between long-term and short-term memory.

focus of conscious awareness. The part of our experience that is happening right now, the focus of conscious awareness usually consists of a vivid sensory aspect and an activated memory aspect. Its capacity is one to three items at most. The focus of consciousness is different from short-term memory. Items that are currently unrehearsed can be present in short-term memory, but are not in consciousness. *See also* **rehearsal; short-term memory.**

form. In music, any grouping longer than 3–5 sec, the time limit of short-term memory, to include all kinds of sections, movements, and whole pieces. The significance of the concept of musical form is that it cannot be perceived directly, unlike events, groupings, and phrases, but must be built up from representations in long-term memory. Formal (section-length) proportion and long-term thematic associations must be established by comparing different materials through long-term memory; these become clearer as long-term memory strength increases with repeated listening. Indeed, a large part of the recognition of musical form depends on repeated listening. *See also* **grouping.**

frequency. In acoustics, the rate at which a sound-producing body vibrates, generally measured in cycles per second (cps). Human beings hear mechanical vibrations between 20 and 20,000 cps as sound. Relative frequency is related to musical pitch; the sense of "high" or "low" position that we assign to a sound is called its "pitch height." Frequency is measured on a linear scale, whereas pitch, which is constructed from frequency ratios, not equal frequency intervals, is represented logarithmically. *See also* **pitch.**

gist. A general model of what happened in a particular place at a particular time, generally in relation to a fixed set of expectations, or schema, and one of the ways our semantic memory categories and schemas interact with episodic memory. Most often, we do not remember exact details of situations, but only the gist of what went on. Exactly what constitutes a musical gist remains an open question. *See also* **schema.**

grouping. In cognitive psychology, the tendency for individual elements in perception to seem related and to bond together into units; the result of such a process. Grouping may be either innate or learned. Innate grouping appears to happen automatically in perception and occurs without any contribution from long-term memory, whereas learned grouping requires the use of long-term memory. Grouping can occur on multiple levels. Those discussed in this book are basic grouping, phrases, and sections. *See also* **phrase.**

hierarchy. In cognitive psychology, a multileveled structuring of associations in long-term memory, where each higher level includes all the lower ones. Hierarchical memory structuring facilitates moving through large bodies of knowledge stored in the form of small chunks. *See also* **chunking; semantic memory.**

image schema. A type of schema that forms expectations based on fundamental aspects of our embodied physical existence, such as gravity, and motion. Image schemas are believed to be the basis for the consistency of many systems of everyday metaphors. More like implicit than explicit memories, image schemas are not easily translatable into simple statements in language, and can have a physical kinesthetic component. Our earliest, most basic (prelinguistic) memories, which form the foundation of all our later thinking, are believed to be image schematic. *See also* **explicit memory; implicit memory; schema.**

implicit memory. A type of long-term memory whose contents are not available to consciousness. Implicit memories include, most notably, memories of physical skills and memories for distributions of things. Emotional memories may also be implicit. Unlike other kinds of long-term memories, implicit memories are established slowly, with repeated practice, and are often not easily modified. Playing a musical instrument may involve both explicit and implicit memory. For example, reading a particular notated pitch on a page and knowing its fingering on an instrument involve explicit memory, whereas correctly performing all of the other physical actions required to produce that note reliably involves implicit memory. *See also* **explicit memory; long-term memory.**

information.   As used in a technical sense in this text, information is equivalent to the novelty in a message. This novelty exists in relation to a memory context. That is, information is that which is not expected. Every situation brings with it some sort of expectations, and it is primarily when events deviate from these expectations that we are informed in this technical sense. Clichés contain little information, and total nonsense contains the most information of all, because it deviates from our expectations completely. Human cognition has a certain information capacity. Information is the opposite of redundancy. *See also* **context; redundancy.**

intensity.   As used in this book, an increase in neural activity. Intensity can be caused by an increase in any of a variety of physical variables such as speed, pitch, timbre, and loudness. An increase in intensity usually increases musical tension and can help establish linearity. *See also* **linearity.**

interference.   In cognitive psychology, an effect that can occur between long-term memories that are similar. Similar memories can confuse association, interfering with the cuing process, and creating irrelevant pathways that hinder recall. *See also* **association.**

interval.   In music, the relation between two pitches. Intervals can be divided into two general categories, small intervals called "steps" and large intervals called "leaps." Intervals occurring across time (as opposed to simultaneously) may also move in one of two directions, up or down. Sequences of intervals changing across time form the melodic dimension known as pitch "contour." *See also* **contour; pitch.**

linearity.   Progressive musical motion toward one or more goals, achieved by control of musical tension through a progression of the average values of one or more parameters in a particular direction, either increasing or decreasing. Directed linear passages move toward goals of maximum tension, called "climaxes," and toward goals of minimum tension, called "cadences" or "resolutions." Linearity in interesting music is usually not simple, that is, not all parameters change at the same speed, or even in the same direction. By no means is all music linear. *See also* **intensity.**

long-term memory.   A very large, possibly permanent memory, whose contents are usually unconscious. Meaning and understanding are derived by processing present perception through long-term memory. Long-term memory is often divided into explicit memory, available to consciousness, and implicit memory, not available to consciousness. Explicit long-term memory is further divided into semantic and episodic memory. Long-term memory is essential to the comprehension of large-scale musical form. *See also* **episodic memory; explicit memory; implicit memory; semantic memory; schema.**

melody.   A "horizontal" sequence of pitches or approximately pitched sounds similar enough to seem related. Melody is metaphorically described as a kind of spatial motion, and moves upward or downward in steps (small intervals) or leaps (large intervals). The pattern that intervallic motion makes over time is called melodic contour. *See also* **contour; interval; pitch.**

metaphor. In cognitive psychology, a connection between correlated features of two different representations in long-term memory. Metaphors allow memory to "jump" between different memory structures and form new types of associations. *See also* **association.**

meter. A cyclically repeating pattern of accents ("strong" and "weak" beats) that can be inferred from events in music. Meter acts as a temporal frame of reference. When actual rhythmic groupings differ from the standardized grouping patterns of meter, metrical tension results. Because it acts as a norm against which current expectations are compared, meter acts as a schema at the rhythmic level. *See also* **accent; metric tension; schema.**

metrical hierarchy. A distribution of related tempos in a piece of music. These tempos are usually whole-number multiples and subdivisions of a basic pulse, which is the salient tempo that listeners respond to physically (e.g., by tapping their feet).

metrical tension. Tension generated by a mismatch between the distribution of accents implied by meter and actual accents. When accented events fall on weak beats of the meter, metrical tension is the result. This type of tension is completely dependent on a metrical structure. *See also* **meter; rhythmic tension.**

nontonal. Said of music that is constructed without reference to a central pitch. *See also* **pitch, tonality.**

nuances. In music, the changes in musical parameters that take place within a category; for example, small fluctuations in pitch which do not result in a pitch being perceived as belonging to a different pitch category. Nuances, because they exist within a category, are much harder to remember than the categories themselves. Because they exist within a category, nuances are not part of syntax, that is, they do not contribute to pattern differentiation. Nuances do, however frequently represent emotional or expressive information. *See also* **category; syntax.**

objective set. The aspects of organization in a piece that are established by being learned while the piece unfolds, such as various kinds of constancies and pattern relations. In contrast to subjective set, objective set refers only to factors directly present objectively. It refers to detail of an individual piece, and is established by comparisons of details only within that piece. As a collection of evolving schemas, objective set is part of semantic memory. *See also* **schema; semantic memory; subjective set.**

octave. A pitch interval where the frequencies of the two component pitches are in a ratio of 2:1. A special interval in that its pitches can seem closely related (similar) even though fairly far apart in pitch height. The octave is the basis of almost all tuning systems, which use it as a basic interval, that is subdivided into smaller intervals. *See also* **interval; tuning system.**

ornamentation. A kind of structured "noise" introduced into music to provide a blurring of categorical structure. Musical tuning systems with small numbers of pitches often have highly ornamented styles of playing and singing to provide interest and uncertainty. *See also* **category; nuances; pitch.**

parallel process. A process in which many activities take place simultaneously, rather than one by one, as they do in a serial process. Because we are most often able to quickly retrieve memories from the enormous amount of information stored there, the activation of long-term memory is believed to be a large-scale parallel process. *See also* **serial process.**

parameter. A musical variable. Aspects of a sound that can change and have different values, parameters are divided into primary parameters, which can be scaled into discernible proportional series of discrete recognizable values (e.g., scales), and secondary parameters, which cannot. *See also* **primary parameter; secondary parameter; syntactical parameters.**

perceptual binding. A psychological process whereby the elementary features of perception are bound together into objects and events. *See also* **feature extraction.**

perceptual category. *See* **categorical perception.**

phrase. In music, the largest grouping of events that can fit within the limits of short-term memory. Phrases usually consist of several smaller groupings of events held together by temporal proximity. Phrase length is often correlated with some human physiological variable, such as the length of a breath or the length of time it takes to move a bow completely across a string. Phrases are often separated from each other by pauses. *See also* **grouping.**

pitch. The aspect of musical sounds that is correlated with frequency and gives them the quality of "highness" and "lowness," referred to as "pitch height." To display this quality, a sound has to have a certain basic minimum of repetition in its microstructure. The opposite of pitch in this sense is a sound with no repetition in its microstructure, which is called noise. Differences in height between pitches are called pitch intervals. Different pitches that have equal differences in pitch height (the same interval) between them have their frequencies in the same ratio. *See also* **frequency; interval.**

primary parameter. An aspect of musical sound that can be represented as a system of categories, and used in musical syntax to create identifiable patterns. Primary parameters are pitch, harmony, and duration. *See also* **category; syntax; syntactical parameter.**

priming. A process whereby the recall of a particular memory causes the low-level activation of other associated memories (a context), without this process necessarily becoming conscious. Priming, which makes it more likely that some of those semiactivated memories will also be recalled, is a type of implicit memory. *See also* **association; context; implicit memory.**

proximity. In cognitive psychology, the principle that groupings form from perceptual elements close to each other in time. The principle of proximity is believed to be innate (i.e., not learned). *See also* **echoic memory; feature extraction; similarity.**

pulse. In music, a uniform succession of identical, unaccented time points, or beats, inferred from musical events percieved to be equidistant in time. The beats of a pulse form a temporal frame of reference for the time intervals of rhythmic patterns. The rate at which the beats of a pulse occur is referred to as a tempo. *See also* **beat.**

recognition. In cognitive psychology, a process whereby something in current experience, cues its own long-term memory. *See also* **long-term memory.**

redundancy. As used in this book, the repetition common to all structured messages. Because of limitations of short-term memory and other cognitive factors, messages we can easily comprehend are constructed out of fairly small numbers of basic elements formed into many different patterns, which themselves display redundancy on a higher level. Messages displaying no redundancy, even though they contain a maximum of information, are incomprehensible, as are messages that are totally redundant and therefore contain no information. Redundancy is the opposite of information. It is worth noting that at higher cognitive levels, involving individual knowledge, what constitutes redundancy and information becomes much more contextual. *See also* **information.**

rehearsal. In cognitive psychology, the active maintenance of elements in short-term memory. Conscious rehearsal consists of repeating something to ourselves to remember it for a longer amount of time. Rehearsal is the primary way of remembering small amounts of information by keeping them active in the short term. *See also* **short-term memory.**

rhythmic grouping. In music, a grouping of events in time, whose boundaries are defined by a relatively large change in some parameter. Several such groupings may form a phrase. *See also* **grouping; phrase; rhythmic tension.**

rhythmic tension. In music, tension created by the contour of different time intervals within a rhythmic grouping. Rhythmic tension differs from metric tension in that it is not dependent on meter for its existence. It is rather based on the tension of changing temporal distances between events. Rhythmic tension may also exist in free rhythm, where there is no pulse. *See also* **contour, intensity; metric tension; rhythmic grouping.**

scale. In music, a particular set of pitches, drawn from a tuning system for use in a particular section, movement, or piece. Whereas a tuning system may consist of a succession of intervals all of equal size, a scale usually consists of several different-sized intervals, some of which can act as cognitive "markers" to orient listeners as to the scale position of a particular pitch. Scales are usually a subset of a tuning system, which bring its pitch resources within the range of short-term memory. Many scales have a focal (most important) pitch, usually notated at the "bottom" of the scale. *See also* **interval; pitch; short-term memory; tuning system.**

schema. A particular set of associations in long-term memory. Schemas are sets of expectations about how things usually are. They generally apply to particular kinds of situations in time and space, and enable us to move through these situations without having to pay attention to every detail. Indeed, if details conform to our expectations, we do not notice them at all. Schemas form our expectations about many aspects of a piece of music, and our initial long-term memories (after a few hearings) will be primarily schematic, that is, not of specific details, but of the gist of the piece. Traditional musical forms are essentially preconstructed schemas, which can provide a sense of knowing where we are in a piece. Schemas describe what listeners bring to the musical experience. Hence both subjective and objective set are collections of schemas. A musical culture could be defined as a particular collection of schemas. *See also* **context; gist; musical culture; objective set; subjective set.**

secondary parameter. An aspect of musical sound that cannot be divided into a series of perceptible proportions, hence cannot be used syntactically. Secondary parameters cannot be formed into reidentifiable patterns, but may be used in relations of "more of" or "less of." Secondary parameters include loudness, tempo, timbre, pitch range, and number of instruments. Unlike primary parameters, they are not limited in number, and new ones may be created. *See also* **primary parameter; syntactical parameter; syntax.**

semantic memory. A type of long-term memory for abstract categories, rules, principles, and the like, and not concerned with specific events or their time order as are episodic memories. Semantic memories seem to be related; not by their time order, but in conceptual hierarchies of various types, and seem not to be vulnerable to the same types of transformations or distortions that episodic memories are. Our general knowedge of music would consist of semantic memories. *See also* **episodic memory; objective set; schema; subjective set.**

serial process.   A process in which activities take place sequentially, one after the other. Most current computers are serial machines, processing information one step at a time, with the steps following each other in very rapid succession. *See also* **parallel process.**

short-term memory.   A type of temporary memory that persists for a short time (3–5 sec on average; 10–12 sec maximum) and whose capacity is limited to around 5–9 elements, or one "chunk." There appear to be multiple short-term memories, for different aspects of experience. Items may be maintained for a longer time in short-term memory through the process of conscious rehearsal. Short-term memory length is one of the limitations on the size of small-scale groupings, and accounts for local musical structures such as phrases. *See also* **chunking; echoic memory; focus of consciousness; long-term memory; phrase; rehearsal.**

similarity.   In cognitive psychology, the principle that groupings form from perceptual elements that are qualitatively similar. Some aspects of the principle of similarily seem to be innate. *See also* **feature extraction; proximity.**

stream.   A coherent grouping of acoustical events that is formed by their basic similarity and proximity to each other. When several streams of events occur simultaneously, we can only attend to one of them in detail at a time. The formation of streams is one of the basic ways in which we identify different sound sources in the environment. *See also* **event; grouping.**

subjective set.   The aspects of groupings in a piece of music established through knowledge listeners bring to the piece in their long-term memory, such as knowledge of music-historical styles and performance practices. In contrast to objective set, subjective set consists of factors established at a scale larger than a particular piece. As a collection of schemas, subjective set is part of semantic memory, and would also constitute part of a listener's musical culture. *See also* **musical culture; objective set; schema; semantic memory.**

synapse.   A gap between two nerve cells. Electrical impulses that travel through nerves cells are converted to a wave of chemical activity which travels across the synaptic gap. The specialized molecules that accomplish this conversion are similar in all organisms with nervous systems and are called "neurotransmitters." It is currently believed that long-term memory consists of lasting chemical changes (referred to as "long-term potentiation") that occur at synapses and that alter the ability of the synapses to transmit neural pulses. The chemical changes that accomplish this take some time to become fixed, a process referred to as the "consolidation of memory."

syntax.   As used here, refers to sets of relations between identifiable patterns. This is a very general definition, and includes both traditions of rules for the use of particular kinds of functional patterns in particular styles and relations between patterns that are unique to a particular piece. The essence of syntax as defined here is the ability to recognize and identify patterns as similar. This has been referred to as musical structure, as opposed to expressive nuance. Not all parameters of music seem to support these kinds of patterns. *See also* **nuances; primary parameters; secondary parameters; syntactical parameters.**

syntactical parameters.   Aspects of musical sound that can be divided up into proportional relations, such as the intervals of a tuning system or the time lengths of a duration system.

These proportional relations make it possible to form patterns that may be recognized and identified in different contexts. Only pitch, duration, and harmony are considered syntactical parameters. Also called "primary parameters." *See also* **primary parameters; syntax.**

timbre.   A secondary parameter of musical sound, related primarily to its overtone structure and often referred to as "sound color." Examples of timbres are the different sounds of different instruments playing the same pitch. *See also* **secondary parameter.**

time interval.   The distance between the onset of one musical event and the onset of the next event. Rhythmic patterns consist of groupings of events at different time intervals with different accents. Note that this is different from duration, which is defined here as the length of time from the onset of an event to the end of that event. *See also* **accent; duration.**

tonality.   The arrangement of pitches in a piece of music so that one pitch predominates, usually accomplished by repeating the pitch and placing it in important locations, such as the downbeat of the metrical cycle. *See also* **nontonal; meter; pitch.**

top-down processing.   Information processing that is primarily memory driven. Unlike bottom-up processing, which deals primarily with immediate perceptual experience, top-down processing involves the past. Most information processing in the nervous system is both bottom-up and top-down. *See also* **bottom-up processing.**

tuning system.   A way of dividing up the range of possible perceptible musical pitches into a series of intervals large enough to be reliably perceived as categories. Tuning systems often form one of the foundations of a musical culture, and are frequently built into the physical structure of instruments in order to make it easier to play them "in tune." Tuning systems are one of the mechanisms (along with scales) of introducing redundancy into the vast acoustical resources available for music. A tuning system forms a basic set of interval categories, which are learned, and which can vary between cultures. Almost all tuning systems use the octave as a basic interval, which is then subdivided into smaller intervals. *See also* **category; frequency; interval; musical culture; octave; pitch; scale.**

working memory.   The ensemble of memory components used in conscious thought. Working memory includes the focus of conscious awareness, visual and acoustical short-term memories, and a central executive component that maintains immediate plans and goals. As defined here, not all of the contents of working memory are conscious. Currently unrehearsed elements in short-term memory, for example, are not conscious, but are part of working memory. Working memory shades off into the unconscious context that is currently semi-activated. *See also* **context, focus of conscious awareness, short-term memory.**

References

Abel, Ted, et al. (1995). "Steps Toward a Molecular Definition of Memory Consolidation." In Daniel L. Schacter (Ed.), *Memory Distortion*. Cambridge: Harvard University Press.

Aiello, Rita (1994). "Can Listening to Music be Experimentally Studied?" In Rita Aiello and John Sloboda (Eds.), *Musical Perceptions*. New York: Oxford University Press.

Anderson, John R. (1990). *Cognitive Psychology and Its Implications*. New York: Freeman.

———. *Rules of the Mind*. (1993). Hillsdale, NJ: Erlbaum.

Arom, Simha, G. Léothaad, and Frédéric Voisin (1997). "Experimental Ethnomusicology: An Interactive Approach to the Study of Musical Scales." In Irene Deliege and John Sloboda (Eds.), *Perception and Cognition of Music*. East Sussex, U.K.: Psychology Press.

Atkinson, R. C., and R. M. Shiffrin (1968). "Human Memory: A Proposed System and Its Control Processes." In K. W. Spence and J. T. Spence (Eds.), *The Psychology of Learning and Motivation, vol. 2*. Orlando: Academic Press.

Baars, Bernard (1988). *A Cognitive Theory of Consciousness*. New York: Cambridge University Press.

———. (1997). *In the Theater of Consciousness*. New York: Oxford University Press.

Bagchee, Sandeep (1998). *Nad: Understanding Raga Music*. Mombai, India: Eshwar.

Barbour, J. Murray (1972). *Turning and Temperament: A Historical Survey*. New York: Da Capo Press.

Barlow, H. B., and J. D. Mollon (1982). *The Senses*. New York: Cambridge University Press.

Barnett, H. G. (1953). *Innovation: The Basis of Cultural Change*. New York: McGraw-Hill.

Barsalou, Lawrence (1992). *Cognitive Psychology: An Overview for Cognitive Scientists*. Hillsdale, NJ: Erlbaum.

———. (1993). "Flexibility, Structure, and Linguistic Vagary in Concepts: Manifestations of a Compositional System of Perceptual Symbols." In Alan Collins et al. (Eds.), *Theories of Memory*. Hillsdale, NJ: Erlbaum.

Bechtel, William (1988). *Philosophy of Mind: An Overview for Cognitive Science*. Hillsdale, NJ: Erlbaum.

von Bekesy, Georg (1970). "Improved Musical Dynamics by Variation of Apparent Size of Sound Source." *The Journal of Music Theory*, vol. 14.

Berger, Harris M. (1997). "The Practice of Perception: Multi-Functionality and Time in the Musical Experiences of a Heavy Metal Drummer." *Ethnomusicology*, vol. 41, no. 3.

Berliner, Paul (1994). *Thinking in Jazz*. Chicago: University of Chicago Press.

Berz, William L., and Anthony E. Kelly (1998). "Research Note: Perceptions of More Complete Musical Compositions: An Exploratory Study." *Psychology of Music*, no. 26.

Bharucha, Jamshed J. (1999). "Neural Nets, Temporal Composites, and Tonality." In Diana Deutsch (Ed.), *The Psychology of Music*. 2d ed. San Diego: Academic Press.

Bigand, Emmanuel (1993). "Contributions of Music to Research on Human Auditory Cognition." In Stephen McAdams and Emmanuel Bigand (Eds.), *Thinking in Sound: The Cognitive Psychology of Audition*. New York: Oxford University Press.

Black, Ira (1991). *Information in the Brain: A Molecular Perspective*. Cambridge, MA: MIT Press.

Blacking, John (1995). *Music, Culture, and Experience*. Chicago: University of Chicago Press.

Block, Richard A. (1990). "Models of Psychological Time." In Richard A. Block (Ed.), *Cognitive Models of Psychological Time*. Hillsdale, NJ: Erlbaum.

———. (1985). "Contextual Coding in Memory: Studies of Remembered Duration." In *Time, Mind, and Behavior*. New York: Springer-Verlag.

Bolinger, Dwight (1978). "Intonation across Languages." In J. P. Greenburg et al. (Eds.), *Universals of Human Language*. Vol. 2, *Phonology*. Stanford, CA: Stanford University Press.

———. (1986). *Intonation and Its Parts: Melody in Spoken English*. Stanford, CA: Stanford University Press.

———. (1989). *Intonation and Its Uses: Melody in Grammar and Discourse*. Stanford, CA: Stanford University Press.

Bregman, Albert S. (1990). *Auditory Scene Analysis: The Perceptual Organization of Sound*. Cambridge, MA: MIT Press.

———. (1993). "Auditory Scene Analysis: Hearing in Complex Environments." In Stephen McAdams and Emmanuel Bigand (Eds.), *Thinking in Sound: The Cognitive Psychology of Audition*. New York: Oxford University Press.

Brewer, William F. (1986). "What is Autobiographical Memory?" In David C. Rubin (Ed.), *Autobiographical Memory*. New York: Cambridge University Press.

Brinner, Benjamin (1995). *Knowing Music, Making Music*. Chicago: University of Chicago Press.

Broadbent, Donald (1958). *Perception and Communication*. Oxford: Pergamon Press.

Brown, Gordon D. A. (1997). "Formal Models of Memory for Serial Order." In Martin Conway (Ed.), *Cognitive Models of Memory*. Cambridge, MA: MIT Press.

Brugman, Claudia (1983). *The Story of Over*. Bloomington: Indiana University Linguistics Club.

Burnham, Scott (1999). "How Music Matters: Poetic Content Revisited." In Nicholas Cook and Mark Everest (Eds.), *Rethinking Music*. New York: Oxford University Press.

Burns, Edward M. (1999). "Intervals, Scales, and Tuning." In *The Psychology of Music.* 2d ed. San Diego: Academic Press.

Burns, Edward M., and W. Dixon Ward (1978). "Categorical Perception: Phenomenon or Epiphenomenon: Evidence from Experiments in the Perception of Melodic Musical Intervals." *Journal of the Acoustical Society of America,* February 1978, vol. 63, no. 2.

————. (1982). "Intervals, Scales, and Tuning." In Diana Deutsch (Ed.), *The Psychology of Music.* Orlando, FL: Academic Press.

Buser, Pierre, and Michel Imbert (1992). *Audition.* Cambridge, MA: MIT Press.

Butler, David, and Helen Brown (1994). "Describing the Mental Representation of Tonality in Music." In Rita Aiello and John Sloboda (Eds.), *Musical Perceptions.* New York: Oxford University Press.

Carterette, Edward C., and Roger A. Kendall (1999). "Comparative Music Perception and Cognition." In Diana Deutsch (Ed.), *The Psychology of Music.* 2d ed. San Diego: Academic Press.

Chafe, Wallace (1994). *Discourse, Consciousness, and Time: The Flow of Conscious Experience in Speaking and Writing.* Chicago: University of Chicago Press.

Clark, Andy (1993). *Associative Engines.* Cambridge, MA: MIT Press.

————. (1997). *Being There.* Cambridge, MA: MIT Press.

Clarke, Eric F. (1987a). "Categorical Rhythm Perception: An Ecological Perspective." In Alf Gabrielsson (Ed.), *Action and Perception in Rhythm and Music.* Stockholm: Royal Swedish Academy of Music Publication 55.

————. (1987b). "Levels of Structure in the Organization of Musical Time." *Contemporary Music Review,* vol. 2.

————. (1999). "Rhythm and Timing in Music." In Diana Deutsch (Ed.), *The Psychology of Music.* 2d ed. San Diego: Academic Press.

Classen, Constance (1993). *Worlds of Sense.* New York: Routledge.

Clynes, Manfred (1986). "When Time is Music." In J. R. Evans and Manfred Clynes (Eds.), *Rhythm in Psychological, Linguistic, and Musical Processes.* Springfield, IL: Charles C. Thomas.

Cohen, Dalia, and Ruth Katz (1997). "Attitudes to the Time Axis and Cognitive Constraints: The Case of Arabic Vocal Folk Music." In Irene Deliege, and John Sloboda (Eds.), *Perception and Cognition of Music.* East Sussex, U.K.: Psychology Press.

Cook, Nicholas (1990). *Music, Imagination, Culture.* New York: Oxford University Press.

————. (1994). "Perception: A Perspective from Music Theory." In Rita Aiello with John Sloboda (Eds.), *Musical Perceptions.* New York: Oxford University Press.

Cooper, Grosvenor, and Leonard B. Meyer (1960). *The Rhythmic Structure of Music.* Chicago: University of Chicago Press.

Corbett, John (1995). "Ephemera Underscored: Writing around Free Improvisation." In Krin Gabbard (Ed.), *Jazz among the Discourses.* Durham, N.C.: Duke University Press.

Cowan, Nelson (1988). "Evolving Conceptions of Memory Storage, Selective Attention, and Their Mutual Constraints within the Human Information-Processing System." *Psychological Bulletin*, vol. 104, no. 2.

————. (1995). *Attention and Memory: An Integrated Framework.* New York: Oxford University Press.

Crick, Francis (1994). *The Astonishing Hypothesis: The Scientific Search for the Soul.* New York: Simon and Schuster.

Crowder, Robert G. (1993a). "Auditory Memory." In Stephen McAdams and Emmanuel Bigand (Eds.), *Thinking in Sound: The Cognitive Psychology of Audition.* New York: Oxford University Press.

————. (1993b). "Systems and Principles in Memory Theory: Another Critique of Pure Memory." In Allan Collins et al. (Eds.), *Theories of Memory.* Hillsdale, NJ: Erlbaum.

Cruttenden, Alan (1986). *Intonation.* New York: Cambridge University Press.

Cuddy, Lola L. (1993). "Melody Comprehension and Tonal Structure." In Thomas J. Tighe and W. Jay Dowling (Eds.), *Psychology and Music.* Hillsdale, NJ: Erlbaum.

Damasio, Antonio R. (1994). *Descartes' Error: Emotion, Reason, and the Human Brain.* New York: Putnam.

D'Andrade, Roy (1995). *The Development of Cognitive Anthropology.* New York: Cambridge University Press.

Danielou, Alain (1995). *Music and the Power of Sound: The Influence of Tuning and Interval on Consciousness.* Rochester, VT: Inner Traditions.

Davis, Michael, and M. David Egger (1992). "Habituaion and Sensitization in Vertebrates." In Larry R. Squire (Ed.), *Encyclopedia of Learning and Memory.* New York: Macmillan.

DeBellis, Mark (1995). *Music and Conceptualization.* Cambridge, UK: Cambridge University Press.

Deliège, Irene (1987). "Grouping Conditions in Listening to Music: An Approach to Lehrdahl and Jackendoff's Grouping Preference Rules." *Music Perception*, vol. 4, no. 4.

————. (1989). "A Perceptual Approach to Contemporary Musical Forms." *Contemporary Music Review*, vol. 4.

————. (1996). "Cue Abstraction as a Component of Categorization Processes in Music Listening." *Psychology of Music*, no. 2.

Deliège, Irene, and Abdessadek El Ahmadi (1990). "Mechanisms of Cue Extraction in Musical Groupings: A Study of Perception on Sequenza VI for Viola Solo by Luciano Berio." *Psychology of Music*, vol. 18, no. 1.

Deliège, Irene, et al. (1996). "Musical Schemata in Real-Time Listening to Piece of Music." *Music Perception*, vol. 14, no. 2.

Dennett, Daniel C. (1991). *Consciousness Explained.* Boston: Little, Brown.

Deutsch, Diana (1999). "The Processing of Pitch Combinations." In Diana Deutsch (Ed.), *The Psychology of Music.* 2d ed. San Diego: Academic Press.

Dibben, Nicola (1994). "The Cognitive Reality of Hierarchic Structure in Tonal and Atonal Music." *Music Perception*, vol. 12, no. 1.

Donald, Merlin (1991). *Origins of the Modern Mind*. Cambridge, MA: Harvard University Press.

Doty, Robert W. (1990). "Time and Memory." In James McGaugh, Norman Weinberger, and Gary Lynch (Eds.), *Brain Organization and Memory*. New York: Oxford University Press.

Dowling, W. Jay (1978). "Scale and Contour: Two Components of a Theory of Memory for Melodies." In *Psychological Review*, vol. 85, no. 4.

———. (1982). "Melodic Information Processing and Its Development." In Diana Deutsch (Ed.), *The Psychology of Music*. Orlando, FL: Academic Press.

———. (1993). "Procedural and Declarative Knowledge in Music Cognition and Education." In Thomas J. Tighe and W. Jay Dowling (Eds.), *Psychology and Music*, Hillsdale NJ: Erlbaum.

———. (1999). "The Development of Music Perception and Cognition." In Diana Deutsch (Ed.), *The Psychology of Music*, 2d ed. San Diego, CA: Academic Press.

Dowling, W. J., and Dane L. Harwood (1986). *Music Cognition*. San Diego: Academic Press.

Dreyfuss, Hubert L. (1992). *What Computers Still Can't Do*. Cambridge, MA: MIT Press.

Eagle, Robert (1996). "Working Memory and Retrieval." In John Richardson et al. (Eds.), *Working Memory and Human Cognition*. New York: Oxford University Press.

Edelman, Gerald (1987). *Neural Darwinism: The Theory of Neuronal Group Selection*. New York: Basic Books.

———. (1989). *The Remembered Present: A Biological Theory of Consciousness*. New York: Basic Books.

———. (1992). *Bright Air, Brilliant Fire: On the Matter of the Mind*. New York: Basic Books.

Edelman, Gerald, W. E. Gall, and W. M. Cowan (1988). *Auditory Function: Neurobiological Bases of Hearing*. New York: Wiley.

Eddins, David A., and David M. Green (1995). "Temporal Integration and Temporal Resolution." In Brian C. Moore (Ed.), *Hearing*. San Diego: Academic Press.

Eichenbaum, Howard (1994). "The Hippocampal System and Declarative Memory." In *Memory Systems, 1994*. Cambridge MA: MIT Press.

Elman, Jeffry, et al. (1998). *Rethinking Innateness*. Cambridge MA: MIT Press.

Erickson, Robert (1975). *Sound Structure in Music*. Berkeley: University of California Press.

Fassbender, Christoph (1996). "Infants' Auditory Sensitivity Towards Acoustic Parameters of Speech and Music." In Irene Deliege and John Sloboda (Eds.), *Musical Beginnings*. New York: Oxford University Press.

Feld, Steven (1982). *Sound and Sentiment: Birds, Weeping, Poetics and Song in Kaluli Expression*. Philadelphia: University of Pennsylvania Press.

————. (1996). "Waterfalls of Song: An Acoustemology of Place Resounding in Bosavi, Papua New Guinea." In Steven Feld and Keith Basso (Eds.), *Senses of Place*. Santa Fe: School of American Research Press.

Fink, Robert (1999). "Going Flat: Post-Hierarchical Music Theory and the Musical Surface." In Nicholas Cook and Mark Everist (Eds.), *Rethinking Music*. New York: Oxford University Press.

Fotheringhame, David K., and Malcolm P. Young (1997). "Neural Coding Schemes for Sensory Representation: Theoretical Proposals and Empirical Evidence." In Michael D. Rugg (Ed.), *Cognitive Neuroscience*. Cambridge, MA: MIT Press.

Fraisse, Paul (1963). *The Psychology of Time*. New York: Harper and Row.

————. (1982). "Rhythm and Tempo." In Diana Deutsch (Ed.), *The Psychology of Music*. Orlando, FL: Academic Press.

————. (1987). "A Historical Approach to Rhythm Perception." In Alf Gabrielsson (Ed.), *Action and Perception in Rhythm and Music*. Royal Swedish Academy of Music Publication 55.

Francès, Robert (1988). *The Perception of Music*. Trans. W. Jay Dowling. Hillsdale, NJ: Erlbaum.

Fraser, J. T. (1987). *Time: The Familiar Stranger*. Amherst: University of Massachusetts Press.

Fuster, Joaquin M. (1995). *Memory in the Cerebral Cortex*. Cambridge, MA: MIT Press.

Gallistel, Charles R. (1990). *The Organization of Learning*. Cambridge, MA: MIT Press.

Gärdenfors, Peter (2000). *Conceptual Spaces*. Cambridge, MA: MIT Press.

Garner, W. R. (1974). *The Processing of Information and Structure*. Hillsdale, NJ: Erlbaum.

Gazzaniga, Michael S., Richard B. Ivry, and George R. Mangun, (1998). *Cognitive Neuroscience*. New York: W. W. Norton.

Gell, Alfred (1992). *The Anthropology of Time*. Providence: Berg.

Gibbs, Raymond (1994). *The Poetics of Mind*. New York: Cambridge University Press.

Gibson, Eleanor J. (1953). "Improvement in Perceptual Judgements as a Function of Controlled Practice or Training." *Psychological Bulletin*, vol. 50, no. 6.

Gjerdingen, Robert O. (1988). "Shape and Motion in the Microstructure of Song." *Music Perception*, vol. 6, no. 1.

————. (1994). "Apparent Motion in Music?" *Music Perception*, vol. 11, no. 4.

Globus, Gordon (1995). *The Postmodern Brain*. Philadelphia: Benjamins.

Goldstein, E. Bruce (1989). *Sensation and Perception*. Belmont, CA: Wadsworth.

Goldstone, R. L., and Lawrence W. Barsalou (1998). "Reuniting Perception and Conception. In Steven A. Sloman and Lance J. Rips (Eds.), *Similarity and Symbols in Human Thinking*, Cambridge, MA: MIT Press.

Gopnik, Alison, and Andrew Meltzoff (1997). *Words, Thoughts, and Theories*. Cambridge, MA: MIT Press.

Goschke, Thomas (1997). "Implicit Learning and Unconscious Knowledge: Mental Representation, Computational Mechanisms, and Brain Structures." In Koen Lamberts and David Shanks (Eds.), *Knowledge, Concepts, and Categories*. Cambridge, MA: MIT Press.

Grimes, John (1996). "On the Failure to Detect Changes in Scenes across Saccades." In Kathleen Akins (Ed.), *Perception*. New York: Oxford University Press.

Guck, Marion (1981). "Musical Images as Musical Thoughts: The Contribution of Metaphor to Analysis." *In Theory Only* vol. 5, no. 5.

————. (1997). "Two Types of Metaphoric Transference." In Jenefer Robinson (Ed.), *Music and Meaning*. Ithaca, NY: Cornell University Press.

Hahn, Ulrike, and Nick Chater (1998). "Similarity and Rules: Distinct? Exhaustive? Empirically Distinguishable?" In Stevan A. Sloman and Lance J. Rips (Eds.), *Similarity and Symbols in Human Thinking*. Amsterdam, the Netherlands: Elsevier Science Publishers.

Hajda, John M., et al. (1997). "Methodological Issues in Timbre Research." In Irene Deliège and John Sloboda (Eds.), *Perception and Cognition of Music*. East Sussex, U.K.: Psychology Press.

Handel, Stephen (1989). *Listening: An Introduction to the Perception of Auditory Events*. Cambridge, MA: MIT Press.

Hardin, C. L. (1988). *Color for Philosophers: Unweaving the Rainbow*. Indianapolis: Hackett.

Harnad, Stevan (1987). "Psychophysical and Cognitive Aspects of Categorical Perception: A Critical Overview." In Stevan Harnad (Ed.), *Categorical Perception*. New York: Cambridge University Press.

————. (1993). "Symbol Grounding Is an Empirical Problem: Neural Nets Are Just a Candidate Component." In *Proceedings of the Fifteenth Annual Meeting of the Cognitive Science Society*. Hillsdale, NJ: Erlbaum.

Harwood, Dane L. (1976). "Universals in Music: A Perspective from Cognitive Psychology." *Ethnomusicology*, no. 22.

Higgins, Kathleen Marie (1997). "Musical Idiosyncrasy and Perspectival Listening." In Jenefer Robinson (Ed.), *Music and Meaning*, Ithaca, NY: Cornell University Press.

Hirsh, Ira J., and Carl E. Sherrick (1961). "Perceived Order in Different Sense Modalities." *Journal of Experimental Psychology*, vol. 62, no. 5.

Hirschfeld, Lawrence A., and Susan A. Gelman (1994). "Toward a Topography of the Mind: An Introduction to Domain Specificity." In Lawrence A. Hirschfeld and Susan A. Gelman (Eds.), *Mapping the Mind: Domain Specificity in Cognition and Culture*. New York: Cambridge University Press.

Hochberg, Julian (1998). "Gestalt Theory and Its Legacy." In Julian Hochberg (Ed.), *Perception and Cognition at Century's End*. San Diego: Academic Press.

Holyoak, Keith J., and Paul Thagard (1995). *Mental Leaps: Analogy in Creative Thought*. Cambridge MA: MIT Press.

Hopkins, Pandora (1982). "Aural Thinking." In Robert Falck and Timothy Rice (Eds.), *Cross-Cultural Perspectives on Music*. Toronto: University of Tornoto Press.

Hopkins, Robert (1990). *Closure and Mahler's Music*. Philadelphia: University of Pennsylvania Press.

Howard, James, and James Ballas (1981). "Feature Extraction in Auditory Perception." In *Auditory and Visual Pattern Recognition*. Hillsdale, NJ: Erlbaum.

Imberty, Michel (1993). "How Do We Perceive Atonal Music? Suggestions for a Theoretical Approach." In *Contemporary Music Review,* vol. 9, parts 1 and 2.

Jackendoff, Ray (1987). *Consciousness and the Computational Mind.* Cambridge, MA: MIT Press.

Jackson, Janet, L. (1990). "A Cognitive Approach to Information Processing." In Richard A. Block (Ed.), *Cognitive Models of Psychological Time.* Hillsdale, NJ: Erlbaum.

Jacoby, L. L., et al. (1989). "Memory Attributions." In H. C. Roediger and F. I. M. Craik (Eds.), *Varieties of Memory and Consciousness.* Hillsdale NJ: Erlbaum.

Jahnke, John C., and Ronald H. Nowaczyk (1998). *Cognition.* Upper Saddle River, NJ: Prentice Hall.

Jenkins, James J. (1980). "Remember that Old Theory of Memory? Well, Forget It!" In John G. Seamon (Ed.), *Human Memory.* New York: Oxford University Press.

Johnson, Mark (1987). *The Body in the Mind.* Chicago: University of Chicago Press.

———. (1997). "Embodied Meaning and Cognitive Science." In David Michael Levin (Ed.), *Language beyond Postmodernism.* Evanston, IL: Northwestern University Press.

Jones, Mari Reiss (1993). "Dynamics of Musical Patterns: How do Melody and Rhythm Fit Together?" In Thomas J. Tighe and W. J. Dowling (Eds.), *Psychology of Music: The Understanding of Melody and Rhythm.* Hillsdale, NJ: Erlbaum.

Jonides, John (1995). "Working Memory and Thinking." In Daniel Osherson (Ed.), *Thinking.* Cambridge MA: MIT Press.

Jonides, John, and Edward E. Smith (1997). "The Architecture of Working Memory." In Michael Rugg (Ed.), *Cognitive Neuroscience.* Cambridge, MA: MIT Press.

Kagan, Jerome (1994). *Galen's Prophecy.* New York: Basic Books.

Karno, Mitchell, and Vladimir J. Konecni (1992). "The Effects of Structural Interventions in the First Movement of Mozart's Symphony in G Minor K. 550 on Aesthetic Preference." *Music Perception,* vol. 10, no. 1.

Keefe, Douglas H., Edward M. Burns, and Nguyen Phong (1991). "Vietnamese Modal Scales of the Dan Tranh." *Music Perception,* vol. 8, no. 4.

Keil, Charles, and Steven Feld (1994). *Musical Grooves.* Chicago: The University of Chicago Press.

Kivy, Peter (1989). *Sound Sentiment: An Essay on the Musical Emotions.* Philadelphia: Temple University Press.

Kramer, Jonathon (1988). *The Time of Music.* New York: Schirmer.

Kraut, Robert (1992). "On the Possibility of a Determinate Semantics for Music." In Mari Reiss Jones and Susan Holleran (Eds.), *Cognitive Bases of Musical Communication.* Washington, DC: American Psychological Association.

Krumhansl, Carol L. (1990). *Cognitive Foundations of Musical Pitch.* New York: Oxford University Press.

Lachman, Roy, Janet Lachman, and Earl C. Butterfield (1979). *Cognitive Psychology and Information Processing.* Hillsdale, NJ: Erlbaum.

Lakoff, George (1987). *Women, Fire, and Dangerous Things*. Chicago: University of Chicago Press.

Lakoff, George, and Mark Johnson (1980). *Metaphors We Live By*. Chicago: University of Chicago Press.

Langacker, Ronald W. (1987). *Foundations of Cognitive Grammer*. Standford, CA: Stanford University Press.

———. (1997). "The Contextual Basis of Cognitive Semantics." In Jan Nuyts and Eric Pederson (Eds.), *Language and Conceptualization*. New York: Cambridge University Press.

LeDoux, Joseph (1996). *The Emotional Brain*. New York: Simon and Schuster.

Lee, Christopher S. (1991). "The Perception of Metrical Structure: Experimental Evidence and a Model." In Peter Howell, Robert West, and Ian Cross (Eds.), *Representing Musical Structure*. New York: Academic Press.

Leppert, Richard, and Susan McClary (1987). *Music and Society: The Politics of Composition, Performance, and Reception*. New York: Cambridge University Press.

Lerdahl, Fred (1987). "Timbral Hierarchies." *Contemporary Music Review*, vol. 2.

———. (1988). "Cognitive Constraints on Compositional Systems." In John Sloboda (Ed.), *Generative Processes in Music*. New York: Oxford University Press.

———. (1997). "Composing and Listening: A Reply to Nattiez." In Irene Deliège and John Sloboda (Eds.), *Perception and Cognition of Music*. East Sussex, U.K.: Psychology Press.

Lerdahl, Fred, and Ray Jackendoff (1983). *A Generative Theory of Tonal Music*. Cambridge, MA: MIT Press.

Levinson, Jerrold (1997). *Music in the Moment*. Ithaca, NY: Cornell University Press.

Levy, Mark (1982). *Intonation in North Indian Music*. New Delhi: Biblia Impex.

Linton, Marigold (1982). "Transformations of Memory in Everyday Life." In Ulrich Neisser (Ed.), *Memory Observed*. New York: Freeman.

Llinas, Rodolfo, and D. Pare (1996). "The Brain as a Closed System Modulated by the Senses." In Rodolfo Llinas and Patricia Churchland (Eds.), *The Mind-Brain Continuum*. Cambridge, MA: MIT Press,

Locke, David (1987). *Drum Gahu: The Rhythms of West African Drumming*. Crown Point, IN: White Cliffs Media.

Logie, Robert (1996). "The Seven Ages of Working Memory." In John Richardson et al. *Working Memory and Human Cognition*. New York: Oxford University Press.

Lynch, Gary, and Richard Granger (1994). "Variations in Synaptic Plasticity and Types of Memory in Corticohippocampal Networks." In Daniel Schacter and Endel Tulving (Eds.), *Memory Systems, 1994*. Cambridge MA: MIT Press.

Mandelbaum, Mayer Joel (1961). "Multiple Division of the Octave and the Tonal Resources of 19 Tone Temperament." PHD Dissertation. Ann Arbor, MI: University Microfilms Inc.

Mandler, George (1967). "Organization and Memory." In K. W. Spence and J. T. Spence (Eds.), *The Psychology of Learning and Motivation*. Vol. 1. Orlando, FL: Academic Press.

———. (1984). *Mind and Body: Psychology of Emotion and Stress*. New York: Norton.

Mandler, Jean M. (1979). "Categorical and Schematic Organization in Memory." In Richard C. Puff (Ed.), *Memory Organization and Structure.* Orlando, FL: Academic Press.

——. (1984). *Stories, Scripts, and Scenes: Aspects of Schema Theory.* Hillsdale, NJ: Erlbaum.

——. (1992). "How to Build a Baby: 2. Conceptual Primitives." *Psychological Review*, vol. 99, no. 4.

Mann, Thomas (1966). *The Magic Mountain.* New York: Knopf.

Massaro, Dominic, and Geoffrey R. Loftus (1996). "Sensory and Perceptual Storage." In Elizabeth Ligon Bjork and Robert A. Bjork (Eds.), *Memory.* San Diego: Academic Press.

Massey, Reginald, and Jamila Massey (1996). *The Music of India.* New Delhi: Abhinav Publications.

McAdams, Stephen (1989). "Psychological Constraints on Form-Bearing Dimensions in Music." *Contemporary Music Review*, vol. 4.

——. (1993). "Recognition of Sound Sources and Events." In Stephen McAdams and Emmanuel Bigand (Eds.), *Thinking in Sound: The Cognitive Psychology of Audition.* New York: Oxford University Press.

McClelland, James L. (1995). "Constructive Memory and Memory Distortions: A Parallel-Distributed Processing Approach." In Daniel L. Schacter (Ed.), *Memory Distortions.* Cambridge, MA: Harvard University Press.

Medin, Douglas L., and Lawrence Barsalou (1987). "Categorization Processes and Categorical Perception." In Stevan Harnad (Ed.), *Categorical Perception.* New York: Cambridge University Press.

Mehler, Jacques, and Emmanuel Dupoux (1994). *What Infants Know: The New Cognitive Science of Early Development.* Cambridge, MA: Blackwell.

Merzenich, Michael M., and R. C. deCharms (1996). "Neural Representations, Experience, and Change." In Rodolfo Llinas and Patricia Churchland (Eds.), *The Mind-Brain Continuum.* Cambridge, MA: MIT Press.

Metcalfe, Janet (1995). "Monitoring and Gain Control in an Episodic Memory Model: Relation to the P300 Event Potential." In Alan F. Collins et al. (Eds.), *Theories of Memory.* Hillsdale, NJ: Erlbaum.

Meyer, Leonard (1973). *Explaining Music.* Chicago: University of Chicago Press.

——. (1989). *Style and Music: Theory, History, and Ideology.* Philadelphia: University of Pennsylvania Press.

——. (1994). *Music, the Arts, and Ideas.* Chicago: University of Chicago Press.

Michon, John A. (1985). "The Compleat Time Experiencer." In John A. Michon and Janet Jackson (Eds.), *Time, Mind, and Behavior.* New York: Springer.

——. (1990). "Implicit and Explicit Representations of Time." In Richard A. Block (Ed.), *Cognitive Models of Psychological Time*, Hillsdale, NJ: Erlbaum.

Mikumo, Mariko (1992). "Encoding Strategies for Tonal and Atonal Melodies." *Music Perception*, vol. 10, no. 1.

Miller, George [A.] (1956). "The Magical Number Seven, Plus or Minus Two: Some Limits on Our Capacity for Processing Information." *Psychological Review*, vol. 63, no. 2.

Miller, George A., and Philip N. Johnson-Laird (1976). *Language and Perception*. Cambridge, MA: Harvard University Press.

Minsky, Marvin (1985). *The Society of Mind*. New York: Simon and Schuster.

Monahan, Caroline B. (1993). "Parallels between Pitch and Time, and How They Go Together." In Thomas J. Tighe and W. Jay Dowling (Eds.), *Psychology and Music*. Hillsdale, NJ: Erlbaum.

Moore, Brain C. J. (1997). *An Introduction to the Psychology of Hearing*. San Diego: Academic Press.

Mountcastle, Vernon B. (1998). *Perceptual Neuroscience: The Cerebral Cortex*. Cambridge, MA: Harvard University Press.

Murphy, Gregory L., and Mary E. Lassaline (1997). "Hierarchical Structure in Concepts." In Koen Lamberts and David Shanks (Eds.), *Knowledge, Concepts and Categories*. Cambridge, MA: MIT Press.

Nairne, James S. (1996). "Short Term/Working Memory." In Elizabeth Ligon Bjork and Robert A. Bjork (Eds.), *Memory*. San Diego: Academic Press.

Narmour, Eugene (1989). "The Genetic Code of Melody: Cognitive Structures Generated by the Implication-Realization Model." *Contemporary Music Review*, vol. 4.

———. (1990). *The Analysis and Cognition of Basic Melodic Structures*. Chicago: University of Chicago Press.

———. (1992a). "The Influence of Embodied Registral Motion on the Perception of Higher-Level Melodic Implication." In Mari Riess Jones and Susan Holleran (Eds.), *Cognitive Bases of Musical Communication*. Washington, DC: American Psychological Association.

———. (1992b). *The Analysis and Cognition of Melodic Complexity*. Chicago: University of Chicago Press.

Nattiez, Jean-Jacques (1990). *Music and Discourse*. Princeton, NJ: Princeton University Press.

Neisser, Ulrich (1976). *Cognition and Reality*. New York: Freeman.

———. (1986). "John Dean's Memory: A Case Study." In Daniel Goleman and D. Heller (Eds.), *The Pleasures of Psychology*. New York: New American Library.

———. (1988). "What is Ordinary Memory the Memory Of?" In Ulrich Neisser and E. Winograd (Eds.), *Remembering Reconsidered*. New York: Cambridge University Press.

Norton, Richard (1984). *Tonality in Western Culture*. University Park: Pennsylvania State University Press.

Noth, Winfried (1990). *Handbook of Semiotics*. Bloomington: Indiana University Press.

Ohala, John J. (1994). "The Frequency Code Underlies the Sound-Symbolic Use of Voice Pitch." In Leanne Hinton, Johanna Nichols, and John J. Ohala (Eds.), *Sound Symbolism*. New York: Cambridge University Press.

Orbach, Jack (1998). *The Neuropsychological Theories of Lashley and Hebb*. Lanham, MD: University Press of America.

Ornstein, Robert (1997). *On the Experience of Time*. Reprint, New York: Westview, 1969.

Palmer, Gary B. (1996). *Toward a Theory of Cultural Linguistics*. Austin: University of Texas Press.

Papousek, Mechthild (1996). "Intuitive Parenting: A Hidden Source of Musical Stimulation in Infancy." In Irene Deliège and John Sloboda (Eds.), *Musical Beginnings*. New York: Oxford University Press.

Parncutt, Richard (1987). "The Perception of Pulse in Musical Rhythm." In Alf Gabrielsson (Ed.), *Action and Perception in Rhythm and Music*. Stockholm: Royal Swedish Academy of Music Publication 55.

———. (1994). "A Perceptual Model of Pulse Salience and Metrical Accent in Musical Rhythms." *Music Perception*, vol. 11, no. 4.

Pashler, Harold E. (1998). *The Psychology of Attention*. Cambridge, MA: MIT Press.

Pederson, Eric, and Jan Nuyts (1997). "Overview: On the Relationship Between Language and Conceptualization." In *Language and Conceptualization*. New York: Cambridge University Press.

Peretz, Isabelle (1993). "Auditory Agnosia: A Functional Analysis." In Stephen McAdams and Emmanuel Bigand (Eds.), *Thinking in Sound: The Cognitive Psychology of Audition*. New York: Oxford University Press.

Petrie, Hugh, and Rebecca Oshlag (1993). "*Metaphor and Learning*." In Andrew Ortony (Ed.), *Metaphor and Thought*. New York: Cambridge University Press.

Pierce, John M. (1988). "Stimulus Generalization and the Acquisition of Categories by Pigeons." In Lawrence Weiskrantz (Ed.), *Thought without Language*. New York: Oxford University Press.

Pollard-Gott, Lucy (1983). "Emergence of Thematic Concepts in Repeated Listening to Music." *Cognitive Psychology*, vol. 15.

Poppel, Ernst (1978). "Time Perception." In *Handbook of Sensory Physiology*. Vol. 8, *Perception*. New York: Springer.

———. (1988). *Mindworks: Time and Conscious Experience*. Boston: Harcourt Brace Janovich.

Povel, Dirk-Jan (1981). "Internal Representation of Simple Temporal Patterns." *Journal of Experimental Psychology: Human Perception and Performance*, vol. 7, no. 1.

———. (1984). "A Theoretical Framework for Rhythm Perception." *Psychological Research*, vol. 45.

Povel, Dirk-Jan, and Peter Essens (1985). "Perception of Temporal Patterns." *Music Perception*, vol. 2, no. 4.

Povel, Dirk-Jan, and Hans Okkerman (1981). "Accents in Equitone Sequences." *Perception and Psychophysics*, vol. 30, no. 6.

Progler, J. A. (1995). "Searching for Swing: Participarory Discrepancies in the Jazz Rhythm Section." *Ethnomusicology*, vol. 39, no. 1.

Raffman, Diana (1993). *Language, Music, and Mind*. Cambridge, MA: MIT Press.

Rakowski, Andrzej (1990). "Intonation Variants of Musical Intervals in Isolation and in Musical Contexts." *Psychology of Music*, no. 18.

Randel, Don Michael, Ed. (1986). *The New Harvard Dictionary of Music*. Cambridge, MA: Harvard University Press.

Reber, Arthur (1993). *Implicit Learning and Tacit Knowledge*. New York: Oxford University Press.

Reddy, Michael J. (1993). "The Conduit Metaphor." In Andrew Ortony (Ed.), *Metaphor and Thought*. New York: Cambridge University Press.

Rieke, Fred, et al. (1997). *Spikes: Exploring the Neural Code*. Cambridge, MA: MIT Press.

Roederer, Juan G. (1979). *Introduction to the Physics and Psychophysics of Music*. Berlin: Springer.

Rosenfield, Israel (1988). *The Invention of Memory*. New York: Basic Books.

Royal, Matthew (1994). "The Detection of Rhythm and Tempo Change in Simple Drum Patterns." Paper delivered at the June, 1994 Conference of the Society on Music Perception and Cognition, Berkeley, CA.

Rubin, David C. (1995). *Memory in Oral Traditions*. New York: Oxford University Press.

Rumelhart, David E. (1980). "Schemata: The Building Blocks of Cognition." In Bruce Spiro and Lawrence Brewer (Eds.), *Theoretical Issues in Reading Comprehension*. Hillsdale, NJ: Erlbaum.

Saslaw, Janna (1996). "Forces, Containers, and Paths: The Role of Body-Derived Image Schemas in the Conceptualization of Music." *Journal of Music Theory*, vol. 40, no. 2.

Schacter, Daniel L., Ed. (1995). *Memory Distortions*. Cambridge, MA: Harvard University Press.

Schacter, Daniel L., and Endel Tulving (1994). "What Are the Memory Systems of 1994?" In Daniel L. Schacter and Endel Tulving (Eds.), *Memory Systems, 1994*. Cambridge, MA: MIT Press.

Schaller, Susan (1991). *A Man without Words*. Berkeley: University of California Press.

Schank, Roger C. (1982). *Dynamic Memory*. New York: Cambridge University Press.

———. (1990). *Tell Me a Story*. New York: Scribner.

———. (1991). *The Connoisseur's Guide to the Mind*. New York: Summit.

Schank, Roger C., and Robert Abelson (1977). *Scripts, Plans, Goals, and Understanding*. Hillsdale, NJ: Erlbaum.

Schenker, Heinrich (1969). *Five Graphic Music Analyses*. New York: Dover Publications.

Scherer, Klaus R., and Paul Ekman (1984). *Approaches to Emotion*. Hillsdale, NJ: Erlbaum.

Schiff, David (1983). *The Music of Elliot Carter*. New York: Eulenburg.

Schvanevelt, Roger W. (1992). "Coding Processes: Organization of Memory." In Larry R. Squire (Ed.), *The Encyclopedia of Learning and Memory*. New York: MacMillan.

Scruton, Roger (1997). *The Aesthetics of Music*. New York: Oxford University Press.

Selfridge-Field, Eleanor (1998). "Conceptual and Representational Issues in Melodic Comparison." In Walter B. Hewlett and Eleanor Selfridge-Field (Eds.), *Melodic Similarity: Concepts, Procedures, and Applications*. Cambridge, MA: MIT Press.

Semal, Catherine, and Laurent Demany (1990). "The Upper Limit of Musical Pitch." *Music Perception*, vol. 8, no. 2.

Sethares, William (1998). *Tuning, Timbre, Spectrum, Scale*. New York: Springer.

Shannon, Claude, and Warren Weaver (1949). *The Mathematical Theory of Communication*. Urbana: University of Illinois Press.

Shapiro, Matthew L., and David S. Olton (1994). "Hippocampal Function and Interference." In Daniel L. Schacter and Endel Tulving (Eds.), *Memory Systems, 1994*. Cambridge, MA: MIT Press.

Shepard, Roger N. (1982). "Geometrical Approximations to the Structure of Musical Pitch." *Psychological Review*, vol. 89.

———. (1987). "Evolution of a Mesh between Principles of the Mind and Regularities of the World." In J. Dupré (Ed.), *The Latest on the Best*. Cambridge, MA: MIT Press.

Sibley, Frank (1993). "Making Music Our Own." In Michael Krausz (Ed.), *The Interpretation of Music*. New York: Oxford University Press.

Singer, Wolfe (1996). "Neuronal Synchronization: A Solution to the Binding Problem?" In Rodolfo Llinas and Patricia Churchland (Eds.), *The Mind-Brain Continuum*. Cambridge, MA: MIT Press.

Sloboda, John (1985). *The Musical Mind*. New York: Oxford University Press.

Sloboda, John, and Jane Davidson (1996). "The Young Performing Musician." In *Musical Beginnings*. New York: Oxford University Press.

Smith, J. David (1997). "The Place of Novices in Music Science." *Music Perception*, vol. 14, no. 3.

Smith, Linda B., and Larissa K. Samuelson (1997). "Perceiving and Remembering: Category Stability, Variability and Development." In Koen Lamberts and David Shanks (Eds.), *Knowledge, Concepts, and Categories*. Cambridge, MA: MIT Press.

Sperber, Dan (1996). *Explaining Culture*. Malden, MA: Blackwell.

Squire, Larry R. (1994). "Declarative and Nondeclarative Memory: Multiple Brain Systems Supporting Learning and Memory." In Daniel Schacter and Endel Tulving (Eds.), *Memory Systems, 1994*. Cambridge, MA: MIT Press.

Squire, Larry, and Eric Kandel (1999). *Memory: From Mind to Molecules*. New York: Scientific American Library.

Stein, Barry E., and Alex M. Meredith (1993). *The Merging of the Senses*. Cambridge, MA: MIT Press.

Sternberg, Saul, and Ronald Knoll (1994). "Perception, Production, and Imitation of Time Ratios." In Rita Aiello and John Sloboda (Eds.), *Musical Perceptions*. New York: Oxford University Press.

Stockhausen, Karlheinz (1989). *Stockhausen on Music*. Compiled by Robin Maconie. New York: Marion Boyars.

Summers, Jeffery, Simon Hawkins, and Helen Mayers (1986). "Imitation and Production of Interval Ratios." *Perception and Psychophysics*, vol. 39, no. 6.

Swain, Joseph P. (1997). *Musical Languages.* New York: Norton.

Swain, Rodney A., et al. (1995). "Speculations on the Fidelity of Memories Stored in Synaptic Connections." In Daniel L. Schacter (Ed.), *Memory Distortion.* Cambridge: Harvard University Press.

Sweetser, Eve (1990). *From Etymology to Pragmatics: Metaphorical and Cultural Aspects of Semantic Structure.* New York: Cambridge University Press.

Talmy, Leonard (1988). "Force Dynamics in Language and Cognition." *Cognitive Science,* vol. 12.

Tenny, James (1988). *Meta Hodos and Meta Meta Hodos: A Phenomenology of 20th Century Musical Materials.* Oakland, CA: Frog Peak Music.

Thomson, William (1991). *Schoenberg's Error.* Philadelphia: University of Pennsylvania Press.

Tobias, Betsy, John F. Kihlstrom, and Daniel F. Schacter (1992). "Emotion and Implicit Memory." In Sven-Ake Christianson (Ed.), *The Handbook of Emotion and Memory.* Hillsdale, NJ: Erlbaum.

Tolaas, Jon (1991). "Notes on the Origin of Some Spatialization Metaphors." *Metaphor and Symbolic Activity,* vol. 6, no. 3.

Trehub, S., and L. Trainor (1993). "Listening Strategies in Infancy: The Roots of Music and Language Development." In Stephen McAdams and Emmanuel Bigand (Eds.), *Thinking in Sound: The Cognitive Psychology of Audition.* New York: Oxford University Press.

Tulving, Endel (1972). "Episodic and Semantic Memory." In Endel Tulving and W. Donaldson (Eds.), *Organization of Memory.* Orlando, FL: Academic Press.

———. (1983). *Elements of Episodic Memory.* New York: Oxford University Press.

———. (1995). "Varieties of Consciousness and Levels of Awareness in Memory." In Alan Baddeley and Lawrence Weiskrantz (Eds.), *Attention, Selection, Awareness, Control.* New York: Oxford University Press.

Varela, Francisco, Evan Thompson, and Eleanor Rosch (1991). *The Embodied Mind: Cognitive Science and Human Experience.* Cambridge, MA: MIT Press.

Velmans, Max (1991). "Is Human Information Processing Conscious?" *Behavioral and Brain Sciences,* vol. 14.

von der Marlsburg, Christoph (1996). "The Binding Problem of Neural Networks." In Rodolfo Llinas and Patricia Churchland (Eds.), *The Mind-Brain Continuum.* Cambridge, MA: MIT Press.

Wade, Bonnie C. (1991). *Music in India: The Classical Traditions.* Westwood, MA: Riverdale.

Wagenaar, William A. (1986). "My Memory: A Study of Autobiographical Memory over Six Years." *Cognitive Psychology,* vol. 18.

Walker, Robert, et al. (1996). "Open Peer Commentary: Can We Understand the Music of Another Culture?" *Psychology of Music,* no. 24.

Warren, Richard M. (1993). "Perception of Acoustic Sequences: Global Integration versus Temporal Resolution." In Stephen McAdams and Emmanuel Bigand (Eds.), *Thinking in Sound: The Cognitive Psychology of Audition.* New York: Oxford University Press.

————. (1999). *Auditory Perception A New Analysis and Synthesis.* Cambridge, UK: Cambridge University Press.

Waterman, Christopher A. (1995). "Response." *Ethnomusicology,* vol. 39, no. 1.

Wells, Gary, and Donna Murray (1984). "Eyewitness Confidence." In G. L. Wells and E. F. Loftus (Eds.), *Eyewitness Testimony.* New York: Cambridge University Press.

Weinberger, Norman M. (1999). "Music and the Auditory System." In Diana Deutsch (Ed.), *The Psychology of Music.* 2d ed. San Diego: Academic Press.

Weiskrantz, Lawrence, Ed. (1988). *Thought without Language.* New York: Oxford Science.

Yates, Francis (1966). *The Art of Memory.* Chicago: University of Chicago Press.

Zbikowski, Lawrence M. (1991). "Large-Scale Rhythm and Systems of Grouping." Ph.D. diss. Ann Arbor, MI: University Microfilms.

————. (1998). "Metaphor and Music Theory: Reflections from Cognitive Science." *Music Theory Online: The Online Journal of the Society for Music Theory,* vol. 4, no. 1. http://smt.ucsb.edu/mto/issues/mto.98.4.1/mto.98.4.1.zbikowski_frames.html

Index

Abatements, 63
Accents
  defined, 159–160
  meter and, 170–171, 174–175
  metrical, 170
  phenomenal, 170
  rhythm and, 159–160, 170–171
  structural, 170
  types of, 170–171
Accompaniment, 145
Acoustical grouping, 42
Adjacent tones, 127–128
Ametrical rhythm, 189. *See also* Free
  rhythm
Amnesia, 75
Arch, melodic, 154–155
Articulation, 198
Associations, 56, 69–71, 96, 224–225
Associative memory, 107
Attack point, 159
Auditory events, 4
Auditory memory. *See also specific
  processes*
 associations and, 224–225
 form and, musical, 212–213
 hierarchy and, 217–219
 model, simplified, 5–12
 overview, 3–4
 physiological perspective of, 4
 pitch discrimination and, 127–128
 processes
  echoic memory and early processing,
  3–4

functional view of, 3
long-term memory, 3–5
short-term memory, 3–5
time and, 212–213
Auditory nerves, 6–7
Axial melody, 154

Basic pulse, 159, 168
Beats, 159–163, 165
Beats per minute (bpm), 167
Blacking, John, 205
Bottom-up processing, 21–22, 32–33,
  104
Boundary effects, 225–226
bpm (beats per minute), 167
Brain processes, 25–27

Cadences, 63, 201, 232
Categories
  conceptual, 4–5, 8, 82–85, 128, 195–
  196
  implicit memory and, 81, 87–90
  nuances and, 85–87
   implicit memory and, 87–90
  overview, 81–82
  perceptual, 4, 7–8, 19–23, 82–83, 128,
  144, 202
  pitch, 247
   blurring, 143
  scale and, 140–143
  schemas vs., 95
Categorization, 81, 86. *See also* Categories
Causality metaphors, 63–65